D0959106

Mastering Family Therapy

Other Books by Salvador Minuchin

Families and Family Therapy

Family Healing: Tales of Hope and Renewal from Family Therapy
(with Michael P. Nichols)

Family Kaleidoscope: Images of Violence and Healing

Family Therapy Techniques
(with H. Charles Fishman)

Institutionalizing Madness
(with Joel Elizur)

Psychosomatic Families: Anorexia Nervosa in Context
(with Bernice L. Rosman and Lester Baker)

Families of the Slums
(with Braulio Montalvo, Bernard G. Guerney, Bernice L. Rosman, and Florence Schumer)

Mastering Family Therapy

Journeys of Growth and Transformation

Salvador Minuchin

Wai-Yung Lee
George M. Simon

John Wiley & Sons, Inc.

New York • Chichester • Brisbane • Toronto • Singapore • Weinheim

This text is printed on acid-free paper.

Published by John Wiley & Sons, Inc.

Though this book is nonfiction, the names and distinguishing traits of all clients mentioned in the book have been changed.

Library of Congress Cataloging-in-Publication Data:

Minuchin, Salvador.
Mastering family therapy : journeys of growth and transformation / by Salvador Minuchin, Wai-Yung Lee, George M. Simon.
p. cm.
Includes index.
ISBN 0-471-15558-6 (cloth : alk. paper)
1. Family psychotherapy. I. Lee, Wai-Yung. II. Simon, George M. III. Title.
RC488.M56 1997
616.89'156—dc20 96-22887

Printed in the United States of America

10 9 8 7 6 5 4 3 2 1

To Andy Schauer (1946–1994), a friend who was open
and lovable, lived his life without grudges, and
left us long before his time.

Foreword

This book is a bottomless bag of tools. Part I is a pathbreaking contribution, in which Salvador Minuchin offers his unique perspective on the major ideas of the field's luminaries, selecting some of the most exciting conceptual and clinical tools for helping troubled families.

In Part II, we hear the individual voices of nine therapist-supervisees as they struggle to transform themselves and the families in their care, under their supervisor's masterful guidance. We watch them improve the complexity and accuracy of their interventions, and we observe them learning to abandon unworkable goals. We see how they use Minuchin's catalyzing reactions, and we share their pain and joy as they sharpen their skills and enhance their styles.

The manner in which each therapist's story is told, as well as Minuchin's ongoing comments on their work, make reading this book become, in effect, like sitting in on a "master class." We follow both the teacher's and students' perspectives and see how they intersect and how those perspectives affect the therapy. This work is especially impressive in light of the examples presented: a formidable gallery of *Diagnostic and Statistical Manual* casualties of high difficulty levels.

For the beginner searching for new approaches to problems that at first appear to be inside the individual only, *Mastering Family Therapy* is a remarkably rich resource. For the experienced therapist seeking to cultivate fresh ways of unbalancing pathologic systems, to amplify divergences, and to challenge the usual, the harvest has never been so abundant. This book will be particularly valuable in stimulating the supervisor's imagination. All of us who have found ourselves in conflict with a supervisee's chosen direction will learn from the ingenious ways Minuchin finds to resolve clashes and promote growth. He shows how a supervisor can thrive on the differences between himself and the supervisees, and the supervisee and the family he or she works with, turning those differences into productive conflict, unexpected problem solving, and healing. He teaches how to make efficient use of the supervisor's most fundamental instrument: the ability to join the supervisee in a tough and honest dialogue in which both search avidly for ways of anticipating and creating scenarios.

These ideas do not fit in a field inclined to sacrifice the use of the evocative and probing conversation in the planning and carrying out of therapeutic interventions. These ideas do not accommodate the quick and automated protocol as a principal means of training. They do belong, however, in any professional setting that employs a family-based therapy, delivered by providers who value the relevance and usefulness of interventions above all. These clinicians will heartily embrace the book's main point: discovering feasible goals and improvising a flexible trajectory for therapy by gaining a systemic understanding of families. Minuchin's guidance in achieving such an undertaking cultivates and releases the therapist's protean imagination—the endless capacity to shape new options. He teaches how to assume different forms depending on what the case requires.

In the future, when the field of family therapy is examined and the tools in its workshop are inventoried, *Mastering Family Therapy* will be counted as more than the work of a brilliant craftsman from whose forge came an extraordinary collection of tools that go on shaping the structure of family therapy. It will be remembered as the source book on inspiring therapists to fire their own imaginations and forge their own tools to better serve the families they work with.

BRAULIO MONTALVO

Preface

> Once upon a time, a wise old rabbi listened fondly as his two brightest students engaged in a polemical discussion. The first presented his argument with passionate conviction. The rabbi smiled approval. "That is correct."
>
> The other student argued the opposite, cogently and clearly. The rabbi smiled again. "That is correct."
>
> Dumbfounded, the students protested. "Rabbi, we can't both be right!"
>
> "That is correct," said the wise old man.

Like the wise old rabbi, the authors are of two minds concerning the making of a family therapist. Meyer Maskin, a brilliant and caustic training analyst at the William Alanson White Institute, used to tell his supervisees how once, when he wanted to build a summer house, he asked an architect to show him the plans of homes he had previously designed. Then he went to see how they looked when they were finished. Here Maskin would pause for dramatic effect. "Shouldn't we take an equally rigorous approach when we are searching for an analyst? In other words, before we start the arduous psychological trek together, shouldn't we look at how a potential analyst has constructed her life? How well does she understand herself? What kind of spouse is she? Even more important, how well did she parent her children?"

An equally critical observer of clinicians, the family therapist Jay Haley, would disagree with this point of view. Haley says that he knows many good people and excellent parents who are mediocre or miserable therapists; he also knows good family therapists who have made a mess of their personal lives. Neither life skills nor self-knowledge via psychoanalysis or psychotherapy improves the capacity of therapists to become better clinicians. Clinical skill, he would observe, requires specific training in the art of therapy: how to plan, how to give directions, how to rearrange hierarchies. It can be achieved, he would say, only via supervision of therapy itself. For Haley, to know how good a family therapist is, one would need to interview her previous patients. Even a therapist's written work, he would say, tells us only about her writing skills, not about her therapeutic skills.

So here we find ourselves in a quandary because, as in the rabbi's story, the two sides absolutely disagree, and we agree with both of them. In previous writings, I have indicated how I respond to the specific needs of patients by using different facets of myself. My experiential understanding of the pulls that the family exerts on me shapes my responses to them. This aspect of therapy certainly requires self-knowledge. But Haley is right when he says that therapeutic responses are not guided by self-knowledge but by knowledge of the processes of family functioning and the interventions directed toward changing them.

To escape this paradox, a number of schools of family therapy require their trainees to undergo psychotherapy while they are trained in family therapy. In fact, this is a licensing requirement in some European countries. We remember the early strategies of Virginia Satir on family reconstruction and Murray Bowen sending his students to change their relationships with their families of origin. Carl Whitaker used to have his students and their spouses in therapy as part of their training. More recently, Harry Aponte and Maurizio Andolfi have developed supervisory techniques that aim at self-knowledge *as* therapists.

The supervision strategy with which we confront this paradox is to focus on the therapist's preferred style—that is, his or her use of a narrow set of predictable responses under a variety of diverse circumstances. One therapist may be very involved with content; another may perceive behavior in the light of a particular ideology, such as feminism. Sometimes style relates to the therapist's basic characterological responses, such as conflict avoidance, a hierarchical stance, fear of confrontation, an exclusive focus on emotions or on logic, or a preference for happy endings. But for the most part, the therapist's style manifests itself in elements that are less visible to the therapist himself, like focusing on small details, remaining aloof, being indirect, talking too much, lecturing, or not owning one's ideas.

Thus, two therapists with a similar understanding of a family situation and the same therapeutic goal will respond to the family in two different, idiosyncratic ways. This difference in style may have considerable effect on the course of therapy; some responses are better than others. My approach to supervision therefore is to begin by working with the therapist to understand her preferred style. Which responses in her repertoire does she use most frequently? I accept them. They are okay. Then I declare them wanting. The therapist's style is all right as far as it goes, but it can be expanded. The therapist who focuses on content can learn to direct her attention to the transactions occurring between family members; the therapist who is captivated by the story line can learn the art of discontinuous intervention.

Whatever we identify in the beginning becomes the point of departure. We challenge the therapist to expand her repertoire, to be able to respond from a variety of perspectives in ways that are complementary to the family's needs. The goal is a clinician who can manipulate herself on behalf of therapeutic change and nonetheless be spontaneous.

Carl Whitaker, who was a colorful, idiosyncratic therapist, communicated in his teaching the need to take a variety of universal role functions while working with a family. He enjoyed telling stories about when he was a little "girl." It is this freedom to be protean while remaining true to yourself that we try to impart to our students.

Successful supervision results in a therapist who is different from the supervisor but also different from the person he was before the supervision. The trick is to respect the boundaries of the supervisee's private life during the process of self-transformation.

About the Book

We have divided this book into two parts. In Part I, we examine the contrasting theories of family therapy and describe an interventionist model of therapy, the model that is the basis of our supervision of practicing therapists. This portion of the book was written jointly by the three authors listed on the title page, who share the views on families and family therapy that are expressed throughout the book. The authorial voice in these discussions is therefore "we" and refers to all three. Much of the discussion of the therapeutic encounter and its supervision refers to the individual work done by Minuchin and when the authorial "I" is used, it refers to him.

Part II is a response to Haley's suggestion that the way to know if the therapist is successful is to ask the families. We asked nine supervisees in an advanced training course with Minuchin to talk about their experiences in supervision and its effect on their therapeutic practice. The author/supervisees begin their stories by describing themselves as members of their families of origin. (Such an account is not a part of their training course; it was assigned only for the purpose of this book.) We have a whole gallery of family therapists, all of them working with one supervisor, meeting with a diverse group of families. It will be easy to see that none of them are Minuchin clones.

Supervisor and supervisee were caught in the same experience. They were joined in the goal of producing a complex, flexible therapist, a therapist having a successful experience with a family in therapy. The process affected everyone. The teacher not only responded on an intellectual level but was an active participant. And in the end, both supervisor and student gained an understanding of their own expertise as well as their limitations.

In Chapters 7 through 15, italic passages reflect Minuchin's commentary on the cases.

We hope that the two parts of this book—the theoretical and the experiential—will convey the complex and rewarding process of mastering family therapy.

SALVADOR MINUCHIN

Acknowledgments

To begin with, we owe a deep debt of gratitude to the therapists whose chapters constitute Part II of this book. Were it not for their courageous willingness to expose their clinical work to mass perusal, this book would have become a dry, academic affair, with lessened utility for those who are involved in the flesh-and-blood work of doing and supervising family therapy.

We would like to acknowledge the contributions of Richard Holm, our fellow faculty member at the Minuchin Center for the Family. Richard is present everywhere in this book, albeit invisibly. His contributions ranged from the sublime to the meticulous—from helping us crystallize some of the theoretical ideas to working with the analysis of videotapes.

Authors can count themselves blessed if they find an editor who can understand their material and make it better. In writing this book, we were fortunate; we had three such editors. Frances Hitchcock worked the basic transformations when the material first emerged from our word processors. Nina Gunzenhauser alerted us to the flaws in the manuscript when we believed it was already flawless. And Jo Ann Miller, Executive Editor at John Wiley, brought an understanding of the field and an ability to integrate the work of many writers into a coherent volume.

Our profound thanks also to Lori Mitchell, Jenny Hill, and Gail Elia. They labored tirelessly and with tactful patience to type the numerous revisions through which the manuscript passed.

Finally, we would like to thank our spouses: Patricia Minuchin, Gail Elia, and Ching Chi Kwan. They accompanied us through this book, and they represent the best of complementarity in work and marriage.

Contents

PART I

Families and Family Therapy

Chapter 1

Family Therapy
A Theoretical Dichotomy

MOTHER *(eagerly)*: Do you want to tell him what you did?
DAVID: Oh, yeah, my eye, I rubbed it a little. I didn't have to. The urge didn't last that long.
GIL *(softly)*: David, where were your parents, just before the urge? What were they doing?

The Wednesday class, behind the one-way mirror, is attentively watching Gil struggle with David's family. David, 24 years old, has spent the last year of his life on a psychiatric ward. When the compulsive rubbing of his eye threatened to leave him blind, there seemed to be no alternative to hospitalization. Gil was, at first, his individual therapist, but for the last four months he has been working with David and his parents.

During these four months, Gil has been presenting videotapes of the therapy to the group. Today for the first time we are observing the family session "live." We feel as if we know these people well. We are familiar with the parents' hovering attention to David. Every detail of his behavior becomes invested with meaning and is a matter of concern to them. He cannot hide.

The father, a figure in gray, seems hesitant, pleading to be useful. The mother's round and jovial face seems always closer to David's than we, the group members, think necessary. David's stumbling explanations are divided evenly between them; he tries first to satisfy his mother, then his father. It is clear his mission is to please.

Gil, a psychologist born and raised in the South, tends to relate to people from a respectful distance. As a therapist, he has a preference for low-key interpretations delivered in a soft voice.

MINUCHIN *(the supervisor, to the group)*: I think that Gil is telling them that David's rubbing of his eyes is triggered by the mother's proximity. He is so respectful of the power of words that he thinks they got it. But they are on a different wavelength. Gil will need to learn to shout before they can hear him.

I have been working with Gil on his style with this family since the beginning of the year, and while he has recognized the limitations of his style and seems invested in expanding his way of working, he has kept his narrow cognitive focus and his reliance on softly delivered interpretations. I decide to join Gil on the other side of the mirror and to work with him as a supervisor/cotherapist for a short while.

As I enter, Gil says simply "Dr. Minuchin." I sit down. The family knows that I have been supervising the therapy for the last few months.

MINUCHIN *(to the father):* If you want to help your son, you must keep your wife from dealing with him like that. Talk to your wife.
FATHER: I can't. There's no talking to her.
MINUCHIN *(to David):* Then you should continue blinding yourself.
DAVID: I'm not going to blind myself.
MINUCHIN: Why not? Good children do nice things like that for their parents. Your father has decided that he cannot handle your mother. She feels lonely and alone. You have decided to be a healer. So you will blind yourself to give her a job in life, to be a mother.

Later, in Chapter 10, Gil will describe in detail his experience of being supervised by me in this case. In my introduction to Gil's chapter, and in my comments on his narrative, I will describe the thinking that led me to intervene in the consultation session in the way that was just described. The case of David and his family is such a fascinating one that it would be tempting at this point to delve into the details of my supervision of the case. Before beginning this exploration of family therapy supervision, however, a more general point must be made.

The way in which I intervened during the consultation session—in fact, the way in which I supervise in general—is rooted in my vision of the therapeutic encounter. It is based on a particular understanding of people and why they behave in the way that they do, how they change, and what kind of context invites change. This intimate connection between one's therapeutic vision and one's way of doing supervision and training is not peculiar to structural family therapy. Since the field of family therapy began, in every one of the so-called "schools" of family therapy, how one supervises has been driven by how one sees therapy.

Thus, an exploration of family therapy supervision must begin with a look at how family therapy is done. It must, however, be a look that sees through the welter of techniques in use in the field. To ground an exploration of supervision in a solid understanding of what happens in family therapy, we must penetrate to the thinking that underlies the techniques and discern the fundamental assumptions and values that give birth to techniques. When one looks at the practice of family therapy in this way, many of the apparent differences among the "schools" of family therapy disappear. As will soon be clear, however, what differences remain are crucial ones.

Going back to my supervision of Gil's work with David's family, it is important to note that my focus as a supervisor was based not so much on family dynamics as it was on Gil's therapeutic style. We think that this focus on the person of the therapist is essential. Unfortunately, the literature of family therapy has all too often displayed a much greater interest in therapeutic technique than it has in the therapist himself as an instrument of change. This division between therapeutic techniques and the therapist's use of self began to occur quite early in the development of the field. In part, this was simply an unintended by-product of family therapy's historical need to differentiate itself from psychodynamic theories. Consider, for example, the psychodynamic concepts of transference and countertransference, concepts that very much involve the person of the therapist. The early theorists of family therapy dismissed these concepts as irrelevant. Since the patient's parents and other family members were right there in the therapy room, it did not seem necessary to consider how the patient might be projecting feelings and fantasies associated with family members onto the therapist. But with the dismissal of these concepts, the therapist as a person began to become invisible in the writings of the family therapy pioneers. As the therapist disappeared, all that was left behind was his or her techniques.

As the field developed, family therapists accepted, copied, and modified techniques innovated by other practitioners. For example, Jay Haley's restraint of change reappeared in the Milan school's notion of paradox and counterparadox. Virginia Satir's sculpting was taken over and modified in Peggy Papp's technique of choreography. And the genogram, developed by Bowen and Satir, became a common way for almost all family therapists to map families.

Of course, in practice, the way in which therapists applied techniques was of concern for families, therapists, and supervisors. For the most part, however, this concern was not reflected in the literature of the field; at most it was an afterthought. For instance, in *Families of the Slums* (Minuchin, Montalvo, Guerney, Rosman, & Schumer, 1967) I wrote:

> The therapist's choice of intervention is decidedly limited because he must operate under the organizational demands of the family system.

> But this has the advantage that awareness of himself in the midst of these "system pulls" allows him to identify the areas of interaction which require modification and the ways he may participate in them to change their outcome. . . . The therapist loses distance and is fully in when he enters the role of reciprocating the family members with complementary responses which tend to duplicate what they usually elicit from each other. (p. 295)

This is a rather complex description of the process by which the therapist experiences and knows the family by using his awareness of self in the therapeutic context. Nonetheless, the major focus of my early books was not on the therapist's self, but on the techniques of influencing families. As I focused on *them* (the families) rather than *us* (the therapists), the therapist as the carrier of techniques became universal, while families became increasingly idiosyncratic.

Another example of this process of the disappearance of the therapist can be seen in the way my concept of joining reappeared in modified ways in the Milan school's concept of positive connotation. In *Family Therapy Techniques* (Minuchin & Fishman, 1981), I described joining in the following way:

> The therapist is in the same boat with the family, but he must be the helmsman. . . . What qualifications must he have? What can he use to guide the craft? . . . [He] brings an idiosyncratic style of contacting and a theoretical set. The family will need to accommodate to this package in some fashion or other and the therapist will need to accommodate to them. (p. 29)

The overriding concept in joining had to do with two idiosyncratic social systems (the family and the therapist) accommodating to each other.

When joining was transformed into positive connotation, it simply became a technique of responding to families.

> The best known of these attempted solutions was undoubtedly the *tactic* we called positive connotation, which implied not only abstaining from criticizing anyone in the family but also pointedly playing up everyone's commendable behavior. . . . As we think back on it today, we note that the idea of positive connotation, originally designed as a means of guarding the therapist against both counterproductive clashes with the family and dropouts . . . was a *strategically flimsy device*. . . . (Selvini-Palazzoli, Cirillo, Selvini, & Sorrentino, 1989, pp. 236–237; emphasis added)

The difference between these two concepts is not primarily at the level of content. A large part of joining does have to do with positively connoting family members' way of being, though it is not limited to that. But while joining acknowledges the therapist as an active, idiosyncratic therapeutic instrument, positive connotation sees her only as a passive, universal carrier of meaning and technique.

As we have noted, the disappearance of the person of the therapist from the family therapy literature can be partly attributed to the historical context in which family therapy developed. For a large segment of the field, however, the disappearance of the therapist has been intentional rather than accidental, the result of deliberate theoretical choice. It is, in fact, one of the central contentions of this book that the field of family therapy has organized itself over time into two camps, characterized by two very different views of the role that the therapist should play as an instigator of change. We will discuss later in the chapter the theoretical concerns that have led some family therapists deliberately to seek a kind of invisibility in the therapy room. First, however, let us see what family therapy looks like when it is done by a member of that group of practitioners who, in their practice if not always in their writings, see the person of the therapist as the primary instrument of change in the therapeutic encounter. This kind of family therapy is exemplified in the following description of a session conducted by Virginia Satir.

Activist Family Therapy

In the 1970s, the Philadelphia Child Guidance Clinic sponsored several extremely interesting workshops in which two therapists would separately interview the same family on successive days. The sessions were observed from behind a one-way mirror and videotaped. (The secrecy that characterized psychoanalysis was one of the concepts against which family therapy was in full revolt at the time.) The idea behind the format was that since each therapist's interventions would be guided by his theoretical premises, the audience could observe the way these concepts about the nature of families and the process of change took shape in the therapist's style.

One of the first participants was Virginia Satir, who interviewed a blended family. The father and his eighteen-year-old daughter by his first marriage lived with his second wife and her sixteen-year-old daughter. His ten-year-old son of the first marriage lived with his first wife. Both families had been in treatment for about a year because of disagreements about the boy. The father felt that his first wife was an unfit mother, and he had taken her to court to fight for custody. Their legal battles were reflected in bitter and acrimonious arguments between the families. The daughter had not spoken to her mother in a year, and the boy was having severe problems in school.

Satir was tall and blond, a goddess of a woman who filled a room with her presence. As she entered the interview room, she shook each person's hand, seated herself comfortably, and asked the boy to go to the blackboard and draw a genogram of the family. She chatted easily, asking questions and making personal comments: "I don't know why I can't remember that name." "When I feel this way . . . ." Within minutes she had created an atmosphere of openness in which both sides felt free to talk. Clearly *pro*-everybody, Satir proceeded to engage each family member, tracking the content of each exchange and punctuating everything with friendly comments.

Her remarks seemed random, but she had soon organized the family's information into a unified narrative. She got the husband and his second wife to describe their style of resolving conflicts and asked them to act out a fight for her. Then she created two family sculptures. She asked the boy to sit on his mother's lap and asked his sister to sit on his lap. She seated the other subsystem mirror-fashion, putting the second wife on her husband's lap and her daughter on top of her. Then she asked the son to move out, leaving the 18-year-old daughter alone on her mother's lap. She moved a chair very close to the mother and asked the daughter to sit in it. Then, kneeling on the floor next to them, she encouraged the mother and daughter to describe their resentment, betrayal, loving, and longing. Through sympathy, teaching, and direction, she moved the two women to express how much they missed each other. Then she asked the ex-husband to sit with them. The session ended with the possibility that these two families could reconnect in love instead of conflict.

There is no way that a narrative can convey the very warm quality of the session or the process by which Satir moved from what seemed a random involvement with each individual to the reconciliation of daughter and mother. It was clear that her goal was connection. She targeted the areas of contact, using herself with such emotional proximity that it would have been quite difficult for the family members to resist her direction. Stylistically, one could argue that her level of involvement was smothering and that her push for positive emotion inappropriately overrode and suppressed the honest expression of conflict. Nonetheless, in the space of one hour, she was able to help the family move away from a year of destructive interactions and begin a process of more cooperative parenting.

The therapy of Virginia Satir was nothing if not highly idiosyncratic. But in its very idiosyncrasy, it serves as a worthy exemplar of the work of the activist group of family therapists.

A Dissenting View of Family Therapy

At the same time that Satir was developing her approach to family therapy, very different ideas were also being explored in the field. Gregory Bateson, at the Mental Research Institute (MRI) in Palo Alto, was bringing the combined sensibilities of an anthropologist and a cybernetician to the endeavor of helping families. As an anthropologist, Bateson was deeply and correctly concerned with the dangers of imposing one's cultural values on another. He knew from history as well as from theory that in this domain, it is impossible to predict the direction of change; introduce any perturbation into a culture, however minute and well intentioned, and from then on you have a bear by the tail. Bateson's strong aesthetic preference for letting things be is given endearing expression in his "Metalogue: Why Do Things Get in a Muddle?"

DAUGHTER: Daddy, why do things get in a muddle?
FATHER: What do you mean? Things? Muddle?
DAUGHTER: Well, people spend a lot of time tidying things, but they never seem to spend time muddling them. Things just seem to get in a muddle by themselves. And then people have to tidy them up again.
FATHER: But do your things get in a muddle if you don't touch them?
DAUGHTER: No—not if *nobody* touches them. But if you touch them—or if anybody touches them—they get in a muddle and it's a worse muddle if it isn't me.
FATHER: Yes—that's why I try to keep you from touching the things on my desk. Because my things get in a worse muddle if they are touched by somebody who isn't *me*.
DAUGHTER: But do people *always* muddle other people's things? Why do they, Daddy? (Bateson, 1972, p. 3)

As a cybernetician, Bateson carried an epistemological outlook that reinforced and amplified his aesthetic preference for letting things be. When cybernetics seeks to explain an event, it does not search for positive explanations of the event. Rather, it considers all the alternative events that could have happened and then asks, "Why didn't they happen?"

> In cybernetic language, the course of events is said to be subject to *restraints,* and it is assumed that, apart from such restraints, the pathways of change would be governed only by equality of probability . . . . The cybernetic method of negative explanation raises the question: Is there a difference between "being right" and "not being wrong"? (Bateson, 1972, pp. 399, 405)

When Bateson's aesthetic and intellectual sensibilities were brought to bear on the task of helping families, the predictable result was an extreme concern on his part about introducing any change that might distort family balance in unpredictable ways. He rejected psychoanalytic theory, but his posture during family interviews, as the data-collecting anthropologist, mirrored the psychoanalytic concern for avoiding intrusion into the patient's psychological field. Thus, Bateson introduced a very different tradition into the field of family therapy, a tradition of a cautious, restrained interviewer, who over time became more focused on what not to do in therapy ("not being wrong") than on what should be done ("being right").

The work of the MRI group, which included Virginia Satir among its founders, started its family therapy with the interventionist fervor of the time. But later, especially under the influence of Paul Watzlawick, the concerns raised by Bateson about the potentially disruptive aspects of intervention grew. Watzlawick taught that attempts at solutions are precisely what create human problems in the first place. Thus, therapy should be brief and minimally interventive.

Bateson's introduction of a neutral, reflective therapeutic stance instantly posed a conundrum for those family therapists who wished to pursue this approach to doing therapy. How could the influence of the therapist in the session be controlled?

For the psychoanalyst, the tool for controlling countertransferential responses was the self-awareness developed via the training analysis. No equivalent to the training analysis was available to the family therapist. So those in the field who wished to pursue Bateson's restrained therapeutic posture had no choice but to create external controls on the therapist's interventions. In this effort, the most ingenious group was the Milan School, whose methods will be described in more detail in Chapter 4. To control the therapist's intrusiveness, they created the "therapeutic team" of observers behind the one-way mirror, to whom the therapist in the session was responsible. They changed the "I" of the therapist to the "we" of the team and worked to activate a process of change in family members when they were away from the session and the therapist's influence. The therapists saw themselves as objective interveners at a distance, tossing psychological pebbles that would create ripples in the family.

Interventionist versus Restrained Therapy

Our look at how family therapy is done has revealed that throughout its brief history, the field has been populated by two kinds of therapists. The difference between the groups involves the extent to which they advocate the therapist's use of self as an instrument for producing change. On one side is the interventionist therapist, who practices the "try, try again" active therapy of self-commitment that is a product of the 1960s, with all its optimism and energy, experimentalism, creativity, and naivete.

FATHER: Jimmy is very, very wild. I can't control him.
THERAPIST: Ask Jimmy to bring his chair over here, and talk to him. Jimmy, I would like you to listen to him. Then tell him what you think. And Mother, don't interrupt!

The therapist creates a transaction between father and son that allows her to observe how they interact, in her presence, without the mother's monitoring. Her next intervention will be organized by what she observes.

On the other side is the restrained therapist:

FATHER: Jimmy is very, very wild. I can't control him.
THERAPIST: Why do you think that is?

The therapist may ask other questions, encouraging the exploration of meaning. She will be attentive and respectful, careful not to impose her own biases on father and son. It is a therapy of minimalism.

The restrained therapist has sought intellectual justification for a minimalist therapeutic style from a number of sources. During the 1980s, Bateson's founding intellectual contribution was supplemented with ideas imported from the work of the Chilean scientists Humberto Maturana and Francisco Varela (1980). Their research had demonstrated that an organism's perception of the outside world is largely determined by its internal structure. Much was made in some circles of an experiment in which a newt's eye was rotated 180 degrees. When a moving insect was placed in front of the newt, the newt jumped around and tried to pick it up as though the insect were behind the newt (Hoffman, 1985). The trifling objections on biological grounds—that the mammalian eye, and brain for that matter, are of a different order than the reptilian—and on human grounds—that human beings and their interactions are not confined to questions of neurobiology—did not deter some restrained therapists from their triumphal march to the logical conclusion: There is no objectively knowable "reality." If each organism is primarily responsive to its own internal structure, then no organism can directly bring about any given state of affairs in another. To practitioners of restrained therapy, a therapeutic corollary seemed self-evident: It is impossible for a therapist to produce specific targeted changes in a family. Thus, therapy should be noninterventionist, a simple conversation among people.

In the 1990s, the restrained therapist turned to social constructionism (Gergen, 1985) and to the postmodernism of Michel Foucault (1980) for support and inspiration. Social constructionism highlights the fact that knowledge is not a representation of external reality but a consensus constructed by individuals who are "in language" together. Foucault's postmodernism adds the observation that local conversations are governed by larger sociocultural discourses that privilege certain perspectives while submerging and marginalizing others. Under the influence of these schools of thought, the restrained therapist has come to focus on language and narrative. The therapist asks his clients questions that provide them with the opportunity to reconsider meanings and values that up until then they had considered as "given" and normative. The therapist thus creates a context in which clients are invited to "re-story" their lives, throwing off, in the process, the oppression of constraining cultural discourses.

We do not question the importance of social constructionism and postmodernism for understanding social phenomena, but in our view, therapy should not be primarily an exercise in understanding, especially the kind of abstract, academic understanding that is produced by postmodernist analysis. Instead, therapy should be oriented toward action. It is a relatively brief, ad hoc arrangement between a family and a therapist, with the explicit goal of alleviating stress. To apply constructionist and postmodernist ideas in an unmodified fashion to such an arrangement appears to us to be an instance of what Bateson would call a category error, a misapplication of a concept from one level of abstraction to another.

Nonetheless, the restrained therapist of the 1990s remains wary of our brand of therapeutic interventionism. Emphasizing the ways people are governed by, and limited to, the stories that they have coconstructed in conversation with others, the restrained therapist continues to call both therapeutic expertise and norms into question. Harlene Anderson (1994) has described the shifting in the theoretical basis of therapy that accompanies a constructionist practice:

From	*To*
Knowledge as objective and fixed—knower and knowledge as independent	**Knowledge** as socially created and generative—interdependent
Language as representational, accurate picture of reality	**Language** as the way we experience reality, the way we give meaning to it

From	*To*
Social systems as cybernetic, order-imposing, social units defined by role and structure	**Social systems** as layered social units that are a product of social communication
Therapy as a relationship between an expert and people who need help	**Therapy** as a collaboration between people with different perspectives and experience

Source: AAMFT Conference, Washington, DC, 1994.

In neither column is the word "family" included. The conceptualization of the family as the significant social unit that creates idiosyncratic definitions of self and others virtually disappears. The workable idea of the family as a social system, in which patterns of experiencing are molded, is replaced by the notion of language system as a social unit. Meanwhile, the therapist is robbed of her flexibility by an ideological mandate that she operate only in collaborative, symmetrical postures. Gone is her latitude to challenge, to play, to give opinions, to be in the therapy room the complex, multifaceted person that she is outside of it. All that remains for her in her role as therapist is to be a distant, respectful questioner.

As a group, the constructionist therapists have tried hard to create a therapy of support and respect for their patients. In their practice, pathology is pushed outside the family into the culture that surrounds the family. The therapist confines himself to language that is governed by the imperative to be respectful. In these approaches, the therapist becomes the collector of family stories. He serves as the person to whom all family members direct their narratives and as the person who connects the various narratives.

The restrained therapists have traveled far since Bateson championed a democratic therapy of meaning and, in the process, they have arrived at a totally different conceptualization of the position of people in context. In Bateson's systems thinking, family members' transactions maintain family functioning and their view of themselves and the other. Though expressed in scientific terms of systems and ecology, this view is profoundly moral. It implies mutual responsibility, commitment to the whole, loyalty, and protection toward each other—belonging. It forces both clinician and social scientist to focus on the relationships among individual, family, and context. Contemporary constructionist practice, however, has taken a different moral stance. It focuses on the individual as a victim of constraining language that carries the invisible yet prevalent dominant discourse. The response to cultural constraint is a stance of political liberation, of challenging the culture by questioning accepted meanings and values.

This position eschews the mutual responsibility of members of a group in favor of a philosophy of individual freedom. To those who hold this position, therefore, the optimal contact between people is characterized by mutual respect but disengagement. We think this position reflects the postmodern pessimistic view of our culture, the disenchantment with government, and the conviction that social constraints are detrimental to the individual.

From an interventionist family therapist's point of view, the restrained therapist's focus on content and the technique of sequentially interviewing individual family members from a central position rob the therapeutic context of its greatest resource: the direct engagement of family members with each other. All the nonverbal elements, all the irrationality, and all the affect of family interaction are lost. As a result, some of the most important gains of the family therapy movement are abandoned.

For the interventionist therapist, the family is the privileged context in which people can most fully express themselves in all their complexity. So family interaction, with its potential for both destruction and healing, continues to occupy center stage in practice. To us, family life is as much drama as it is story. Like drama, family life unfolds in time. It has a past, expressed in stories told by the characters. But it also has a present, realized in the characters' interactions. And like drama, family life is also spatial. Family members communicate with each other by gesture and affect as much as by words.

The process of change occurs through the engagement of the therapist with the family. The therapist is a catalyst for family change (though unlike a physical catalyst, he may also change in the process). Whatever therapeutic events occur during therapy happen because of this mutual engagement. Thus, the therapist brings the family drama into the therapy room, creating a context in which family members are encouraged to interact directly with each other. The therapist listens for content, themes, stories, and metaphors, but he also looks. Where are people sitting? What is the relative position of family members? He watches movement—the various entrances and exits, the shifting of family members toward each other and away. He looks at gestures—subtle changes in posture, seemingly casual touches by which family members signal each other. Slowly the map of family organization becomes visible; the boundaries that define affiliations, alliances, and coalitions begin to appear. As this happens, the therapist begins to experience the family forces. The family pushes and pulls, inducting the therapist into the role of judge, mediator, ally, opponent, spouse, parent, and child. The therapist develops an experiential understanding of the family's chosen transactional patterns and also begins to sense the submerged alternatives that might become accessible. Now he can use his personal responses to guide his interventions, perhaps by purposefully inserting himself into the family drama.

Intervening in this way has its dangers. It adds another force to an interpersonal field already riddled with forces. But the answer to this problem is not to avoid engagement but to monitor it.

The therapist must operate both as a participant in the family drama and as an observer. It is important to engage, and it is also vital to move out, encouraging family members to interact directly with each other. It is important to be pulled by the emotionalism of the field, but it is also important to observe. It is this modulation of distance that gives the therapist's interventions the effect of a catalyst. He triggers the family to respond, then watches their response. If the therapist's interventions have been useful, family members will find themselves interacting in novel ways that produce expansion and enrichment. Healing happens in these moments, and the healers are both the therapist and the family members themselves.

The interventionist family therapist accepts the responsibilities of intervening. He needs to be aware of his ignorance and of his knowledge. He needs to know how social norms mold families. He needs to be conscious of the physiological, the cultural, the economic. He needs to know that he is limited by his own history. But all these necessary constraints notwithstanding, he must do more than just listen.

Whether interventionist or restrained, and with whatever conceptual framework, the family therapist is an agent of change. She modulates the intensity of her interventions according to the needs of the family and her own personal style. A restrained therapist operates at the low intensity end of this spectrum, contenting herself with helping family members understand how they construct their stories. Her goal is to provide a neutral context for "therapeutic conversations." An interventionist therapist, by contrast, may operate at the high-intensity end of the spectrum, perhaps enacting family conflict by having lunch with an anorectic patient and the patient's family (Minuchin, Rosman, & Baker, 1978).

But whether the therapist is carefully neutral or the opposite, she is always an "improver." She joins families, as healer, teacher, and resonator, for an experiential journey. And inevitably, she will bring her preconceptions about families with her. How do families get stuck? What resources may this family have for resolving conflicts? These preconceptions may be formulated or remain unexamined, but explicit or not, they will organize the content the therapist hears and determine which transactions she sees and how she responds to them. Furthermore, the personal style that she has developed through traveling the byways of her own life will give shape to the manner of her interventions.

The family, too, has its own preconceptions and styles. It is a social system that inevitably reflects the historical, cultural, and political systems in which it is nested like a set of Russian dolls. The family shares some universals with the therapist; they hold language, certain social concepts, and some values in common because of their shared space and time. Were it otherwise, family and therapist could not understand each other. But the mindsets they share can also lead to shared blind spots.

It is important to acknowledge what we do not know. However, it is also important for the therapist to know what she knows and to own her knowledge. The restrained therapist's position of not knowing cannot evade the biases, experience, knowledge, and ignorance without which no human being can travel; it can only obscure them. Therapists cannot escape being guided by their notion of a functional family and, more often than not, by their notions about a correct (or at least better) fit between family and society.

Our culture may well be changing faster than our awareness, but it does seem that a practitioner who claims to be a family therapist should have some idea of what a family is. If we are to intervene in a family to increase the flexibility of family members' repertoire or alleviate pain and stress, our interventions must be guided by an informed understanding of the context in which we are intervening. The next two chapters turn to a consideration of families, which, in a paradox that recalls the story of the rabbi in the Preface, are all different and all alike.

Chapter 2

Family Particulars

All Families Are Different

Most definitions of a family focus on the composition of a small group related by blood or commitment. But what wording could include all the possibilities? Traditional concepts instantly bring exceptions to mind:

> *Family:* A group consisting of parents and their children.
>
> *Exception:* What about a childless couple, devoted to each other for decades?
>
> *Family:* The children of two parents, a group of people closely related by blood.
>
> *Exception:* What of a blended family, composed of remarried parents and step-siblings?

Families in a kibbutz extend their boundaries to include the community. A Mormon family composed of a man, his four wives, and their children consider themselves a nuclear family, whatever sociologists or the state may say. With today's biotechnology, a family may include a couple's biological child, conceived of her ovum and his sperm but gestated in the body of a stranger. In a recent instance, a lesbian couple was brought to family court by the biological father of their child, a homosexual friend whom they had asked to donate sperm. When their daughter was two years old, the donor sued, seeking parental rights. The judge ruled that the daughter already had two parents and that it was in the best interests of the child not to upset her concept of a family.

What, then, is a family? The sociologist Stephanie Coontz (1992) would ask at what date and in what culture? A family is always some segment of a larger group, in a particular historical period.

People today tend to think of "the" family as the nuclear unit. But according to the sociologist Lawrence Stone (1980), the British family of two centuries ago would not have been the nuclear unit but the kin unit. In the open lineage system of that time, Stone has said, marriage was concerned more with the combination of properties and the continuation of family lines than with an attempt to unite soulmates. As late as Napoleonic France, the marriage contract of Pierre Rivière's parents shows the economic basis of the union (Minuchin, 1984). The children were as much a part of the assets of the marriage as were the land and livestock.

Moreover, two of the tasks that today are considered fundamental to the family unit—the rearing of the children born to the union and the emotional support of the spouses—were then much more the business of the kin system. In fact, according to Stone, relatively little importance was attached to the spouse unit at all. If a husband and wife grew to care for each other, there was certainly no harm done, but if mutual affection did not develop, no one considered the marriage a failure.

Today a woman's nurturing response to her child is assumed to be so fundamental that we call it instinct. The French historian Elizabeth Badinter (1980), however, has argued that centuries ago the "maternal response" was rare. Children were customarily reared away from their parents—sent to wet nurses as infants, apprenticed as children. Perhaps one reason for this detachment was that so many children died in infancy. Until the level of infant and child mortality began to decline toward the beginning of the modern age, it was unwise to love a baby. Stone has pointed out that in the Middle Ages parents often gave several of their children the same name, hoping that at least one might live to bear it into adulthood.

The nuclear family as we know it became common with urbanization and industrialization and as a consequence of the improved hygiene and medical care of the scientific revolution. As European society began to change, so did family norms. By the mid-18th century, the nuclear family had become the accepted ideal of the middle classes. For the first time, the interdependence of the spouses and the rearing of children were considered major tasks for the nuclear unit. Stone has estimated that this change in family norms took about 200 years.

Moreover, the autonomy and authority of today's nuclear family are recent acquisitions. Before this century, the community played much more of a role in what we consider family business. In colonial America, as in 17th-century Europe, matters that today would be considered private, such as unruly children, were directly and explicitly regulated by the community. Tale-bearing was discouraged by the use of stocks. The ducking stool disciplined women who scolded their husbands.

During the colonial period, law, like religion and custom, concerned itself intimately with family matters. A woman who complained of abuse might well be ordered to return to her husband to preserve the social order (Skolnick, 1991). For the same reason, women and children were legally under the control of the husband/father or guardian. A boy legally became a person on coming of age. As for a woman, the influential English jurist William Blackstone expressed the opinion that the law provided that husband and wife were one, and the husband was that one.

We are taking this historical detour because family therapists must understand that families are different in different historical contexts. Imagine traveling through time to do therapy with a family in colonial America or with the family of Pierre Rivière in 19th-century France (Minuchin, 1984). Our traveling therapist would have to change his view of families with every place and time in which he touched down. The requirements of therapy in different times and cultures would force him to re-evaluate the norms he might hitherto have considered universal.

Our exploratory therapist would want to pay particular attention to the large forces that shape families in a given era, especially the public policy of the time. For example, in the Union of Soviet Socialist Republics, laws changed with the changing needs of the state. The early laws concerning marriage and abortion, relatively egalitarian as befit allegiance to a Marxist feminism, were made less liberal during the 1930s, when the population was declining (Bell & Vogel, 1960). Jacques Donzelot's *Policing of the Family* (1979) explores a similar phenomenon in France. When industrialization created the need for a steady workforce, institutions appeared that supported family preservation (and a concomitant rise in population). Similarly, when France was establishing overseas colonies, family-centered philanthropic societies became common. Child-rearing became the concern not only of physicians and educators but also of politicians like Robespierre, who attacked the practice of turning infants over to wet nurses. Policy changes followed accordingly, in response not to family needs but to the purposes of the dominant political class.

Public policy has its impact on the American family today, as do the rapid economic and social changes Western culture is experiencing. As a result, family arrangements that only a few years ago were taken for granted seem irrelevant. As always during times of significant social change, a sense that the social fabric has become dangerously frayed is finding expression in fear of family changes. Some people have made an icon of "the American family" according to the ideal of the 1950s: the gracious suburban home, that warm refuge for highly valued children and the breadwinning husband and father, who could look forward to coming home to a wife and mother in her proper sphere. But beneath the bland surface of the self-styled golden age of the 1950s were tension and discontent that fueled the cultural revolutions of the 1960s, which were inevitably succeeded by the backlash of the 1980s. With the stagflation of the 1980s, the liberated, "greened" America of the 1960s and 1970s became a land of "sexual fear, television evangelists, and antidrug and antipornography crusades" (Skolnick, 1991, p. 5). Now, in the 1990s, it is becoming clear that the New Right's dream of restoring the male-headed nuclear family to dominance faces enormous challenges.

Where will the family go from here? One thing we can predict with certainty is change. Families, like societies and individuals, can and must change in response to changing circumstances. Rushing to label adaptive change as deviant and pathogenic is the product of hysteria, not of history or reason.

The social psychologist Arlene Skolnick delineates three areas that may govern family change in the 1990s and beyond. The first is economic. For example, the shift from the factory to the office means that high-paying blue-collar jobs are disappearing as low-paying pink-collar jobs increase. This shift has been accompanied by the large-scale movement of women into the workforce. In today's economy, many women do not have the option of remaining at home, even if they wished to. The impact of women working outside the home, together with feminist ideas, has shifted the cultural ideal of marriage in a more egalitarian direction.

The second factor influencing family change is demographic. Rearing children in a technological society poses such a crushing economic burden that families are becoming smaller. Families that two generations ago would have expected to have many children now plan to pour enormous resources into rearing and educating just one or two. At the same time, life expectancy is increasing, and for the first time in history people expect to grow old. Even with the increasing length of "childhood," a couple can plan on many years together after completing their parenting function (though they may well need to "parent" their own aging parents).

The third major structural change that Skolnick delineates, which she calls "psychological gentrification," also has profound implications for the family. Because of rising levels of education and leisure time, Americans have become more introspective, more attentive to inner experience. Above all, they have become more interested in the emotional quality of relationships, not only in the family but at work. This emphasis on warmth and intimacy has been of great significance to the development of family therapy, partly because it can create discontentments unthought of when family life was more a matter of conformity with social roles. It is no longer enough for a husband and father to be a good provider. A woman cannot prove her wifely virtues by the contents of her pantry. A child can no longer be merely dutiful and obedient. When family life is expected to provide happiness and fulfillment, perceived family problems are to be expected.

Socioeconomic Perspectives on the Family

While Skolnick's description of the family offers a sociological overview of white middle-class families in the United States, it stops short of reflecting the lives of many other American families. The experiences of poor families are often very different in ways that go beyond economic deprivation and have enormous impact on family functioning. The intrusion of institutions is a good example. Many institutions, although very respectful of the family boundaries of the middle class, feel free to intervene in poor families. On behalf of the children, they enter the familial space, creating not only dislocation of family organization but affiliations between children and the institutions, empowering the children to challenge the parents. Schools, departments of welfare, housing authorities, and mental health institutions have all created pseudosolutions to the problems of the poor family that contribute to family fragmentation. The effect of this intrusion is felt in cases like those of the Harrises and Jimmy Smith.

The Harrises: A Family without Doors

Let's enter the home of the Harris family. It's easy to enter; in a sense, their apartment has no doors. Steven and Doris Harris, married for 10 years, have four young children. They struggled for years to maintain their own apartment on Steven's paycheck as a truck driver. But six months ago, he was laid off. During the past month, they have been homeless. So the apartment they live in now is not theirs; it belongs to a government-funded social service agency.

For as long as they can recall, the Harrises have been involved with governmental and social services. They have seen so many social workers, child welfare workers, case managers, and therapists that in the Harrises' memory, these helpers have all blended into one. All of them have shared the assumption that the Harrises' need for social services entitles workers to enter, unannounced and uninvited, into the family's space, both physical and psychological.

The Harrises have learned that when helpers enter their domain they invariably bring very well-defined ideas about how the family should be functioning. The drug counselor tells Doris that she should focus exclusively on her recovery from drug addiction. At the same time, the child welfare worker tells Doris to be less self-absorbed and devote more energy to being a good mother. The drug counselor reports to Doris' probation officer, while the child welfare worker has the ear of the family court judge, before whom a complaint of child neglect has been entered. As a result, both drug counselor and welfare worker are in a position to coerce Doris into accommodating their agendas, despite the fact that these agendas are diametrically opposed.

The drug counselor and child welfare worker never talk to each other. Neither of them speaks to Steven, who is virtually invisible to them. Doris spends more time and effort dealing with the drug counselor and child welfare workers than she does dealing with Steven. He is becoming invisible to her, too, spending more and more time away from the apartment. He is still looking for work, but he is getting fewer positive responses now than at any time since he was laid off. Doris feels overwhelmed and overburdened. Steven feels like a failure, a third wheel.

Over the years, the Harrises, both young and old, have developed ways of coping with the intrusions of the helpers. The children have grown used to the presence of strangers in their home. Responding to the fact that these strangers tend to assume a benign, interested stance toward them, the children have developed an open, welcoming posture with which they greet and charm these strangers. Superficially engaging, at a deeper level, this pseudointimate posture is disturbing for the lack of boundaries it bespeaks.

Doris and Steven have developed their own version of their children's pseudointimate posture. They have learned that their helpers value disclosure ("dealing with their issues"), so they have developed a stereotyped "rap." At the content level, it is sufficiently steeped with intimate details to create the illusion of openness and acceptance of expertise. But in its ritualized delivery, it serves as a buffer between the family and their unsought helpers.

To placate these would-be helpers, at least for a time, the couple have learned to proclaim the wisdom and eminent good sense of any advice or directive their helpers may offer. But to preserve some sense of autonomy, they drag their feet in implementing the suggestions. This foot-dragging invariably earns them labels like "resistant," "passive aggressive," and "manipulative," but the Harrises can see no other way to protect their shredded sense of dignity and privacy. Unfortunately, as the number of such labels grows, so too does the number of helpers who parade into their home without doors.

While the Harrises are African American, the important aspects in their case are generic: They are among the homeless families who are subjected to the unpredictability of life and the necessity of dealing with multiple helpers.

Jimmy Smith

The way the foster care system impinges on families is another example of distortions in context that affect family shape. Jimmy, age two, was an African-American child born with positive toxicity from his addicted mother. He is neurologically impaired. At his birth, the court automatically declared his mother abusive, and Jimmy was sent to an agency that worked with toxic babies and then to foster care. He was placed with a homosexual couple who were extremely nurturing and provided him with all possible care.

Jimmy was thriving, and his foster parents wanted to adopt him. The mother, who at this point was drug free, contacted the agency to establish some connection with her child. She recognized that Jimmy's foster parents were excellent, and she did not oppose the adoption, but she wanted to have some contact with her child. The agency was concerned that contact with Jimmy might give the mother presumptive parental rights, so they entered to defend the foster parents. It was the agency that created an antagonistic, polarized relationship between the foster parents and the mother, handicapping any possibility of creative compromise in which the foster parents and the biological mother might collaborate.

Ethnic Perspectives on the Family

Unfortunately, family therapists have often accepted white middle-class norms, distorting their perspectives out of expediency or sheer ignorance. Yet issues such as minority status are critical determining factors in family problems. The influence of ethnicity on families has been extensively studied (McGoldrick, Pearce, & Giordano, 1982). Although issues of ethnicity are often lumped with economic status, they cut across class lines. Surprisingly, the attainment of middle-class status by ethnic group members can bring unexpected problems.

According to Nancy Boyd-Franklin (1989), middle-class African-American families stand on a tripod of three cultures. There are cultural elements that may be traced to African roots, those that are part of the dominant American culture, and finally the adaptations that people of color have to make to racism in the dominant culture. The multiple demands may strengthen identity, but they also may lead to a confusion of values and roles and to a sense of powerlessness in the face of cultural complexity.

A therapist working with an African-American family may need to explore the extended family. The importance of the kin network may stretch all the way back to African roots as well as laterally into the contemporary necessity of coping with poverty and racism. But a black family that has attained middle-class status may be facing a stressful choice between helping the extended family or disconnecting from them.

Other areas influenced by minority status may include the family power structure. Power is shared more equally by some black spouses than is common in white middle-class families, perhaps because black mothers have historically been more likely than white mothers to be employed outside the home; most of today's middle-class black women had working mothers. In a particular family, however, a Muslim ethic may dictate that the woman remain in an elaborately circumscribed domestic role.

In Latino families, as in black families, an extended family network with relatively flexible boundaries may be important. Godparents (*compadres*) may be very much part of the significant family. Cooperation may be stressed and competition discouraged. Hierarchies may be extremely clear, with roles explicitly organized around generation and gender. Women may be expected to be submissive, and men expected to protect their women. A mother may be expected to be self-sacrificing and devoted primarily to the children. The couple's relationship with their children may well be considered more important than their relationship to each other; in fact, the partners may have little freedom from parental functions.

Like the Harrises and Jimmy Smith, Maria and Corrine also belong to the group of families who have to deal with the Department of Welfare. But since they are Puerto Rican and the therapist in their case was Hispanic, the issues of ethnicity and language became an integral part of the therapeutic encounter.

TRIBES AT WAR: MARIA AND CORRINE

Maria, a Puerto Rican woman in her late twenties, had two children, Peter, age three, and Juana, six. Maria's mother and stepfather, an evangelical minister, threw her out of their apartment when she was 18, when they caught her smoking marijuana. She found a relatively stable relationship with Juan about six years ago, though both of them were in and out of drugs.

When Maria had her second child, Juan's mother invited them to live with her. That was a golden period for Maria. She flourished under the support and care of Juan's mother and his older sister, Corrine. She had always felt unwanted, the deviant. Now Juan's mother and sister were like family to her. She felt protected, guided, cared for. But her relationship with Juan turned sour, and he moved out. Soon after, Juan's mother asked Maria to leave.

Maria began to do drugs again, and Juan called the Department of Welfare seeking to remove their children from her. The court declared Maria an unfit mother and, because she refused to cooperate with agency workers, issued an injunction barring her from seeing the children. Juan's mother became a kinship foster mother, in effect, giving the children to the care of Juan's sister, Corrine.

Expelled from the only benign experience she had ever had, Maria moved to a shelter for drug-addicted women, where she stopped using drugs. She won the right to see her children once every two weeks. Corrine brought the children to visit her at the shelter. At one visit they got into a fight, and Maria slapped Corrine. The court issued a restraining injunction, and Maria was no longer allowed to be near her children.

What the court achieved was a disrupted and immobile family organization. Corrine stopped working in order to devote herself completely to the rearing of the children, curtailing both her social life and her career. Still a young woman, she became the full-time mother of two children who were not hers. Maria was in a shelter for homeless women, where she had an ersatz family, mostly addicted women, although she was not addicted at this point. She was not allowed to see her children or help with their care, while Corrine was becoming a socially isolated young mother. In other words, the court had judicially frozen a situation in which conflict among family members had separated them, creating a no-woman's-land and making natural negotiation among family members impossible.

I (Minuchin) was able to arrange family consultations that included Maria, Corrine, and the children. I joined with both women by speaking Spanish as well as English with them. I complimented Corrine, praising her excellent care of the children. At the same time, I pointed out how frequently she found herself bribing them. I joined with Maria's love and responsibility for her children, although I observed how frequently she found herself rejecting them when they misbehaved. Both were excellent mothers, I concluded, but it would be better for everybody if their different skills could be linked. We talked about the importance of mothering and the mutual support of family members. We talked about family loyalty, highlighting the strong value the Latino culture places on family solidarity. We talked about how the court, not understanding Latino families, had imposed the dominant culture's values. It was not difficult for the two women, who fundamentally cared for each other as well as for the children, to reach an agreement that the court, in its rigid stance, had precluded.

In working with any minority family, it is important for the therapist to assess whether and how the stresses of racism are brought into the family from the outside world. In some families, a family member who feels helpless in the face of racist pressures at work may displace that rage and frustration into interpersonal abuse in the home environment, where he or she feels powerful. It may be necessary to address the anger in therapy, to distinguish between neuroticism and a response to real racism, and help the family member and the entire family to deal with it.

In order to ensure that therapy itself does not become an exercise in racism or classism, some family therapists have suggested that the field should emphasize the influence of all the multicultural contexts in which families are embedded. Celia Falicov (1983) has proposed an ecological definition of culture:

> . . . [Those] sets of common adaptive behaviors and experience derived from membership in a variety of different contexts: ecological settings (rural, urban, suburban), philosophical or religious values, nationality and ethnicity, types of family organization, social class, occupation, migratory patterns and stage of acculturation; or values derived from partaking of similar historical moments or particular ideologies. (pp. xiv–xv)

She has proposed that each individual family's membership in each context be paramount in a therapist's view.

An approach to families in all of their cultural contexts seems theoretically correct, but the multiplicity of possible contexts makes workable generalizations difficult if not impossible. Furthermore, cultural norms of what "ought to be" do not necessarily coincide with the norms held by a particular family. Falicov has argued for a culture-bound approach precisely because it highlights diversity and challenges the tendency of the dominant culture to impose its values on minorities. But as she points out in regard to ethnicity, cultural norms always have to be examined in the case of each individual family to ensure that the therapist, albeit with the best of intentions, is not wedging the family into an ethnic stereotype.

Family therapists have often been too comfortable with making the dynamics of a family explicit and leaving the social determinants formulated only vaguely, if at all. But study of the cultural matrix is not an end in itself. The concern for ethnicity is one of many elements contributing to family therapy theory and practice. While valuable in itself, it should be recognized as but one of many contributing elements.

We are uneasy, too, about the oversimplification inherent in many of the currently popular efforts to develop well-rounded, "culturally competent" therapists. Culture contains more than can be captured in laundry lists of concepts that purport to describe the values and worldview of a particular ethnic group. The difficulties involved in understanding culture can be seen in Wai-Yung Lee's experiences while attempting to teach family therapy in Hong Kong and in my attempts to train paraprofessionals in family therapy during my tenure at the Philadelphia Child Guidance Clinic.

When Wai-Yung Lee, who was brought up in Hong Kong but works primarily with Caucasian families in North America, began to teach in Hong Kong four years ago, the usual "West meets East" encounter had an interesting twist. Introducing family therapy to her old cultural group was more confusing for her than it might have been for an outsider. An outsider would have taken for granted his or her ignorance of local expertise on traditional values. But for Lee, her exploration or reexploration of the Hong Kong culture in relation to her teaching contained one surprise after another.

Lee's supervisees had fixed notions about what works and what does not work with Chinese families, notions that she herself shared. But she found that if she accepted these notions, her teaching had the effect of confirming rather than challenging her students and the families they were working with to expand and to explore novelty.

Lee found that the greatest challenge of her job in working with a cultural group to which she had once belonged was to free herself from a culturally imposed straitjacket in order to become effective. The fact that she was Chinese created an interesting distortion in her teaching. Her supervisees' expertise in their own culture was threatened by her challenges to their view of families and to their usual responses to what works in therapy and what does not. She found herself caught between her American and her Chinese cultures, a feeling that she had not been conscious of in her training of Western students or her work with Caucasian families. Only after getting past the cultural "guardians" among her students and her own internal cultural guardians was she able to lead her supervisees into an exploration of the clinical implications of working with this particular group of families.

I had a similar experience of the vagaries of bringing cultural consciousness to the practice of family therapy three decades ago when, along with Jay Haley, Braulio Montalvo, Marianne Walters, Rae Weiner, and Jerome Ford, I began a program at the Philadelphia Child Guidance Clinic to train paraprofessionals.

We were trying to repair an obvious skew. In the clinic, white middle-class clinicians were working with a population composed in large part of African-American and Hispanic families from lower socioeconomic levels. We therefore recruited a group of intelligent, highly motivated but academically undereducated community people, African American and Hispanic, and trained them in family therapy. Our assumption was that since they were members of the cultural groups with which they would be working, they would have an instinctive knowledge of the cultural terrain that they would be traversing in their clinical work. It turned out, however, that we were naive. In addition to living in their own world, our colleagues-to-be had also lived in the dominant culture that had formed us. From this culture, they had absorbed prejudices about their own cultures that mirrored, and sometimes exaggerated, the prejudices of the dominant culture.

The training of these paraprofessionals took three years. The goal of the training was to produce workers who, like every other worker in the clinic, regardless of academic background, race, or socioeconomic level, could be the therapist of any family that came for treatment. Were we idealistic and naive? Was this a blind attempt to blur differences? That would probably be the verdict of the field today, with its current emphasis on diversity.

We welcome today's concern for diversity as a significant raiser of consciousness about the dangers of imposing majority values on minority populations. But we also think that there is an element of danger in that politically correct social attitude—a kind of reverse bigotry. As therapists, we are always working with people who are different from us. So we need to account for our own ignorance, and our assumptions about people who are different. We need to incorporate the present ethos for understanding diversity, but while accepting that, we also need to recognize that there are universals. As Harry Stack Sullivan pointed out years ago, "Anybody and everybody is more human than otherwise."

Chapter 3

Family Universals

All Families Are Alike

A family therapist must understand how ethnicity, class, and other social factors have implications for family structure and functioning and hence for family therapy. But there are certain developmental imperatives that are more universal than context-related. Parents need to take care of children. Certain requirements are appropriate to certain stages of development. The shape and organization of the family determine its dynamics. Family members age at different rates and therefore have needs that may conflict. The list goes on.

The family therapist, while recognizing the diversity of family forms, both historically and currently, believes that there are superordinate principles that guide therapy. This chapter presents a model of family concepts that can form an umbrella under which a variety of therapists can experiment with a variety of procedures and still be able to generalize and communicate usefully.

Constructing the Family

A family is a group of people, connected emotionally and/or by blood, who have lived together long enough to have developed patterns of interaction and stories that justify and explain these patterns of interaction. In their patterned interactions with each other, family members construct each other. This complementary construction in the family web of transaction is both bad news and good news. It means that family members are always underfunctioning. There are aspects of self not activated in the family's current rules and patterns, and that is a loss. But life in common also has the comfort of a certain predictability and the sense of a place to be.

Family members adapt to the family rules that allocate roles and functions. This adaptation fosters smooth functioning, anticipating responses, security, loyalty, and harmony. It also means that grooves become ruts, spontaneity is handicapped and growth is curtailed. It may mean imprisonment in interpersonal molds and boredom. But there are always possibilities for expansion.

The complementary construction of family members requires long periods of negotiating, compromising, rearranging, and competing. These transactions are usually invisible, not only because context and subject constantly change but also because they are generally the essence of minutiae. Who passes the sugar? Who checks the map for directions, chooses the movie, changes the channel? Who responds to whom, when, and in what manner? This is the cement by which family members solidify their relationships. Who is included? What is the level of proximity and intimacy? Who is responsible for whom? Who is excluded, scapegoated, abused? What are the triggers that enhance pleasure or increase strain, and what are the usual mechanisms for defusing conflicts?

In a thousand small ways, family members develop preferred styles of transacting their truths about me and thee and the way we relate. Families maintain some of these truths about their uniqueness while changing others as they evolve. Family members may spontaneously discover alternative ways of relating, and when this happens, the flexibility of family functioning increases. But for the most part, family members remain predictable to each other. The expectation of predictability allows for a parsimonious choreography of life, an economy of the energy it takes to relate. But there is also a coercive element in the demands for loyalty to the family rules, since growth or change by a family member may be experienced as betrayal.

A family therapist, trained to sort out and observe patterns, can anticipate the movement of the pieces on the family board as a master chess player does. The therapist sees the formal characteristics of the game. Who are the players around certain issues? Who joins in a coalition against others? How are nurturing, support, and power played out? These parameters define the family structure.

I have previously developed some concepts about family organization (Minuchin, 1974) that will be summarized here. These concepts do not pretend to offer a comprehensive, scientifically rigorous description of family functioning. They are only an organization I have imposed on my observations.

In truth, there is no such thing as a family structure. Family structure is only a frame the therapist imposes on the data she observes. We think a therapist has to have a framework that offers a way of organizing and thinking about the great bustling, booming family world. But the strategy has all the dangers of strategy. When the therapist observes with a point of view, she tends to see certain data more clearly, the data to which she has already assigned importance. A genogram is another example of this kind of artificial construct. Valuable as an instrument for organizing information, highly useful in its inclusion of historic as well as current participation, it also imposes and maintains its own brand of bias.

Nevertheless, I have found structural constructions useful. Designed to be heuristic and clinically suggestive, they help the therapist organize her perceptions and thinking in ways that lead to useful interventions. They also organize the therapist's observations of transactions, as well as verbal material. They can thus be useful with a range of families who rely more on relationships than on family stories. The concept of family structure addresses some universals of family life: issues of belonging and loyalty, issues of proximity, exclusion and abandonment, issues of power, and issues of aggression as they are reflected in subsystem formation, the permeability of boundaries, affiliation, and coalition. The therapist using a structural frame cannot be objective, but I maintain that no therapist can be. And chance does favor the prepared mind.

Family Systems

Every family system comprises a number of *subsystems.* Each individual in the family is a subsystem of that family. Age differences create family subsystems; the adults in a family constitute one subsystem, the children another. In a culture that prescribes differentiated sex roles, gender creates subsystems—the male subsystem and the female subsystem. In a blended family, the ties of blood and history between parent and children may create subsystems—"his kids," "her kids."

The daily dealings that constitute the stuff of family life lead to accepted ranges of proximity among the various subsystems of the family. Subsystems can thus be thought of as being surrounded by *boundaries* of varying permeability. If a father is very close to his child, the boundary between father and child is said to be permeable. Complementarily, the mother may be relatively uninvolved with father and child; the boundary between the father-child subsystem and the mother is then called rigid. In another family, the boundary between the parental subsystem and the child subsystem may be extremely permeable, reflecting the children's participation in the parents' dealings with each other and/or the parents' intrusion into the children's functioning. The metaphor of the boundary may seem abstract, but it does have its uses in therapy, as we will demonstrate later in the book.

The day-to-day negotiations of family life also establish patterns (or understandings) about the use of power in the family. *Hierarchy* may thus be thought of as an aspect of family organization. Which subsystems wield power over other subsystems? In what style is power wielded? Is it coercive and authoritarian, or does it invite discussion and tolerate dissent? Is the use of authority accepted in the family, or is it resisted and opposed?

FAMILY MAPS

Answers to these questions paint a picture of the family that we call a *structural map.* A structural family therapist evaluates these maps by using concepts of *family shape* and *family development.* Family shape refers to the demographics of a family. Is the family in question a "traditional" nuclear two-parent family? A single-parent family, or a blending family? Perhaps it is an extended family, with members of one or both families of origin living in the household or otherwise playing a very active role in the day-to-day life of the family. Perhaps the couple is gay or lesbian.

Different family shapes make different functional demands on family members. Thus, a family structure that might be adaptive for one family form could be maladaptive for another. A high level of proximity between mother and child that might be maladaptive in a two-parent family as a result of the marginalization of the father might very well be normal and workable in a blending family, in which the mother and child have a history that predates the relationship of the mother and her new husband. Behavior by a grandparent that might be seen as undermining parental authority in a nuclear two-parent family, might very well be necessary and useful in a single-parent or extended family system.

The concept of *family development* is rooted in the fact that cultures invariably prescribe different behaviors for individuals at different stages of the life cycle. Contemporary American culture, for example, expects adolescents to think and behave differently from either younger children or adults. Similarly, there is societal pressure for young adults to develop a certain kind of independence from their parents (a kind of independence that current economic circumstances frequently make impossible).

As the constructor of the identity of its members, the family must organize itself to fit the sociocultural prescriptions for the behavior of its members. As these prescriptions are modified in response to growth and changed circumstances, the family must change its structure to achieve a better fit with the modified needs and revised expectations.

What all of this means clinically is that a family structure that is adaptive at one stage may be maladaptive at another. In the early stage of family development, couple formation requires a quantity and quality of involvement between the two people that must change once a

child comes onto the scene. And families with yc
degree of involvement between parents and ch
smothering for adolescents.

The concepts of family shape and family de
therapist to evaluate the structural map he has dra
provide norms in the light of which the relative ad
ily's structure can be assessed. The therapist know
are not universal. They are specific to a given time a
tural context. Clinical use of these concepts in no wa contradicts the understanding of variety in family forms; what it does assume is that each family has to find a way to come to terms with the sociocultural context in which it is embedded.

Family Conflict

Families are complex systems composed of individuals who necessarily view the world from their own individual perspectives. These points of view keep the family in a state of balanced tension, like the nodes of a geodesic dome. The tension is between belonging and autonomy—between me and us. Tensions are activated daily in every family, in hundreds of interactions, at any point at which significant or even quite minor decisions are made. There is always negotiation. Will we do it my way, your way, or find a compromise? Like the patterns formed by family members' preferred styles of seeing themselves and others, management of conflict also becomes patterned.

Family members accept the expertise of individual family members; she's the accountant, so let her balance the checkbook. The older brother is a deal maker; if you'll let us on the swings, you can ride our trikes. A family may explicitly agree that father's ways are better; we must all try to be like him. Or they may adopt his ways without noticing it; father loathes snakes, so we never go to the reptile house. Alternatively, family members may, in negotiating, develop totally novel ways of reaching decisions, which become *our* way, the family way. But some issues of disagreement are so difficult to resolve that the family tends to create blank spots. Whole chapters of experience are sealed, not to be dealt with, with the result that family life is impoverished.

Sometimes when family members find disagreements unresolvable, they organize hierarchically, using authority as the way of settling the issue. Then content tends to disappear, and family members take polarized positions. Sometimes people from the extended family are recruited as allies in the conflict, strengthening an armed truce that has closed off negotiations.

Hierarchy can be necessary and useful. Differentiation of functions with acceptance of expertise and authority of a member in particular

es for better functioning. In families with children, the par-
uthority, used to resolve conflicts, may be salutary, and the chil-
n learn in the process. But when naked power becomes a way of
imposing solutions, it usually becomes maladaptive.

CASE: STRUCTURE IN THE SMITH FAMILY

To see how these generic descriptions of the family might be expressed in people of flesh and blood, let's enter the home of the Smiths and observe them in their process of negotiating differences. This time we will consider a white family who are upper-middle-class suburbanites. Jean has her MBA. Mark is a lawyer. They are in their forties and have two children, a boy age ten and a girl age six. They have been married for fifteen years. They share similar tastes in art and music, and they have always enjoyed and made a point of reading similar literature and attending concerts together. Politically they are liberal and involved. They value loyalty and responsibility toward each other, their families, and their jobs.

They met as young people in the 1960s, when they were both in the Peace Corps, working in Africa. They lived together for three years, then married, dreaming of a life style and a harmony that they did not remember in their families of origin.

She was attracted, among other things, by his autonomy and his sense of being at home wherever he was. He was like a snail, she said. He carried whatever he needed with him. He was attracted by her sense of order. Troubled waters seemed to calm in her presence, and he thought they could sail forever on sunny seas.

As the idealistic sixties gave way to the sober seventies and they got a little older, they both became a little more career-oriented and a lot more middle class. Mark donned three-piece suits. Jean had a good job in a large corporation but also assumed the responsibility of managing their home. The children came along, and her work at home increased as his work outside increased. He made more money than she did and when they moved to the suburbs, she stopped working to stay home with the children, while Mark began to spend more time in the office to maintain their standard of living.

Mark and Jean have come to therapy at the point of considering divorce. Their life together has remained calm; there are no storms in their sea, but they are not going anyplace. His work is taking more and more of his time. She has gone back to work and is now on double duty, coming home early and taking care of the children.

They feel unconnected. Jean eats with the children and puts them to bed, then waits for Mark to get home. At nine or ten o'clock she prepares his dinner, and when she has put the dishes in the dishwasher, they fall into bed, both tired, he on his side and she on hers.

Jean complains that Mark criticizes her constantly. She feels he is selfish, cold, and detached; he takes proper care of the children only if she watches. He feels she is controlling and obsessively attached to things; in his view the romance of their lives has been sacrificed in a world where continuity and order must reign supreme. He sees himself as invested in the family, loving the children and responsible with them, but given no importance at all in any decisions. At home, he feels superfluous. She sees herself as responsible, concerned, overwhelmed by her two full-time jobs. She feels enslaved.

They are both right. And in their sense of betrayal they have sought allies in their silent struggle. The son has joined his father in his jaundiced view of his mother. The mother pours into the daughter all the love and nurturing that has dried up in the relationship with her husband.

One night when Mark came home late from work and Jean dutifully heated up his dinner, he was worried about how tired she looked. He suggested that she go to bed. He would eat alone. She heard criticism of her sense of order. She went to bed in silence, desolate. He read her silence as lack of affection and felt even more strongly his inability to reach her.

Since both of them avoid open conflict, she got busier around the house. Feeling superfluous at home, he got busier at the office. And as their silent war dragged on, life in the family narrowed and became unexamined routine. To open up the problem was to risk open war.

This schematic rendition of the Smith family is a therapist's construction, a picture cut from the small daily events, the dialogues, the disagreements, and the emotionality of family life. Affiliations, coalitions, loyalties and betrayals, negotiation and conflict, selfhood and belonging—not in the neat dichotomies and temporal sequences that language demands but all mixed up in the confusion of unexplained emotions—have to be reduced to some clearer description of family functioning.

The therapist listens to the family's story, but he also selects observations of transactions in which he himself participates, in the office. The therapist asks them to start talking about their relationship. Mark starts complaining about Jean. He says she is obsessively controlling, attached to things, cold, and stingy. The therapist then asks Jean to describe Mark from her perspective. Jean says he is critical, selfish, cold, detached, and careless whenever he deigns to help at all.

Now the therapist has two stories, both of them true. She is angry and hurt because he is so cold and unfeeling, always criticizing her. He has given up trying to reach her; she always withdraws and never gives him a chance. The therapist is beginning to get a feel for the way they enter conflict, each holding his or her idea of the truth.

To learn about the flexibility of their system, how they trigger each other, and their capacity to find alternative ways of relating, the therapist encourages them to continue talking while he listens closely. He observes the nonverbal: body postures, the affect that accompanies the content, the emotional noise. Jean describes preparing Mark's dinner the night she was exhausted. She was just trying to be a good wife, and he sent her away. Mark responds angrily that all he did was try to get her to rest. But that's typical—she could turn a diamond ring into a grievance. There is silence. As the silence lengthens, they look hopefully at the therapist. He suggests that they keep talking.

Disappointed, and very wary, they obey. During their continued exploration, the therapist enters mostly to keep the dialogue going. He observes that Mark's defense of his view is tentative. Jean is tenacious. Mark is detached, while Jean is emotional and confrontative, though she sees herself as the victim. Mark is rendered silent when Jean insists on engagement. When he insists on his viewpoint, she is the one who is silent.

The therapist now has an initial map of the family and a glimpse of their possibilities for expansion. He also senses some emotional responses. Something about this couple makes him feel protective. He does not yet know why. They are all at the beginning of their experiential journey.

Summary

The Smiths were my patients, and the description of their way of being is the product of my "cookie cutter," the way in which I organized their seemingly random transactions. In Part II of this book, in the stories of nine therapists working with families, we will witness the ways in which each of these families is unique but we will also note the universal characteristics they share as they relate to the therapists, who have idiosyncratic styles but share with me a perspective on the therapeutic process.

There are many different ways of organizing data. Interventionist and restrained therapists observing families from their different corners will see only the segment that will explain and justify their interventions. In Chapter 4, we will explore these partial views and the complex picture they form of the field of family therapy.

Chapter 4

Family Therapies

Clinical Practice and Supervision

The Japanese classic *Musashi Miyamoto* depicts the making of the great samurai Musashi. It begins when Musashi encounters a wise old monk who recognizes the potential and talents in this young rebel, who has been tyrannizing the village.

Determined to educate this wild man, the old monk first challenges Musashi to fight him with all his strength. An experienced street fighter, Musashi laughs at the thought of taking on the frail-looking monk. He soon discovers, however, that even with his physical strength he cannot defeat the monk, who simply avoids direct confrontation with him. In the process of playing hide-and-seek, the monk tricks Musashi into perfecting his swordsmanship in ways that will become clear to him only much later.

Angered by his inability to capture the monk, the ungrateful pupil searches through the temple where the monk resides, only to find himself once again trapped by the monk, this time in a library with no escape. After months of shouting obscenities in vain, Musashi finally settles down and begins to read the many books and rare manuscripts in the room, where he is kept in confinement for ten years. During this period, there are numerous encounters between Musashi and the monk, and with each experience Musashi's skills are more finely polished.

One day, Musashi finds the library door open. Outside the door stands the monk, who tells him that he has taught him everything he knows and that from there on Musashi must continue learning on his own. Thus Musashi begins the great adventure of becoming the finest samurai in history.

The story of this self-appointed teacher and his reluctant student awakens deeply rooted fantasies for both students and teachers. To teachers, the story demonstrates that power struggles are inevitable in the process of interpersonal learning. To those of us who long to find a teacher so committed to our growth and achievement despite our stupidity and resistance, Musashi's experience with the monk is the encounter of a lifetime. To those who are sensitive to hierarchy and control issues, however, this method of samurai training would be a nightmarish learning experience.

The drama of the learning transaction carries different themes and meanings for different people. The family therapy field has always prided itself on its diversity, as reflected in its many different schools of thought. The same diversity occurs in training.

In the 1990s, family therapy is an established practice. The earlier struggles against the psychoanalytic establishment have been replaced by a concern for effectiveness in discrete territories. The training of family therapists is not relegated to specialized institutes but instead takes place in universities, in departments of social work, psychology, psychiatry, and nursing. Programs that give a masters degree in family therapy have sprung up in a number of places in the United States and abroad, as the scope of its potential application continues to expand. There is no longer a theoretical center to the discipline; training programs advertise their adherence to a particular school, and there is high drama in the competing discourses between the interventionist and the restrained therapists. But family therapy in the 1990s, regardless of preferential approaches, accepts as a given that which has become public domain in theory and practice, without even a nod of acknowledgment to its origins.

Our task in this chapter will be to provide an overview of the numerous ways in which family therapy has been conducted and therapists have been trained in its practice. To provide some organization for our overview, we return to the division of the field into interventionist and restrained therapies. This distinction is somewhat artificial and the therapists we have grouped together would not necessarily see themselves as similar, but the grouping helps to highlight important commonalities and differences among the various major approaches to systemic therapy.

Interventionist Therapies

We have selected four therapists among the pioneers in family therapy to represent the interventionist group of therapists. Our selection is somewhat arbitrary, in part based on the fact that we already have tapes of their work from which to describe their clinical styles. Though markedly different, their styles all convey the sense of personal commitment to the therapeutic process that is the hallmark of the group. In Chapter 5, my own style of therapy will be discussed and illustrated, and in Part II, that style will be elaborated in the stories of supervision by nine of my students and colleagues.

Virginia Satir

Virginia Satir's warm and proximate style was described in Chapter 1 as an example of interventionist practice. Satir's goal in therapy was growth, which she measured in increased self-esteem for individuals and increased coherence for the family unit. For Satir, the concept of "people-making" was the same in supervision as in therapy. Therefore, Satir created for her students the same kind of experiences that she created for families, experiences aimed at improving emotional expression and gaining insight.

Satir believed it was essential for therapists to have knowledge of themselves as parts of their own families. In her thinking, therapists needed to work through unresolved issues in their own family relations. She often trained in a group format in which a trainee would sketch a particular period in his life and the familial context of that time. She would then direct people in the group to play the different parts of the family, so that the individual trainee could re-experience his family role for new growth.

Having created student-followers all over the world, Satir would meet with her "beautiful people" in a month-long summertime retreat attended not only by her students but by their families. Part of her teaching format during these retreats involved interviewing her students and their families in front of the large group, in the spirit of growth and sharing. Some people found the way in which Satir involved herself, becoming a "good mother" for her students, to be rather intrusive and overwhelming. She was, in fact, extremely proximal, and she used herself in a way that was highly nurturing. Supervisors who prefer their relationship with the supervisee to be friendly, formal, and at a middle distance might have found her supervisory style too close for independent thinking to take place. But Satir's therapy was a therapy of intimacy, and her supervision had the same quality. Many of the techniques that she developed, such as reframing, the use of the family tree (which preceded the genogram), and family sculpting, to name a few, are still widely used in the field.

Carl Whitaker

Carl Whitaker's style was completely different from Satir's. Where she was warm and engaging, he was gnomic and somewhat off the wall. Whitaker advocated "craziness"—nonrational, creative experiencing and functioning—as integral to the process of therapy. He believed that by allowing themselves to become a little crazy, families could enjoy the benefits of spontaneity and enhanced emotionality.

In order to draw out "craziness" in people and free them from their emotional roadblocks, Whitaker created a technique of spontaneously communicating his own feelings to patients, sharing his emotions and fantasies as well as his own stories. His unique style is well illustrated by a session he once conducted with the family of a ten-year-old boy who had been hospitalized after a suicide attempt. He began by talking with the father, asking for a history of the family. He paid special attention to deaths. A grandparent had recently died. The father's sister has committed suicide using the same method the boy had attempted. Twice Whitaker broke in to say, "I have a crazy thought." He interjected something tangential, to which he did not seem to expect the father to respond. Turning to the mother, he asked about her parents, again paying special attention to the death of her father. He then talked about the death of his own father, saying that he felt like a murderer. He added that probably anyone who survives a family member's death feels like a murderer and he suggested that this family must feel the same way.

The mother said she couldn't understand such an idea. Whitaker replied indignantly that he wasn't trying to teach her how to understand but how to tolerate *not* knowing—"the only way we can cope with this insane world." The woman was startled by the sharp response, but Whitaker seemed absolutely unconcerned. He conveyed a sense that narratives didn't have to go in any particular direction. Again and again he disrupted the logical flow with his "crazy thoughts." At one point he said, "You do me good; your accent makes me remember when I lived in Atlanta," and the Southern flavor of his own accent deepened. At another point, he said again, "I have a crazy thought. I'm thinking about dueling. Would you like to duel?" At the puzzled expression of the family he said, "No, I suppose not" and continued the interview, interposing comments about his own life. He told the boy about a patient of his who had been trained to kill in Vietnam. Back in the States, trying to sell a vacuum cleaner to a woman who didn't want one, the patient had had the impulse to use the cord of the vacuum cleaner to strangle her as he had been taught.

For the observing audience, as well as for the family, Whitaker's interview was puzzling, seemingly directionless. Studying the tape, however, one realizes that in an interview lasting less than an hour, he elicited or suggested discussions of death, suicide, and murder over thirty times. The whole session was permeated with images of death and responses to death, so that the exploration of death and its consequences became something familiar. Whitaker was challenging secrecy in a family that tended not to share internal dialogues. He was encouraging them to present, respect, and validate unconscious elements in their thinking, challenging their overrationality.

Virginia Satir and Carl Whitaker shared at least one goal: to cut through to deeper levels of experience. But Satir's emphasis was on affection and caring, and she involved herself very directly in unearthing those tender emotions. Whitaker's statements were rooted in universal ideas, issues that transcend individuals, families, and even cultures. He was dealing with the perennial elements of death, killing, sex, and discontinuity, not joining the family but rather challenging the family members to join him in a profound and irreverent way of looking at things.

Whitaker saw theory as a hindrance in clinical work (Whitaker, 1976). Therapists who base their work on theory, he felt, are likely to substitute dispassionate technology for caring. It should come as no surprise, then, that Whitaker believed that doing therapy cannot be taught. If one cannot teach therapy, the only thing one can do is to expose students to therapy by doing it with them. Therefore, all of Whitaker's students were his co-therapists. Through doing therapy with him, receiving therapy from him, and talking to him, they were supposed to become not like him, but more of themselves. His was a training by participation and not by instruction.

Although the experiential therapy that Whitaker introduced to his families was not always easy for people to follow, his capacity to "admire people in the field of dreams, and act it out, like Alice in Wonderland" (AAMFT Founders Series, 1991), is a legacy that he wished to leave behind, and he has indeed done so. Learning to play and introduce elements of absurdity into a rigid family system is beneficial to any therapist, whether a follower of Whitaker's or not.

By challenging meaning and logic in people's thinking and role functions in the family, Whitaker predated the constructivist challenge of reality. By committing himself personally to the change process in therapy, he also challenged the cognitive posture of constructionist practice.

Murray Bowen

Whereas Satir and Whitaker were spontaneous, emotional, and instinctive, Murray Bowen was cerebral, deliberate, and theoretical. Bowen viewed symptoms as a product of emotional reactivity within the family, acute or chronic. Since Bowen saw the major problem in the family as emotional fusion, his major goal in therapy was differentiation. In order to create the conditions for increased individual autonomy and growth, he considered it necessary to reopen cut-off family relationships and detriangulate them.

Bowen believed that change can occur only when anxiety is low and that understanding, not feeling, is the critical vehicle for change. Thus, therapists must learn to tolerate the emotionality in families without becoming reactive themselves. In the Bowen approach, the therapist is a coach who remains unsusceptible, calm, and outside the emotional entanglements among family members. If the therapist can withstand the pressure to become triangulated in the family conflict, tension in the family will subside and the fusion among family members will eventually resolve (Nichols & Schwartz, 1991).

In contrast to Satir's warm emotionality and Whitaker's skillful chaos, Bowen's rationality seems overcontrolled and humorless. His approach is well-illustrated by an interview with a couple who were always fighting. The husband and wife would skip from one subject to another, never stopping their bickering and never resolving anything. Bowen took control of the session by asking each of them to talk only to him. He made himself the apex of a triangle, instructing the wife to listen while he and the husband talked, then telling the husband to listen while he talked with the wife. The husband began to describe his anger toward his wife.

Bowen interrupted. "Don't tell me what you *feel,*" he said in his dry, unemotional way. "I'm not interested in what you feel. Tell me what you think." Throughout the session, Bowen inserted himself again and again, exerting cognitive control to monitor the intensity of the couple's exchanges. By the end of the session, the struggle for control that had permeated every transaction between the husband and wife had eased. Within the formal structure Bowen imposed, they were beginning to explore their own and each other's needs, instead of carping at each other.

Bowen's theory guides supervision in the same way that it guides therapy. The goal of supervision is to enhance a therapist's ability to remain reflective and nonreactive in the face of a client family's emotional process. Put in Bowenian terms, this means that the goal of supervision is to enhance the therapist's differentiation of self. Since this goal is identical with that of therapy, the process of supervision will be identical with the process of therapy. The supervisor will function as the supervisee's calm, detriangulated coach, as the supervisee seeks first to understand the relationship between his clinical impasses and his family's multigenerational history and then proceeds to return to his family of origin in order to shift his stance toward key family members.

A problem with Bowen's theory is that it anchors the level of differentiation of people in the childhood experiences in the family of origin. It does not allow for the possibility of change or differentiation based on later life experiences in the new family. In some ways, his theory resembles the psychoanalytic theory of repression, and the potential for growth is dependent on changing early relationships. Still, Bowenian theory offers a comprehensive conceptualization of the relationship between individuals and their families, which is a useful framework for therapists to understand.

Jay Haley*

Jay Haley is more a supervisor than a therapist. But his thinking is so clear and his directives are so easy to transform into therapeutic maneuvers that he can be likened to a master cartographer. With one of his maps, a therapist will always know true north. Haley views human interactions as interpersonal struggles for control and power. The power to which he refers, however, is not necessarily the control of another person; rather, it is the control of the *definition* of the relationship. The goal of therapy, in his view, is to redefine the relationship between family members so that the symptom will be surrendered as a means of exercising power within the family.

For Haley, therapy is an attempt to create conditions in which family members "find" themselves in circumstances in which they need to do something different with each other. The therapist's task becomes a project in social engineering: Given this symptom, this dysfunctionally organized family, this difficulty or stress in life, under what circumstances will family members be inclined to change? And how can the therapist direct them toward such circumstances in such a way that they experience themselves as having come to this solution on their own? Therapy becomes an exercise in "indirect direction."

In the treatment of a couple in which the wife was bulimic, he directed the therapist to explore the areas of mistrust between the

---

*While the work of Jay Haley predates his partnership with Cloe Madanes, and while he and Madanes have both written extensively but never co-authored a book, it seems difficult to write about his work without taking into consideration that for more than a decade Madanes and Haley were codirectors of the Washington Family Institute, teaching and thinking together. In the last decade, they have evolved differently. While Haley has continued to explore strategic techniques, Madanes has moved to a concern for spiritual aspects of therapy.

spouses, saying that the treatment of the bulimia could not start until that problem was addressed. To help the wife trust her husband, she was to ask him to go with her to the supermarket to buy the junk food with which she gorged herself at night. The couple were encouraged to draw up accounts of the amount of food the wife ate and then vomited. At one point, the husband was asked to buy her food. Then they decided together that since it was going to be vomited later on, they could just as well use the blender to chew it. Finally, to save the wife the energy of vomiting, they agreed to buy the food, blend it, then throw it into the toilet.

The increase of collaboration, mutuality, and trust between spouses that was critical for changes in the couple's dynamics and for symptom change remained unhighlighted in Haley's strategic formulation; they seemed almost asides. But they were the essence of Haley's strategies. Haley's strategic therapy has sometimes been described as manipulative and disrespectful, but having watched him for decades, we can testify to the careful and respectful concern for people that invariably undergirds his strategic thinking.

Haley's supervision is also an exercise in "indirect direction." Similar to his concept of therapy, the supervision of a strategic therapist always involves designing a specific and individualized plan (which may or may not be shared with the supervisee) by the supervisor (Mazza, 1988). The context of training is live supervision. Operating behind a one-way mirror, Haley directs the movement of therapy, phoning in directives to the supervisee. These directives are designed to help the supervisee grow in competence as a strategic therapist. She changes by doing something rather than by thinking or talking about it. Learning happens indirectly, largely outside of her awareness. Therefore, while we have included Haley in the interventionist group, his position with respect to the therapist's sense of herself as a therapeutic instrument is different from that of the others in the group.

While the teaching of Jay Haley is often compared to that of other minimalist strategic schools like the Mental Research Institute and the Milan approach, Haley is an interventionist, in our thinking. He uses the presenting symptom to gain entrance into the patient's family or larger system, and his ultimate goal is not only to deal with the symptom but to change the system.

In spite of their differences in style and thinking, all the therapists discussed so far focused on the therapist as the trigger for the change process. Inevitably, they all used themselves as supervisors in ways that directed their supervisees toward their ideal type of therapist. Satir created intense emotional relationships with her students that encouraged their proximity, loyalty, and affection. Whitaker created respect, affection, and puzzlement simultaneously. He gave space to his supervisees' creativity and emphasized the distance necessary for them to be connected to their own individuality, as well as the trust to be connected to him. Bowen kept a whimsical and detached relationship with his supervisees. His ideal of the therapist as a coach was revisited in his supervision of students who were working with their families of origin. Haley, working at middle distance, creates a respectful intellectual atmosphere from which to teach his anti-intellectual approach.

Both Satir and Whitaker assumed that their relationships with clients changed not only the clients but themselves. They therefore felt comfortable in adopting an instrumental role to change their supervisees. Bowen's respect for autonomy and differentiation, however, put supervisees in charge of the change in their work with their families of origin. Haley created a hierarchical relationship in which supervisees experienced the use of therapeutic authority in giving directions.

Each of these interventionist therapists had a preference for a particular corner of the human drama: Satir for nurturance, Whitaker for creativity, Bowen for autonomy, and Haley for power. Their different approaches to therapy show us that it is possible for therapists to operate in a preferred style to increase complexity in their therapeutic work, as long as they understand that that style is not the only possibility.

Restrained Therapies

Restraint in family therapy can take several forms, and various schools of therapy have adopted different ways of restraining their interventions. One group of therapists carefully limits the domain of family functioning into which they intervene; therapy focuses only on the problem as identified by the family. The second group develops a host of techniques to restrain the activities and the stance of the therapist. A third group exercises restraint by limiting the modality of the therapist's responses to the domain of language and story. All three groups, however, share a concern about the imposition of themselves on the family, wary lest intervention become oppressive.

The MRI Group

The Brief Therapy group at the Mental Research Institute in Palo Alto, California, which included John Weakland, Paul Watzlawick, Arthur Bodin, and Richard Fisch, was the first to proclaim a non-normative approach to systemic therapy. The MRI group declared that it did not regard any particular way of functioning, relating, or living to be problematic if the client was not expressing discontent with it (Fisch, 1978).

Once people do define something to be a problem, they invariably attempt some solution to the problem. Sometimes the very solution that is attempted serves only to maintain and to amplify the problem. If, in response, more of the same solution is attempted, a vicious cycle is started. The next stop may be a therapist's office.

If the therapist practices in the MRI model, the therapy will be a self-consciously minimalistic one. The therapist will accept the client's definition of the problem, although he may push the client to describe the problem in behavioral terms. The therapist will then assess the sequences of attempted solutions that appear to be maintaining the problem. The therapist will devise directives designed to interrupt the problem-maintaining sequence and will present the directives by reframing the problem in terms that utilize the client's language, beliefs, and values. The therapist will be activist and strategic, but *only* to interrupt problem-maintaining sequences. When the presenting problem, as defined by the client, is resolved, therapy ends. The MRI therapist expects therapy to be brief, no longer than eight sessions.

The MRI group also believes that training should be brief. Since their model is a simple one, they believe they can teach any reasonably intelligent and interested therapist to use it. The primary goal of MRI training is to get trainees to abandon the perspective of whatever model they worked from before and take on that of the MRI approach. Learning what not to include is considered more important than learning what to include.

The other hurdle is to help trainees to become more active in the one domain in which the MRI model calls for therapeutic activism, that of assessing and interrupting sequences of attempted solutions. To be active in this domain, the trainee needs to acquire the ability to elicit from clients clear problem definitions, to devise and "sell" reframes, and to devise and deliver directives. Live supervision may be used to help the trainee acquire these skills. When it is, the supervisor's main intervention will be to phone in directives to the trainee. She may direct the trainee to ask more questions in a particular area. She may direct the trainee to use a certain reframe. Or she may give the trainee a directive to be delivered verbatim to the client.

This is a training model that requires no history taking, no insight, no going back to the trainee's own family of origin. It is a training model that focuses on planning and technique far more than on the personal style of the therapist.

MRI's insistence that trainees have to abandon whatever they have learned in order to use their model appears to be restrictive and can produce therapists who are technique-oriented and lack the sophistication required to deal with complex human situations. In their concentration on clients' description of their problems and behavior, they frequently dismiss the family as an interactive system and focus on individual phenomena. Therefore, when MRI therapists consider their approach as minimalistic, they are talking about directing their interest to only one aspect of problem solving. With this limited definition, minimalism can be seen as one dimensional.

The contribution of the current MRI development is perhaps not so much its brief model itself but rather its way of addressing problems. It is beneficial to understand that the solution that accompanies a problem can be more problematic than the problem itself—a lesson that is also worthwhile for the MRI group to consider in its attempt to provide a formula for family therapy.

The Solution-Focused Approach

The solution-focused model of Steve de Shazer grew out of the MRI approach. But where the MRI group focuses on the client system's unsuccessful attempted solutions, de Shazer concentrates only on what members of the client system are doing—or have done in the past—that unbeknownst to them has in fact been successful in alleviating the presenting problem. Thus, solution-focused therapists are interested not so much in the problems presented by clients as in the exceptional instances in which clients find themselves better able to handle the problems. The task of solution-focused therapy is to help clients amplify effective solution behaviors of which they are already in possession.

Two techniques are basic to the solution-focused approach to therapy. The first is the "exception question." This question is designed to elicit from clients a search for episodes in the past or present when they were not as affected by their problems. Once such exceptions have been identified, the therapist can explore with clients what it is that they were doing that was effective in alleviating the problems. Plans can then be developed to help clients do more of these behaviors.

De Shazer and his team found that there are clients who, when asked the exception question, are unable to identify any times when they were less beset by their problems. So problem-focused are these clients that they seem completely unaware of anything they are doing or have done in the past that has succeeded at all in alleviating their problems. For these clients, de Shazer devised the "miracle question": "Suppose one night while you were asleep, a miracle happened and your problem was resolved. The next day, how could you tell that your problem was gone? What would you be doing differently?" For the problem-focused client, the miracle question serves the same function as the exception question. It allows them to focus on behaviors that serve to resolve the presenting problem.

Supervision of solution-focused therapy is itself solution-focused. Frank Thomas (1994) has characterized it as "the coaxing of expertise." It is the supervisee who sets the agenda for supervision in this approach, who defines on an ongoing basis what the focus of the supervisory encounter will be.

Supervisees who are new to the solution-focused perspective are likely to define the supervisory agenda in terms of clinical "impasses" or "problems." The supervisor's response to such a definition is informed by her solution-focused assumption that the supervisee is already doing things that represent a solution to the so-called "clinical problem." Thus, the supervisor asks exception questions to help the supervisee focus on and amplify these unidentified solutions. Thomas (1994, p. 14) provides the following sample dialogue between a supervisor and supervisee.

CONSULTANT: When in the session does [the client's] experience change?
THERAPIST: When I keep her on task and hold her to the topic.
CONSULTANT: How do you do that?
THERAPIST: I interrupt her.
CONSULTANT: Could you do more of that?

When this supervisory tack fails to help the supervisee identify exception behaviors, the supervisor is likely to have recourse to the miracle question. As with clients, it is assumed that the supervisee's imagining of a miraculous disappearance of his "clinical impasse" will serve to attenuate his problem focus and empower him to focus on solution behaviors.

Perhaps the greatest obstacle to learning solution-focused therapy is overcoming the preoccupation with problems that dominates the mental health field. By doing a supervision that is informed by the assumptions of the solution-focused approach, the solution-focused trainer provides the supervisee with a firsthand experience of the utility and efficiency of looking beyond problems to solutions. In the end, it is this experience that transforms the supervisee into a solution-focused therapist.

The promise of the solution-focused model is seductive in that it is short term and focuses only on the positive things that work. It offers an optimism that is fine if used to provide an opening to something else. It could, however, be naive and misleading when it becomes the major event. The core concepts of the model—the miracle question and the exception question—are not unique; they are elements in the public domain of psychotherapy, but in this model they have been raised to a high art. Whether they are sufficient to form the basis of a therapeutic model is questionable. This explains the current debate (Journal of systems and strategic therapy, 1994 Nov.) among its own members regarding the need to go beyond the model's defined scope. If it is expanded, it might lose the particular features that the model has promoted. If it is not, its limitations will challenge its therapists to find other solutions. The same is true of its training model. Some therapists, who are already trained in a generic model and wish for something more focused, may benefit from its clear direction. Novice therapists, however, may become too centered on technical procedures at too early a stage and thereby hinder their overall development.

Again, like the MRI brief model from which it has derived, the solution-focused model leads family therapy away from its distinctive focus on family organization and interactive process, to focus on a cognitive process that is more individually based.

The Conceptual Explorations of the Milan Associates

Since its inception, the Milan team has gone through several stages of transformation. It began as a foursome, consisting of Mara Selvini Palazzoli, Luigi Boscolo, Gianfranco Cecchin, and Guiliana Prata. Between 1979 and 1980, the team of four began to split. Boscolo and Cecchin took up teaching and training, while Palazzoli and Prata continued with their research focus and founded the New Center for Family Studies.

It was the original team of four that devised the interview format that has remained the hallmark of Milan therapy in all of its various incarnations. In order to control the therapist's intrusiveness, they created the therapeutic team, a group of colleagues observing behind the one-way mirror, who became an integral part of the therapy. They also modified the language of therapeutic intervention, replacing directives and statements with inquiry and circular questioning, and formulated the now-famous guidelines of hypothesizing, circularity, and neutrality.

The observing team and the guidelines reflect the Milan preoccupation with *thinking*. For the first Milan team, successful intervention required that the therapist formulate a comprehensive, nuanced, systemic understanding of what was happening within the family. The guidelines were devised to restrain the therapist from behaving in ways that might short-circuit the formulation of such an understanding. The interviewing therapist's awareness of his colleagues behind the one-way mirror also served a restraining function, while the observing team's orgy of hypothesizing behind the mirror served to increase exponentially the amount of cogitation that could go into each case.

Sessions were held monthly, and at the end of each session, the therapist presented the family with a message conveying in positive terms the team's understanding of what was happening in the family. The goal of these maneuvers was to activate a process of change in family members when they were on their own, away from the therapy room.

The privileging of epistemology over praxis that characterized Bateson's writing was revisited by the Milan team and explains both their success and their limitations. In Milan practice, the therapist's intervening is more related to her way of thinking than to the family's characteristics or needs; therefore, their therapy is that of a universal family.

Paradoxically, with all the emphasis on the therapist's ways of asking questions, delivering prescriptions, being neutral, curious, or hypothesizing, the therapist as a full human entity seems strangely empty. The therapist should know the correct way of delivering the correct intervention, but who is the therapist? It seems that the creation of a team has diffused the boundaries of the individual therapist, whose identity becomes confused.

Since their adoption of a second-order epistemology, Boscolo and Cecchin no longer accept the notion of a "correct" understanding of what is happening in a family, no matter how systemic the understanding might be. Rather than decreasing their focus on thinking, however, this epistemological turn has actually reinforced it. Cecchin now advocates that therapist and team engage in "curious" hypothesizing about families as a means of keeping aware that any and all hypotheses are nothing more than socially derived constructions.

As the observing team is an integral component of Milan therapy, it is, with an interesting variation, also the key element in Milan supervision. For purposes of training, students of Boscolo and Cecchin are divided into two teams. The first team functions as the observing team for the therapist, also a student, who interviews the family. The second team observes both the interactions occurring in the therapy room and the interactions within the observing team. No interaction occurs between the two teams; their separation is intended to demonstrate the "different levels of analysis of interactive systems" (Pirotta & Cecchin, 1988, p. 53). The presence of a team observing the team that is observing the therapist serves to instill in supervisees the principle that the system that needs to be observed during a therapy session is not just the family system but the therapeutic system as well. By participating over time in both teams, and by functioning as the interviewing therapist as well, supervisees cultivate the intellectual habit of entertaining multiple perspectives that is the hallmark of the thinking of the Milan therapist.

The Milan associates have continued to evolve, replacing one theory with another. However, the first Milan team remains the most influential in that they have provided an alternative to the American interventionist approach. They also paved the way for constructivism by establishing a more restrained position in family therapy.

Michael White's Concept of Externalization

In some ways, the work of Michael White is similar to that of Steve de Shazer. Both are interested in getting clients to explore and expand times when they are free from their problems. While de Shazer prefers to bypass discussion of problems in order to focus on solutions, however, White believes that people feel oppressed by their problems and that before a client's latent resources can be activated, it is necessary to separate the problem from the client and help the client see it as a separate entity.

White sees people entering therapy with problem-focused, problem-saturated stories about themselves, stories in which clients are controlled by their problems. Externalizing begins as the therapist asks clients to explain how it is that they have managed not to be even more dominated by their problems. A new story now emerges, depicting clients as having resources to battle against the externalized villain into which the problem has been transformed.

White's therapy is all about this process of "re-storying," by which clients abandon the dominant, problem-saturated stories about themselves with which they enter therapy and adopt instead alternative empowering stories that had been marginalized by the problem-focused story. Thus, White's therapy is a therapy of narrative, meaning, and language. The only interventive tool he uses is language. In an effort to use language in a way that guides clients toward re-storying, White has devised an extensive catalogue of therapeutic questions: Questions that elicit description of the effects that problems have had on clients, questions that elicit description of "unique outcomes" (what de Shazer calls "exceptions"), "landscape-of-action" questions, "landscape-of-consciousness" questions, "experience-of-experience" questions. Each question is neutral, tentative, and hypothetical. Nonetheless, the overall process of the interview leads inexorably to a challenge of the dominant story.

Supervision in White's narrative therapy has its technical goal as helping the supervisee to learn the process of interviewing just described. Supervisees are asked to copy the therapeutic model provided by the supervisor. White expects this to be a "copying that originates," and so he asks supervisees to identify what it is that they are originating in their attempts to copy. Observation of supervisees' live or videotaped sessions is seen as providing an excellent opportunity to identify that which is unique in each supervisee's rendition of the general narrative model.

Perhaps more important than its technical goal is the opportunity supervision provides for the supervisee to experience firsthand the partial nature of any story. Thus, part of supervision involves interviews with the supervisor, who endeavors to elicit the supervisee's story about herself, her history, her professional career, her work. Through a process of questioning identical to that of therapy, the supervisor leads the supervisee to a "re-authoring" of her autobiography in a way that is richer than the original story. Thus, the supervisee is able to participate directly and personally in a process of re-storying.

Probably the most profound thinker among the pioneers in the constructionist movement, White is infatuated with language and story. Picking up from where the Milan team left off, White has made the most of "question-technique." From that point of view, White is not restrained among the group of restrained therapists. His rapid-fire questioning during therapy puts him in the position of a "director" who is absolutely central.

In externalizing the symptom, White anthropomorphizes it and makes it visible to the symptom bearers so that they can fight it. This is an altogether innovative and very useful therapeutic tool. When White begins to blame the symptoms on "cultural colonization" or social discourse, however, he is at risk of dissolving the enemy that he made visible back into an abstraction and missing the area of interpersonal relationship that makes psychotherapy unique.

THE LINGUISTIC SYSTEMS OF GALVESTON

Like Michael White, Harlene Anderson and the late Harold Goolishian of the Galveston Family Institute developed an approach to therapy that also resolutely focused on language and meaning. Their approach, however, aspires to be less instrumental and more client-focused than White's.

The Galveston system endorses the old MRI premise that a problem is not a problem until people define it to be so. In Anderson and Goolishian's terms, problems exist only in language. Just as problems are consensually defined into existence, they are also consensually defined out of existence. The goal of therapy, from the Galveston perspective, is to bring together the people who have defined the problem into being ("the problem-organizing system"), and to keep them in a well-run conversation, one in which meanings constantly evolve and change. If the problem-organizing conversation is well run, the problem will inevitably be defined out of existence (in Anderson and Goolishian's language, it will "dis-solve"). The movement toward inevitable dissolution of the problem will bog down only if the problem-organizing conversation becomes polarized—that is, if participants become committed to their own particular meanings and invested in making the other participants see the correctness of their meanings.

The task of therapy, in this view, is to endeavor to ensure that the problem-organizing conversation remains well run. Toward this end, the therapist joins the problem-organizing system as the participant manager of the conversation. In an effort to keep the conversation fluid, the therapist shows respect for and takes seriously any position stated, "no matter how astonishing, trivial, or peculiar" (Anderson & Goolishian, 1988, p. 382). The therapist accords plausibility to all ideas voiced in the conversation, even if they contradict each other. He is "slow to understand" any ideas that are presented, asking questions that invite participants to elaborate their ideas. Thus, the therapist tries always to ask questions to which the answers require new questions.

Managing a problem-organizing conversation in this way is not a matter of using specific techniques. (It is Anderson and Goolishian's aversion to techniques that distinguishes their therapy from the equally language-focused therapy of Michael White, which does employ techniques, such as externalization.) What is required to manage a therapeutic conversation this way is a set of *attitudes,* chief among these being an attitude of *not-knowing*. It is this attitude that leads the therapist to accord plausibility to any idea and, at the same time, to consider any idea as needing to be questioned to elicit further elaboration. The attitude of not knowing makes the therapist into a person who "is a respectful listener who does not understand too quickly (if ever)" (Anderson & Goolishian, 1988, p. 382). The not-knowing therapist considers no meaning as self-evident, and is always ready to ask "What do you mean when you say . . . ?"

The task of supervision in the Galveston linguistic systems approach is to help the supervisee cultivate an attitude of not-knowing. A reflective team is used for training, to give a free-form expression about the conversation observed in the session and comment on the meaning team members extract from it.

Among all the schools that privilege language, the Galveston group is perhaps the most "languaging" one. As a practice, it is difficult to understand how their conversation is more therapeutic than a good ordinary conversation. Perhaps this is exactly the point that they are trying to make—therapy is just a good conversation! The way they use a reflective team behind the one-way mirror parallels the unstructured process that they advocate in therapy. Like White's, the Galveston model is basically a cognitive one, minus the kind of elaborated structure that White applies to languaging. Perhaps one needs to understand this group's oversimplified approach in relation to the postmodernism with which the group identifies. Compared with the other, more technically inclined schools in this grouping, Galveston is characterized by a return to basics; empathy and tuning-in to conversation are still the most important elements in the art of healing.

Another Perspective on Therapy: Feminism

Feminist therapy as it exists currently is a philosophy of psychotherapy rather than a particular school. The essence of feminist clinical work lies in the therapists' attitude towards gender and sensitivity to the differential impact that interventions have on men and women. Feminist therapists are accumulating a large body of research and knowledge on disorders of high prevalence in women, such as depression, eating disorders, and the sequelae of interpersonal violence and sexual assault. Treatment focus is generally on empowering clients to change the social, interpersonal, and political environments that have an impact on their relationships with others, rather than helping clients adjust in order to make peace with an oppressive social context (Brown & Brodsky, 1992).

Feminist therapists share with the constructionists an interest in meaning, as they are generally attentive to the belief systems of both males and females and how they developed the role concepts that got them stuck in a particular position. Unlike the constructionists, however, feminist therapists are not afraid of power. On the contrary, many of them see the need to employ power as the only way for women to balance the scale. As a result, they stress solidarity as a way for women to achieve strong influence.

Since feminist therapists vary in their approaches, supervision is also provided in a variety of ways, but always with a common perspective. Marianne Walters, a member of the groundbreaking Women's Project, which included Betty Carter, Peggy Papp, and Olga Silverstein, has described supervision in feminist therapy as "a process of challenging our own assumptions and therapy traditions in order to probe the ways that sex roles and gendered power systems structure family relationships and influence our own thinking about what is happening in the family we see" (Walters, Carter, Papp, & Silverstein, 1988, p. 148). Within this framework, her supervision between therapy sessions is focused on analyzing and critiquing the concepts and assumptions underlying alternative interventions. She stresses the importance of using systemic concepts with reference to the differing meanings that these concepts have for each sex.

The current work of Peggy Papp, with her collaborator Evan Imber-Black (Papp & Imber-Black, 1996), focuses on "multisystemic themes" as a unifying concept in therapy and training. This focus expands their previously articulated interest in gender issues to include the transmission and transformation of family themes. In the training model that they have devised, trainees are asked to explore a significant theme in their family of origin that has affected their own lives, and then to apply the same theme orientation in the analysis of a current case. While retaining a strong feminist orientation, this clinical perspective highlights a sense of family at a time when it seems to be out of fashion in the literature of postmodern therapy.

Though a diverse effort, the feminist therapeutic movement, as exemplified in the work of members of the Women's Project, has opened up new possibilities in the field of family therapy.

While each of the schools of family therapy would like to consider itself as all inclusive, many practitioners consider themselves to be eclectic, taking bits and pieces from various approaches to suit their particular style and the idiosyncrasies of their practice. Therefore, although family therapy has not replaced the individual psychoanalytic approach, as the optimists had predicted thirty years ago, it has evolved into a multibodied practice (like a family itself) that has affected all disciplines of human service.

Most practitioners and trainers today have directed their attention not so much to the development of new theories but to the dissemination of family therapy ideas through the broader mental health delivery system. In doing so, they have enriched the field.

As the different schools and approaches continue to influence one another, ideas that have been considered dated are often revived, while those that are seen as novel are in fact unoriginal. Perhaps in the next decade or so, the need to be original will not be perceived as necessary by the competing schools. The mosaic of family therapy will then be complete.

Chapter 5

The Therapeutic Encounter

Armed with his understanding of families, his knowledge of social norms and family diversity, constrained by his theories of therapy and limited by his own life experiences, the therapist meets a family that is asking for help. The family usually approaches the encounter with hope. In all cases they come with a strong sense that this is an opportunity to make a meaningful statement. They are going to say "We are who we are" in an important way. Because of this sense, and because they are under the observation of this other, they are also under intense self-observation.

The therapist brings his own lifetime of baggage. He too is what he is, and the combination of his character and experience imposes certain limits he cannot transcend. How will he fit with this family? Which of his attributes will this encounter activate?

The therapist has the advantages and disadvantages of training. He has his experiences of previous encounters with other families. Whether he wants to or not, and whether he knows it or not, he carries certain assumptions about families with a profile like this one:

Families with young children need to . . .

Families presenting with psychosomatic illness tend to . . .

Families with incest . . .

Families with adopted children . . .

He understands that holding such assumptions constrains his understanding, but no therapist can transcend the frameworks that organize his thinking. All he can do is recognize them, use them in the best way possible, and know that his expectations must be open to revision according to the data arising from this encounter. While engaging the family, encouraging disclosure, and scanning for problems and possibilities, he associates, tries to fit, probes, modifies assumptions in accordance with the results, and probes again. There is always an intellectual tension between his assumptions about what may be and what he sees in this particular encounter.

The previous chapters have highlighted the concepts that prepare the therapist for the therapeutic encounter. The printed page accommodates concepts easily, but therapy is multidimensional, it is much more than concepts. I wonder how I can communicate the mood of the encounter, the silences that envelop tangential thoughts, the sense of rhythm that alerts me to focus on the emotion that wants to be but cannot be articulated, the mystery of experiencing family members across our differences and finding that we are "more human than otherwise." And then, how do I describe the play, the creative process by which I become audience and participant, leader of the therapy and also a member of the therapeutic system, and the by-ways that family members follow while they experiment with new, better ways of relating?

Four Cases

The teaching of family therapy relies for the most part on observation of families in therapy or videotapes of sessions. In this chapter, I describe what I do and how I think while doing therapy. I will try to deconstruct my practice. For this purpose, I have selected four consultations to use as cases, because consultations carry the tensions of the first encounter.

These four cases embody the search for family patterns, the exploration of avenues for change, and the attempts at joining and challenging. A consultation imposes a demand useful for teaching purposes; the consultant is expected to produce a clear, predictive guide to doing family therapy with this particular family.

THE RAMOS FAMILY: THE TYRANNY OF THE SYMPTOM

I saw the Ramos family in South America. They had been in therapy for five months when I saw them in a two-session consultation.

The therapists said that the family had come because of Mrs. Ramos's severe obsessive compulsive behavior, which completely organized the life of the family. Mrs. Ramos described her life as controlled by *asco* (revulsion). Whenever she touched something dirty, she experienced nausea, palpitations, and sweating until she could wash her hands.

I asked her to show me her hands. They were red and raw from washing. I examined them carefully without touching her.

The children—Sara, eleven; Tomas, thirteen; and Juan, nineteen—and Mr. Ramos listened as Mrs. Ramos described vividly her anxiety attacks when she or someone else in the family touched something dirty.

I expressed surprise when she said that if one of the children or her husband touched their shoes, she could not remain calm until they washed their hands under her supervision. "This is very interesting," I said. "I have seen many people with similar problems. But you are the first I have seen in which anxiety is reduced if family members wash themselves. This is quite interesting," I repeated for emphasis. I then talked with Sara, who told me how her mother asked her to wash and how sometimes she had to wash her hands two to three times before her mother was satisfied. I asked her to stand up and come to me. Without touching her I made a careful observation of both her hands. I explored how each hand and finger felt, repeating frequently, "And this happens to *your* hands."

I went through this procedure with each family member, frequently stating my amazement at the way Mrs. Ramos's revulsion could be calmed by *other* people's washing. Mr. Ramos then said that they couldn't eat eggs any more because they were dirty. I looked baffled. Mrs. Ramos explained to me that it was because of where they came from. I asked what would happen if somebody took the shell off. "Ah," she replied, "then they would be clean."

"Do you buy your chickens without their behinds?" I asked.

"Yes," she replied. "I buy only chicken parts."

My attitude in the first thirty minutes of the interview was one of clinical detachment. I felt I was impersonating some of the great French clinicians of the nineteenth century who could see, smell, hear, and taste an illness. At the same time I was amused by the power of the narrative. How was it possible that the family did not see through the absurdity of my questions? How was it that the symptom expanded to include each and every one of them, so that in the end the entire life of the family was regulated by hand washing?

I asked the children to leave the room and asked the couple about their sexual life. I assumed that sexuality would somehow be dirty and wanted to know how. Mrs. Ramos said that her husband liked to have sex "too much" and that she took pity on him and allowed it every Saturday. He could touch her all over as long as he didn't touch her hands. "My hands are sacred," she said.

We had already spent forty minutes on the consultation, and I was as ignorant about the Ramos family as when we started. Everything had been absorbed in the narration of the symptom.

From some Whitaker memory came a non sequitur: a crazy thought. I asked, "Why don't you trust your husband? Why do you think he lies to you?" It was a long reach, and the result was surprising and satisfactory.

"I frequently dream that I wake up and find him gone." It was as if a faucet had been turned on. She abandoned the symptom and began to describe how critical her husband was—how she tried to please him but whatever she said was wrong, how she cried when he yelled at her, and how the children would come to console her.

I asked her if Sara protected her, and I called Sara back to the room. She described how she felt sorry for her mother and how she would stroke her mother's hair when she cried and kiss her forehead until she was calm. One by one the other two children joined the session to tell similar stories of protecting the mother from the father's criticism. At the same time, they said that their father had never been violent with anybody in the family and that he was very loving.

At this point, the symptom had receded from center stage, and we were in a simple familial drama of children participating in parental conflict. This drama was familiar to me; I have been there many times. I blocked the children, saying that their protection of their mother was not helpful to either of their parents. I encouraged Mrs. Ramos to challenge her husband's lack of understanding. As she did, I supported and amplified her request for fairness.

I asked Mrs. Ramos to tell me about her parents, and which of them was more critical of her. She told me that she had always been considered the least pretty and intelligent of her family. As a child she had always worked harder than her sister to elicit her parents' love, but she had always felt second best.

I finished the session, inviting the spouses to a second consultation in three days. I instructed the husband to find new ways of being supportive of his wife in the meantime. I wanted him to remember earlier times, when he had courted her. He was to buy her a present. I told Mrs. Ramos that she needed to let go of the children's hands so that they could own their own bodies. I asked the children to tell their mother that their hands belonged to *them* and that they would wash them when they thought it was necessary.

As the session finished, I shook everybody's hand. Only after they left did I remember that Mrs. Ramos's hands were sacred and that she didn't touch other people's hands. Both Mrs. Ramos and I had forgotten her symptoms.

What was going on in some vague and complex fashion in my brain circuitry during the session? First, I was impressed by the power of the symptom to control the whole family. I was also amused by the Ramoses' skill—or misfortune—in transforming the meaning of every event into the logic of the narrative around the symptom. At some point I thought that Mrs. Ramos must feel extremely impotent to need all these elaborate forms of control, and almost simultaneously I thought, if she feels so frightened, helpless, defenseless, she and her husband must be living in a context that pushes her to feel and act this way.

I want to make my thinking clear. I didn't think that Mr. Ramos had created his wife's condition. Most probably Mrs. Ramos had brought from her family of origin a propensity to feel wronged. When she married, the conditions for some new forms of relating must have existed, but they hadn't developed. Mr. and Mrs. Ramos were maintaining the old patterns that necessitated her particular response. But instead of a dialogue or a conflict, we had a whole family washing their hands. To induce change, my thinking went, the most promising direction would be to help Mr. Ramos change his relationship to his wife. My non sequitur came at this point: "Why don't you trust your husband? Why do you think he lies to you?" The response to this request for an interpersonal narrative was, I think, predictable.

I was then able to move the session to an exploration of the way the children were recruited into the spouse conflict. After that we were ready for questions about Mrs. Ramos's past and for interventions in the couple's conflict, in which I supported Mrs. Ramos.

At the end of the session, I was feeling excited by the changes and decided to have the next session with the couple alone. I also prepared the stage for a romantic ending and decided to buy a dozen red roses to give to Mr. Ramos for his wife. I didn't have any idea how or even whether I would use these roses.

Three days later the couple returned. Mrs. Ramos had clearly dressed in her Sunday best. She started talking, describing how she had realized that she was damaging the children and had decided to free them from her demands. During these three days, she said, she had at moments felt anxious when she felt they were dirty, but she knew she needed to control herself, and she had.

Her husband said that he had been attentive to her and stopped his criticizing. Mrs. Ramos agreed. As the couple seemed now more emotionally connected, I asked Mrs. Ramos to tell me more about her family, stating that maybe we could discover together the reason for her symptoms. She told of a difficult childhood on her parents' farm. They were poor and had to work hard. She had developed into the child who worked the hardest just to be as good as the rest. The husband joined in, describing how she always needed to please everybody and how she was always available to respond to the needs of her parents and sisters. They talked then about how, when Mrs. Ramos's mother was dying, she spent three weeks nursing her mother day and night. At this point, Mrs. Ramos began to cry and described how her mother would become agitated at night and thrash in her bed. To protect her, she tied her mother's hands, as they had in the hospital. Doing so had been very traumatic for her, she said. She felt guilty for hurting her mother's hands.

Forty minutes into the session, I was called out to get the roses I had ordered. I returned with the flowers and gave them to Mr. Ramos, saying I had bought them for him to give to his wife when he felt loving. He took the flowers and began to give them to her. I stopped him, saying it was for later, when they were alone and in the proper mood. The session finished with a discussion of Cinderella. I suggested to Mrs. Ramos that she had been controlled by her need to work harder just to be accepted. I used the word *fregona* (charwoman) to emphasize my point; maybe, like Cinderella, she could relax and accept her prince.

I really don't know how it happened that the session finished as a fairy tale. Something about this family moved me in simple ways. I felt caught in their drama and in their language. The Ramoses also felt touched. They were grateful, and Mrs. Ramos didn't hesitate to shake my hand. This time both she and I knew that it was a new step, a loosening of the tyranny of the symptom. If I think about the process of change—how such a bizarre symptom began to change in a two-session consultation—I must attribute that to my joining. In my joining with Mrs. Ramos, she felt empowered to make demands. I helped her move from enacting her emotions through the symptom into articulating them in language and in interpersonal challenge.

What were the key elements in this consultation with the Ramos family? The first, I think, was my attention and handling of the symptom. The power of a symptom seems to depend on the unvarying description of the story. It is like children's stories, always told the same way. If in the exploration the therapist expands the story, includes other people, or introduces novelty in any way, the automaticity of the symptom is challenged. Mrs. Ramos's symptom had been strengthened by years of daily repetition, and I felt impelled to explore it in minute detail to give validity to my challenge. (A similar handling of a symptom is presented in Chapter 14.)

From the beginning, I challenged the validity of the story as all-encompassing. My challenges were invisible at first: "I have seen many cases that are similar, but this is the first time I've seen. . . ." When I asked the children to show me their hands, I emphasized they were *their* hands. I explored details: "Are eggs dirty? Is sex clean?" I accompanied my questions with exclamations of amazement that in their repetition challenged the reality of the symptom. These challenges were accompanied with statements of acceptance of the symptom's reality. This is a two-pronged strategy.

Also, I worked with subsystems. I started with the whole family, but when I wanted to challenge the children's intrusion in spouse conflict I asked the children to leave, then asked them to come back when the session again required their participation. In the belief that people construct each other, I concluded that Mrs. Ramos's symptom *had* to be part of the transactions between her and her husband. My question "Why do you think your husband lies?" was triggered by this concept. Once the couple was engaged in the therapy, I encouraged conflict and participated to amplify it, joining with Mrs. Ramos to help her challenge her husband. And since I believe that parents, for the most part, want to help their children, I gave Mrs. Ramos the task of controlling her anxiety for the sake of her children, expecting that she would control her symptom, as she did. The exploration of her history came after we had explored the present and as a way of clarifying the distortions of the present. The second session was dedicated almost entirely to Mrs. Ramos's family of origin.

MARIA AND CORRINE REVISITED

This consultation was technically illegal. As we saw in Chapter 2, Maria's children were in kinship foster care, the legal responsibility of Maria's sister-in-law Corrine, and a restraining order had forbidden the two women to meet. The session was a consultation with a group of supervisors and caseworkers of the Children's Division of the Department of Welfare. They and the children's caseworker were observing from behind the one-way mirror. In the therapy room were Maria and Corrine, both in their twenties, Juana, age six, and Peter, age three, and the women's respective counselors, whose function in the session presumably was to contain aggression.

As the "mothers" sat on a couch, the children proceeded to destroy the toys in my office. Soon there were three decapitated dolls on the floor, and Juana had taken the crayons and was drawing on the coffee table. I observed the mothers, waiting for one of them to control the children as mothers do. Finally I said, "I am confused. I don't know who is the mother, or who is in charge. But I don't want that microphone touched. And I want to talk to both of you, and I can't do that in this racket."

This comment illustrates a very simple but important technique. It has to do with self-restraint when there is family conflict. If I had attempted to control the children and was successful, the results would have been unfortunate. It would have demonstrated to both mothers that they were incompetent. Instead, I gave them the task, and their controlling the children allowed me to observe the resources they brought to parenting.

I waited. Maria went to Peter and talked to him quietly. Corrine bribed Juana with the promise of a trip to McDonald's. I commented on how complementary their styles were and encouraged them to talk with each other, first about the children and then about themselves.

Of course, I could have engaged either one of them in a description of her personal story with the children, while the other listened and observed. But encouraging dialogue between them gave me the advantage of being decentralized; it gave me the freedom to observe the ways in which these women engaged, both the rigidities and the possibilities of alternatives.

It took all my skill to keep them talking, since there was so much bitterness between them. I switched to Spanish, praising their helping each other. I joined with Corrine, complimenting her for her selflessness in taking care of Maria's children, but I also pointed out how her life had been narrowed and how Maria could give her freedom from full-time parenting. I attacked the court, broadly hinting that an Anglo judge could not understand how important it is to Latinos to help each other. I said that the restraining order had prevented the best solution: that they pull together.

Summing up for the staff, I observed that it was natural for the children to be hyperactive in the presence of the two warring mothers. I noted that I had used their behavior to create an enactment of parenting styles and to suggest alternatives that could expand both mothers' lives. Later, the caseworker and I designed a plan to change the court's restraining order.

NINA AND JUAN: HEARING VOICES

Chapter 8 presents a Puerto Rican family composed of Juan, the husband, who was frequently drunk; his wife, Nina, age forty, who had had multiple hospitalizations for multiple diagnoses, and their daughter Juanita, a fifteen-year-old who refused to go to school. They were in therapy with Margaret Meskill, who brought them to my supervisory group for consultation.

I asked Nina to describe her auditory hallucinations. Were her voices male or female? Nina replied hesitatingly that they were female. "What do they tell you?" I asked.

Requesting details about a symptom is part of every psychiatric examination. But my intention here is different from the usual fact-finding. I was using Nina's description of her auditory hallucination as a springboard to transform her individual ownership of the symptom into a more complex web of complementary transactions.

"Your voices can be tamed," I told her. "But they need other voices—voices just as strong—to fight them. Do you hear Juan's voice? Or Juanita's?"

"No, never."

"Ah! Their voices are too soft," I said.

I wondered why Juan's voice was so soft that Nina could not hear him. And why was Juanita's supportive voice inaudible? Then I challenged Juan: "You escape into drinking when your wife needs you." This is an example of one of the most characteristic interventions in family therapy: focusing on the maintenance of the symptom by the other family members.

Throughout the rest of the treatment, Margaret Meskill and I supported Juan's voice, whose strength could challenge his wife's auditory hallucinations. As he changed and became more assertive and responsive to her, their stories changed. Her voices disappeared, and he stopped drinking.

This is a case in which I ignored an individual psychiatric diagnosis of schizophrenia and instead made a diagnosis of hysteric auditory hallucinations in a dysfunctional family context. Using the husband as a cotherapist changed his relationship to his wife, and proved healing to both of them.

"Everybody Fights Everybody Else"

This consultation took place in the outpatient department of a large agency that has a day hospital for children. The family, a divorced mother and her four children, had been in contact with the agency for four and a half years. Harriet, the mother, thirty-eight, had been married twice, both times to physically abusive husbands, and her second husband had been jailed for sexually abusing the children. The family therapist described the family as chaotic. There was a high incidence of violence; fist fights often broke out in the sessions. The therapist dreaded every session, but fortunately the family often broke appointments.

I couldn't elicit any positive comments about this family from the staff, so I decided to speak to a "part" of the family that the staff didn't know. To challenge the staff's emphasis on pathology, I would engage the family around issues of competence and shun areas of aggression. (I assumed, without any data to confirm it, that this family had areas of competence. They could not have survived as a family, if they had been only as the staff described.)

As the session started, the mother said they were coming to therapy "because everybody fights everybody else." As if triggered by this statement, George and Harry began to fight like roosters at a cockfight.

George, age twelve, was much bigger than Harry, age ten. George seemed to me quite controlled, but Richard, sixteen, moved immediately to restrain him and held him forcefully, even though George didn't resist. Suzanne, nineteen, seated near Richard, was in a state of alertness, ready to help him. The mother sat tense in her chair, looking helplessly at the chaotic scene. The whole transaction lasted no more than two minutes; the participants were well rehearsed.

This was clearly the culture of therapy, jelled in previous encounters. Such fights were the family signature, performed to prove to the therapist how impossible they were. I didn't bite. I waited for a pause, then I took a colored pen from my pocket and told Richard that since it was clear he was a helper, I wondered if he could use my magic pen to draw a family that could work better. He remained silent, and fortunately, so did the other family members, who seemed intrigued by my unusual request. After a minute or two, he said, "I would like everybody in the family not to fight, so that my mother won't suffer." Impressed, I asked him what grade he was in. He said he was a senior, had good grades, and wanted to study to become a policeman. He added that for the last two years he had worked at McDonald's after school.

I asked him to pass the pen to his sister. The passing of the pen, as if by ritual magic, got the attention of the other family members, who became audience. This technique is useful in families in which the noise is the content of family transactions. If necessary, the therapist can direct the flow of conversation by insisting that only the family member who holds the pen can talk.

Suzanne told me that after finishing high school she had started working for McDonald's. For the last year she had been a supervisor. She gave her mother a large portion of her salary. I asked her about her responsibilities at work and asked if her mother praised her for being so responsible. She said no. I stood in amazement, then I shook the mother's hand, congratulating her warmly for her competence in having raised children who were so responsible and loyal. This is an intervention suggested by Jay Haley. Congratulating parents on the success of the children (or vice versa) is a systemic intervention that clearly highlights complementarity among family members, emphasizing positive connection.

Fifteen minutes into the session I had engaged each of the family members and observed aggression and attempts at control, which I ignored. I had confirmed the strength of the two older children and the mother. And I had confirmed that the themes of loyalty and of protecting the mother and each other were important and admirable areas, not fully explored.

I now asked George and Harry to stand next to each other. When working with young children, the language of therapy should be the language of action. I often have children stand near each other to see who is taller, who smiles wider, and so on, to help them feel that they are participants. I asked Harry how it was that he provoked George, when he was so much smaller. Suzanne said that George could be very destructive and that he would break Harry's arms and legs unless she intervened. The sequence of violence in the home, which the family was now describing rather amiably, was that Harry provoked George, George stalked Harry, Richard would restrain George, and Suzanne would restrain Richard. It seemed clear to me that this family of abused people had developed a hyperalertness to signals of aggression and a system of immediate responses to squelch the aggression before it became destructive, as it had before.

I asked the mother, Richard, and Suzanne if they could let George and Harry fight without interference. Unanimously they responded that George would kill Harry. I asked George if he could convince his family that he was neither crazy nor criminal. I was thus creating a context in which the family members would interact in my presence and I could observe the usual family patterns and probe for alternatives.

George begged his mother to let him demonstrate that he could control himself, but the mother, Suzanne, and Richard took turns bringing up images of previous destruction and describing scenarios of future horrors. Finally the mother agreed that for two days she would not interfere in George's fights with Harry. Suzanne said she would be watching, but the mother, in what was clearly a new posture, said that this was her decision and Suzanne should butt out.

So there had been a series of changes here. First, I supported George. George, in an unusual but clearly attractive position, asked the family to cooperate as he experimented with self-control. The mother responded in support of his change. Suzanne challenged her mother by reverting to accustomed patterns of control, but the mother changed the family's hierarchical arrangement by assuming responsibility.

The family left surprised that the therapist hadn't seen—or had been conned into not seeing—how destructive they were. But each of the family members was touched, and they enjoyed my confirmation of them as unique, competent, loyal, and loving.

The agency staff didn't understand the transformation of the family into a cooperative group. They promised to observe the next session with the family therapist, who felt very upbeat.

After the session we explored how the staff had focused exclusively on the family's deficits. We also discussed the ways in which the services offered to this family were inefficient, repetitive, and fragmented. The family therapist, the individual therapist, and the staff of the day hospital belonged to different teams and worked with different segments of this family. They had seen no need for integration. Follow-up discussion with the staff six months later indicated that this has been a critical session for the staff, and that the family had continued to show remarkable changes.

Creating the Therapeutic System

I suppose that if one were to attempt a thumbnail description of my work, one would say that what I do is to amplify differences, to the point where the habitual becomes uncomfortable and sometimes impossible. Doing so takes direct self-engagement, and it is a process of challenging family patterns while frequently supporting the individuals caught in them.

In my forty years as a family therapist, I have discovered what many people have discovered before: People prefer not to change. They feel comfortable with the security of the predictable, so they will continue to choose their preferred ways of responding. They have to be pushed to choose responses beyond the established range of the permissible. I therefore almost always work by challenging the customary. But I know that my challenge itself is not very powerful, so what I do is to create an instability among family members that energizes them, forcing them to find new ways to respond. I can then work with this energy, throwing my weight on the side of movement. Families present such beautiful, static pictures. I am the one whose fingers are itching to draw a mustache.

Unlike constructionists, I do not work with individual family members to explore and understand their possibilities for alternative ways of being. I work with changing the family. When I relate to the individual family members, I am frequently joining with them and bolstering self-esteem. In the case of Nina and Juan, I said to Nina, "You are such a together lady; how is it you wind up in the hospital?" and intervened to locate pathology not in her but in her family context.

Continuing my attempt to extract from my idiosyncratic style of therapy some universals that may be useful to other therapists, I have drawn up some guidelines to ways of seeing families and the process of family transformation. I have organized them as a checklist, hoping that it will be read, as the guidelines are intended, as useful simplification.

CONCEPTS ABOUT FAMILIES

1. Families are conservative, constraining social systems that organize their members toward certain predictable functioning with each other. Therefore the alternative ways of relating that

every family member has are marginalized by the family's preferred ways.

2. As families evolve, they move through critical periods in which the demands of new circumstances require change in family members' ways of thinking, feeling, or relating. The birth of a child, aging, childrearing, children's leaving the family, change or loss of job are examples of transitions that contain both danger and opportunity. It is at these junctures that families grow (become more complex) or get stuck (become impoverished). Symptoms in a family member may reflect the ensuing stress.
3. The self is always whole, and at the same time it is always a part of and constrained by the web of family relationships. One can acknowledge a family member's symptom and point out how the control is in the hands of somebody else, in the "ways" of family structure and function.
4. Family members develop ways of negotiating conflict that allow for predictability of interaction but also handicap exploration of novelty.
5. Diagnosis can be seen as being within but also outside of an individual and as occurring in the interactions between family members.
6. Diagnosis of a family, "knowing" the family ways, includes both the visible family organization and functioning and the invisible repertoire of possible transactions suppressed by the family members' reductionist accommodation to life circumstances.
7. While the therapist has ideas and biases about family norms, and about the best family fit, she can only go in the direction that the family indicates when they enact their drama and show possible alternatives.

Transformation in Families

1. Family members present themselves around the symptom and the family definition of the symptom bearer. The therapist's early joining and challenging of the family revolves around the detailed exploration, expansion, and questioning of this definition.
2. Change in family patterns requires the utilization by family members of alternative ways of being and relating that are available only in certain conditions.
3. The therapist is the catalyst of change. As she joins the therapeutic system, she introduces changes in the usual dysfunctional (read "narrow") pattern of family relating.

4. To know where to focus the change process, the therapist needs to observe the drama of the ordinary in the family. She needs to bring the family kitchen into her office; that is what enactment means.
5. The therapist then explores the potential for change by locating areas of conflict and increasing the intensity of conflict beyond the family's usual threshold. The intensity makes the usual transactions difficult or impossible and opens the family members to the exploration—sometimes timid—of new ways of being.
6. In order to respond differentially to the needs of the members of the therapeutic system, the therapist must access different aspects of herself. She must therefore be self-reflective, self-knowing, and comfortable with the manipulation of self on behalf of the family's healing.
7. To encourage and access novelty, the therapist selects a cotherapist from among the family members. This joining with a cotherapist is temporary; one person may be cotherapist over several sessions, but it is also possible to change cotherapists two or three times in one session. All family members should feel recruited into this process at one time or another.
8. Working with agencies that provide services to families, the therapist should consider them part of the family context. She should expand her interventions in the direction of creating organizational changes that are family-friendly.

Any list is arbitrary. Other aspects of my work are also characteristic: my particular techniques of joining, for example, or the ways in which I "stroke and kick" at the same time. Rereading the other vignettes in the cases here and elsewhere in the book should lead to a more complex understanding of these points.

Still other aspects of my thinking and work don't fit the format of a list at all. I need to present them in greater detail. What follows is a discussion of the official story, family memory, and working with enactment.

THE OFFICIAL STORY

Families come to therapy with an official patient and a well-rehearsed presentation of self to strangers. This is the official story; it has been thoroughly organized. One must respect it, but one also needs to know that it is simplistic. Where no alternatives are seen, where no tangents are described, the human richness of a family is being artificially constrained.

Automatically, one can postulate subplots. There must be other stories, like those tantalizing bits of the plot of rich nineteenth-century novels, seemingly random, which turn out to be important in the end. These subplots will appear in the different accounts of various family members, as well as in their actual behavior. The therapist listens to the official story, because it is central to the family concerns. But as she joins and questions, she should be curious about different perspectives. As she tracks the themes the family members present, it is important that she encourage them to talk to each other about them. If she is alert and curious, the official story very soon expands and shows unexpected subplots.

Family stories are told on two levels. They are narrative, and they are drama. The narrative (or narratives) are organized in time. They are linear and coherent. Plot, characters, and conclusions unfold in orderly sequence, and family members play their parts as characters in the story or as storytellers involved in the telling. But the storytelling is always interrupted by something. There is some dissonance. One family member has a different story, or is strangely silent, or is markedly intrusive. This is noise that doesn't fit the script. As the therapist tracks the dissonance, she may amplify it, until its emotional impact becomes apparent. Dormant or unexpressed conflict becomes visible, and its relationship to other elements of the family drama begins to appear.

Individual ownership of the problem is thus shifted to relational patterns. The problem is moved from *inside* individual family members to the transactions *among* family members. When it is seen in this alternative view, the fixed reality of family stories can be questioned. The family members' conviction of autonomous selves is challenged by the therapist's view of selves constrained and constructed by others. For example, if the family story is "Jean is anorectic," the therapist may ask, "Jean, let me ask you an absurd question. How do you think your parents encourage you not to eat? When you don't eat, what do your parents do? Sam, do you think your wife helps Jean eat normally? Diane, how does Sam respond to Jean's eating habits?"

Here the explanation is about how Jean's parents' transactions around her eating invite her not to eat. The goal is to move Jean's eating to the sphere of her relationship with her parents, encouraging an exploration and expression of the interpersonal conflict between parents and child that will move the focus from eating to autonomy. But the therapist could also move the focus to Jean's control over her parents: the mother's story of Jean's demanding that she count calories, the father's story of the way Jean's eating habits organize his dinner, the spouses' stories about their conflicts over the right way to respond to their daughter, or the intensity of their fear that she will starve herself to death.

At this point, the original story of Jean is no longer her story. The therapist has created tension by highlighting the conflicting dramas. As the people in the stories take center stage, issues of how some family members are imprisoned by the others create opportunities for change. So what we have are multiple readings. The goal of the shift in perspective is to encourage exploration of differences and put family members in positions of being potential healers of each other. This concept is different from that of re-storying, in which the exploration is cognitive and the story is from an individual family member. Putting storytellers in dialogues that amplify conflicting stories brings out the controls that family members have on each other and allows them to focus on alternatives.

FAMILY MEMORY

Structural therapists—and interventionist family therapists in general—have given such prominence to our participation in the therapeutic process that we have tended to overlook family history, probably in reaction to the psychodynamic approaches, which overemphasized the past, as though childhood were destiny. We assumed that what is relevant in the past is in the present, salient in today's encounter.

But in clinical practice, a focus on family history often appears in the middle phase of therapy, when any relevant segment of a family's history tends to be uncovered. By now the family and therapist have joined in ways that let them trust each other. Now the history of the parents, their parents, and the extended family becomes a source of curiosity and hypothesis building about the relevance of past events to the present way of relating and to the thinking of family members. Family and therapist explore the constraints that previous experiences impose on present meanings and patterns. Fresh perspectives may come from understanding how old models of relationship carried from childhood are being reenacted anachronistically in current transactions. Today's selves are seen as lashed to old meanings.

For example, John had been promised a dog for his eighth birthday. His father took him to a pet shop where he selected a lovely mongrel puppy. But his father insisted on buying a pedigreed show breed. When discussing the incident in therapy, the father described how his behavior was a carryover of his family of origin's devotion to "the best." This schema, learned in a previous context, constrained him from being responsive to his son's clearly expressed wishes.

In another case, Jim invariably became annoyed whenever his wife felt tired or confused. Questioned by the therapist, Jim realized that he experienced his wife's behavior as a demand to do something. Jim's angry response came to be seen as a carryover of his experience as the parentified, responsible child in his family of origin.

In the process of gathering history, the therapist makes a point of exploring areas of family strength, periods in their past when paths were different. Was their interpersonal repertoire richer, before their problems narrowed their view of themselves and the world? During this phase the therapist may describe the demands he experiences the family members making on him, as a means of helping them identify their ghosts and explore their relevant past. He may share experiences from his own life and past that appear germane to the family's struggles.

WORKING WITH ENACTMENT

In structural therapists' earliest analyses of family therapy skills, enactment was considered a technique. George Simon (1995) has suggested that enactment is more basic than that; it is the essence of structural family therapy.

With very few exceptions, such as the family sculpting of Virginia Satir and Peggy Papp and some of the experiential involvements of Carl Whitaker, therapy relies on speech. The games people play are reduced to the stories they tell. This focus, carried over from individual psychodynamic therapy, dominates family therapy today. It is assumed that some form of cognitive rearrangement will occur during or after the session and that cognitive rearrangement will produce transformation.

This hypothesis is not borne out by results. The lure of the familiar and predictable will almost always outweigh the enticements of the new. We need to touch families at the emotional level and at the level of relationships. The route for these interventions is enactment, bringing the family into action in the therapist's presence. The next step is some form of "I would like to see you behaving in ways that are different from the habitual," which sets up the conditions for observing underutilized resources. In general the therapist creates the context for enactment, but families often engage spontaneously in interactions that, by the magic of bracketing, the therapist can transform into enactment.

For example, a supervisee presented a tape of the case of a thirty-five-year-old single mother, a nurse working in a supervisory position in a nearby hospital. She had three children, including a boy aged seven. The mother had come to the agency seeking to place the seven-year-old, who was disruptive. He had poked a paper clip into an electric socket in school, saying that he wanted to die. The school psychiatrist and the department of welfare were all involved. The child was intelligent and observant. The therapist began to talk with him. She asked him if he remembered when his stepfather hit his mother and how he felt about it. The boy began to talk about how afraid he was for his mother. While the therapist was engaging the boy in the description of these events, the mother, who had been aloof and withdrawn, interrupted the therapist to amplify some points. The child and his mother began to talk. The therapist moved her chair back. She had created a situation in which a rejecting mother and a frightened child were engaging in a concerned conversation, and there was a change of feeling tone.

Now there were two stories. One told of a rejecting mother who wanted to place her child in foster care. The other told of a mother and child remembering a frightening event together. The first one had led to the prospect of dismembering the family. But the therapist bracketed the second story, how the young child felt the need to protect his mother. The story of connection indicated new directions.

I hope I have conveyed something of the way I do therapy today. Now, how do I teach it? This is done very largely through supervision. Academic instruction has a place in teaching family therapy, especially in the opening phases of that process, but training aims at producing a therapist other than an academic family scientist. The trainee's acquisition of new ways of seeing and thinking depends on his development of new ways of being in the therapeutic context. Therefore, the fundamental concepts, values, assumptions, and techniques of structural family therapy cannot be communicated primarily in a cognitive fashion. A trainee whose knowledge of these concepts is acquired solely in the context of didactic, cognitive presentations may find that his reliance on ideas doesn't serve him well in the heat and intensity of the therapeutic encounter.

Similarly, although describing techniques is important in training, the process of creating a therapist goes way beyond that. In *Families and Family Therapy* (Minuchin, 1974) I described therapy in such a clear and simple way that the book became a standard text for students of family therapy. For decades, many students of structural family therapy performed a therapy of techniques. But clearly, therapy involves a great deal more than techniques. The stories of supervision in Part II bring out not only the complexity of therapy but the very complex process by which a journeyman therapist becomes an expert.

PART II

Stories of Supervision

Chapter 6

Supervision of the Therapeutic Encounter

In the chapters to follow, nine therapists relate their experiences in my supervisory group. In addition to the stories of the supervision itself, I asked each author to begin with a personal biographical statement that would illuminate for the reader the values, biases, and constraints that he or she brought to the therapeutic encounter and how they affected both the supervisee's preferred therapeutic style and my work to expand that style. Because my voice is heard throughout their stories in my comments and interactions, it seems appropriate for me to offer a brief personal statement as background to my role in the development of these therapists.

Journey of a Supervisor

Who am I, as a supervisor? I come from a large family. My paternal grandfather, who married three times, had nine children. My mother was one of seven. Both my parents had been taught a strong sense of family responsibility, and I learned it from them. My mother made a point of buying groceries at my Uncle Samuel's store even though it was poorly stocked and some distance away. During the summer, my rich cousins from my father's family in Buenos Aires came to spend vacations at our home in the sticks. My mother brought a distant relative from Russia, who lived with us for five or six years until she married. During the Depression, when we were very poor, my parents regularly sent my mother's elderly father money that we needed for food.

We took it for granted that obligations were mutual. There was no high school in my hometown, with its population of 4,000, so when I finished elementary school I was sent to live with my Aunt Sofia. My father went bankrupt in 1930 and spent the next two years as a gaucho. My Uncle Elias helped him financially, and both of them regarded this assistance as a matter of course. When my parents—by then living in Israel—began to age, I took it for granted that it was my job to take care of them, as they had taken care of me as a child. I cannot vouch for the details of my memories, but I know that what I learned about relationships in my childhood had to do with loyalty, responsibility, and commitment toward the family, the clan, and by extension the Jewish people.

I have started this discussion of supervision by defining myself by my childhood learning because my relationship with my students has been colored by the sense of obligation and commitment I learned as a child. If one thinks about the values one holds most dear as a teacher, one will probably discover that these values are rooted in one's childhood.

I began supervising and teaching in 1952, when I was living in Israel. I was the medical director of five residential institutions for disturbed adolescents. Most of the children were survivors of Hitler's Europe, but there were also children from Morocco, Yemen, Iraq, and India. The staff of the institutions were psychoeducators who followed Adlerian principles modified by their substantial experience in group living, and they knew far more than I did about working with these youngsters.

I was a young psychiatrist, and my training at a residential institution for delinquent adolescents, located near New York City, hardly prepared me for this population or this work. I was naive and ignorant, and I knew it. Yet what I remember best from this experience was my stubborn refusal to be crippled by what I didn't know. As a person, a therapist, and a teacher, this has always been one of my characteristics: I transform obstacles into a challenge to learn. My response to obstacles is in phases. First I get competitive—energized by the problems. Next I get impatient, then depressed, and finally thoughtful. Once I am engaged, the challenge is primary, and obstacles feel like provocation. The underpinning is emotional, but there is also an intellectual response to the adventure of learning.

The years that followed my Israeli experience were restless and productive. I trained as an analyst at the William Alanson White Institute in New York, but basically I was more interested in families. When I moved to the University of Pennsylvania, as professor of child psychiatry and director of the Philadelphia Child Guidance Clinic, I created an institution that worked only with families and with principles of family therapy. Here my persona as a challenger came to the fore. I was a jumper of fences, challenging the rigidities of the psychiatric establishment. Perhaps we created new rigidities in the process, but the challenge to individual treatment and traditional methods was surely appropriate to the times.

It was in the 1960s at the Philadelphia Child Guidance Clinic that I first became a teacher and supervisor of family therapy. Looking back, I am impressed by the discrepancy between my style of therapy and my style of teaching at that time. My therapeutic style was an ensemble of support, confirmation, and challenge. I was careful to join with families, to assimilate their style, and to stay within their acceptable range when challenging. I did not feel that teaching required the same accommodation. I was confrontative and provocative, challenging students to learn. Perhaps I projected my own response to challenge—and my own process for meeting it—onto my students.

My development as a family therapist provided both the building blocks for teaching others and some skills that got in the way. In my therapy, I developed a knack for reading nonverbal communications with great speed and could jump from minimal clues to hypotheses that guided the therapeutic process. I became comfortable with the knowledge that these hypotheses were just instruments for creating experimental contexts, trial balloons that helped make contact with families and that challenged family rigidities by introducing multiple perspectives. I moved by joining and then "stroking and kicking," and during that period the pyrotechnics of such sessions became known as my style of doing therapy.

I transferred that style to my supervision. I would watch videotapes, microanalyze segments, and jump to hypothesis building, excited by the intellectual nature of the enterprise, the way the pieces of the puzzle could be organized into a large framework, and the potential adventure of joining with the family in exploring newness and creating a different gestalt. I think my enthusiasm was catching, but I was impatient with the slowness of other routes through which my students could reach similar or different understandings, and I think this period was difficult for the people I supervised. I did not give them enough space or respect the idiosyncratic talent and difficulties that they brought to the supervisory process.

As I look back on that period and compare it with my current approach, I also see that I emphasized different aspects of supervision. Perhaps influenced by Jay Haley's almost allergic avoidance of instructing from theory, my own teaching was basically inductive and experiential—an emphasis I now consider important but incomplete. I also see as naive the effort of Braulio Montalvo and myself to teach an "alphabet of skills," including how to join, create intensity, enter alliances and coalitions, challenge, create enactments, and so on. Once students had developed these skills, we thought, they would be able to use them in a differentiated, idiosyncratic way. The skills are important, but the alphabet was too mechanical and was probably responsible for the misconceptions that haunted structural family therapy for decades: that structural family therapy required the ability to move people to different chairs, to direct and control, and that it did not deal with people's history and had no place for playfulness or imagination.

Whatever the mistakes and rigidities of my earlier teaching, however, I always felt that the person of the therapist was a therapeutic instrument. Just as families are underfunctioning social systems, so too are therapists. And slowly my supervision changed. My teaching of the alphabet of skills almost disappeared; instead, I worked to enhance the functioning of a therapist as a member of a system. I still think that there needs to be knowledge of bedrock skills, but I now work with students only after they feel that they have enough of a foundation to have developed their own style of therapy.

When I left the Child Guidance Clinic and moved to New York City, my practice changed. Until then most, if not all, of my client families had presented a child as the identified patient. Now I began to see more and more families with adult patients, including middle-aged people with problems and families concerned with their aging parents. My practice seemed to take notice of the fact that I was aging. My style of therapy changed. My quick responses slowed, and I modified the intensity of my encounters. Today I spend more time listening and creating enactments that I comment on. I make the nature of their transactions visible for family members and show the disparity between the content of the transactions and the messages they are sending concerning their relationships. I use myself more fully in my personal responses to family members. I comment on their effects on me and use those effects as a compass to guide us toward understanding family members' impact on each other and their views of themselves.

Since I have a white beard, look old, and have seen a lot, my statements are treated with the respect due to the wise. I work to counter resulting distortions by using humor and absurdity, a freedom I learned from Carl Whitaker. I am also less inclined to explain. I am more skeptical about truth and feel comfortable in introducing discontinuity, leaving to the family the tasks of resolving their confusion and trying solutions.

Working with Family Therapists

My supervision has also changed; today it is a fluid process. I feel comfortable bringing in my impressions of a play I have just seen, my struggles to understand Foucault, the impact of a poem, the esthetic pleasure of watching Borges' characters take both sides of a divide, or the significance of migration for a Puerto Rican family. The goal is to indicate that therapy is a process in which therapists use themselves fully.

I start supervision by asking that supervisees define their styles. Early in the process we watch videotaped segments of therapeutic sessions and create a tentative profile of the maneuvers that each therapist prefers. We make explicit that the goal of supervision is to increase the complexity of the therapist's interventions. This goal makes supervision a very intimate process, because people's preferential styles are tied in with their history and who they are, and I must respect the boundaries that forbid me to enter and tinker with their lives.

To develop that kind of supervision, the supervisees and I have to develop trust. They have to know that we are working on their behalf. I have to know that they will alert me when I cross boundaries. This process is similar to the contract I make with families in therapy. Since my contract with my supervisees mandates that I challenge their limitations and expand their styles, I must depend on them to delimit my scope.

The Context for Supervision: The Group

The supervisee's own work with families provides the content of teaching. The supervisee brings videotapes for supervision or brings families for live supervision or for consultation. The *context* for teaching structural family therapy is group supervision. Optimally, I have six to nine supervisees in a group.

In a well-constructed training group, it is desirable to have clinicians from widely varying work settings. The presence of people working variously in hospital settings, agencies that provide services to the poor, outpatient mental health clinics, drug and alcohol abuse treatment centers, and private practice provides supervisees with an opportunity to observe families that they will rarely, if ever, see in their own work settings. It also provides an object lesson in the way the work setting organizes a therapist's clinical responses. As a supervisee listens to the thoughts and suggestions of colleagues who are not constrained by the culture and organization of his workplace, he comes to recognize the degree to which his own clinical responses are not, in fact, his own but the product of the interplay of forces that organize his setting. Learning this lesson helps therapists appreciate the impact that larger systems, including the ones of which they themselves are members, have on the families that they treat. In the best-case scenario, it also empowers them to become activists within their work setting, advocating for changes that will allow their client families to be better served.

EXPANDING THE THERAPIST'S STYLE

The supervisory process will be seen in detail in the chapters that follow, as my former supervisees describe the ways they experienced it. It is enough, therefore, to give just a brief introduction to the process here.

The first desired outcome of supervision is that the supervisee begin to produce his or her own version of structural family therapy. This rendition will inevitably be marked by the idiosyncrasies of the supervisee's preferred interpersonal style. It is a fundamental assumption of the structurally oriented supervisor that each supervisee, like the families that are treated, is more complex than is initially apparent. There are underutilized resources in his or her interpersonal repertoire that, if activated, will render the therapist a more complex, more effective instrument.

Here the parallels between therapy and supervision become most pronounced. Where therapy seeks to activate underutilized resources in the family's transactional repertoire, supervision seeks to bring out underutilized alternatives in the supervisee's relational repertoire. The therapist uses his relationship with each family member, along with the family processes that he instigates as leader of the therapeutic system, as the mechanisms to produce family expansion. Similarly, the supervisor uses his relationship with each supervisee, together with the group processes that he instigates as leader of the supervision group, as the mechanisms to elicit therapist expansion.

Thus the development of the relationship between me and each supervisee echoes the development of the relationship between that therapist and family members in therapy. On my side, the relationship is a strategic one. From time to time I assume interpersonal postures toward the supervisee that invite him to expand beyond his preferred style of relating. The supervisee's acceptance of this invitation is contingent upon his acceptance of me as an expert, trustworthy guide in this process of expansion; a supervisor earns this trust by showing respect for the supervisee and by supporting what he already does well. I also join the supervisee at times, adopting an interpersonal style that fits the supervisee's preferred style of relating. In doing so, however, I retain the freedom to challenge the supervisee to expand beyond the familiar. Examples of this process will be seen in the chapters that follow.

The mechanisms for change operative in this kind of supervision are complex, and they are layered. Each member of the supervision group experiences an impulse for expansion when he presents a videotape segment and then becomes a participant in the process that is activated in response to the presentation, particularly when the process challenges the limitations of the supervisee's style.

To a certain extent, the process of expansion I instigate for each individual supervisee is dependent upon the particular contours of the supervisee's preferred style and upon my reading of the avenues for expansion that are available to her. Thus, in some ways every story of supervision is unique. It is also true, however, that certain themes reappear with some regularity in the supervision of family therapy. As varied as the journey toward mastery in structural family therapy may be, it seems that there is certain terrain that is traversed again and again. The following are typical expansions of style that I ask supervisees to make:

- *From Story to Drama.* Therapists are almost invariably good listeners, both by temperament and as a result of training. What therapists listen to is the content, the story told by individual family members. The current popularity of narrative approaches to therapy has reinforced therapists' attentiveness to the details of the stories told by family members.

  Supervision must challenge the therapist to *see* as well as to listen—to see transaction, the behavioral, interpersonal subtext that surrounds and suffuses every family story. The supervisee must be challenged to look beyond the *story* to see how the *storytelling* is organized in the family.
- *From Individual Dynamics to the Complexity of Relationship.* The idea that human behavior is driven from the inside out is a cultural "truth" in our society, one that has been elaborated by various theories of individual psychology. Thus, it is common for therapists to enter supervision with a therapeutic style that focuses on individual dynamics.

  Such therapists need to be challenged to explore complementarity—family members' mutual construction and regulation of each other's behavior. I work to get the supervisee to look beyond the individual to see family patterns.
- *From Therapist-Centered to Family-Centered Therapeutic Process.* Therapy is about healing. If the therapist thinks of himself as the healer, he will construct a therapeutic process in which he is central. Family members will speak to him, and he to them, in a process that establishes the therapist as the switchboard of the therapeutic conversation.

  A structural family therapist is not a healer but rather an activator of the client family's own healing resources. Thus, the therapist seeks to construct a therapeutic process in which interaction among family members, not interaction with her, is central.

For the therapist who privileges a highly active, centralized posture in therapy, supervision must create the capacity to withdraw to a middle distance position. I work to help the therapist to become skilled at eliciting enactment and comfortable with the posture of the curious observer.

The authors of the stories that follow are therapists who have, at various times in the last few years, been members of my supervision group. The stories are highly individual, reflecting each author's unique supervision experience. At the same time, they reveal many of the themes just described. Thus, while each story carries the imprint of its author, it can also be read as a type, illustrating how a structurally oriented supervision might go about the business of producing a therapist.

Interwoven with each of these stories is my own commentary. As the story unfolds, I relate my experience of the supervisee, offer my reading of his or her preferred therapeutic style, and discuss how I used myself strategically to try to induce an expansion of that style. What I hope emerges from these stories is an appreciation of the peculiar dance of co-creation that is supervision.

Chapter 7

The Feminist and the Hierarchical Teacher

Margaret Ann Meskill

During the whole first year, Margaret hid. I had supervised her occasionally in a foster care agency, where she was a social worker. I liked her commitment to her families and her street-wise approach. She was direct, and she was impatient with the bureaucratic procedures of the agency. She also had an energy that I liked. To me it is easier to rein in excess energy than to put fire in a disengaged style. I couldn't understand why she avoided supervision or made comments challenging my teaching.

Sometimes her small challenges coalesced into a narrative that was clearly feminist. I would then address her as the expert and ask her for a feminist perspective. This approach is syntonic with my teaching style of assigning expertise to students, who then become the carriers of alternative points of view, but I couldn't seduce Margaret into joining me.

No matter how frequently I stated that she was a good therapist and that I liked her ability to engage her families, joining them where they were and using a directness that they recognized as respectful, Margaret didn't budge from her perspective that I was the *male. Since she could not defeat me, she avoided me.*

The second year began as a continuation of the unrequited love affair, but then she found the Ramirez family, or they found her, and our relationship changed. We joined forces to help them.

Margaret wanted me to jump through hoops that I am constitutionally unable to accept. I couldn't fake a feminist perspective in family therapy.

MARGARET ANN MESKILL holds a master's degree in social work from New York University. She has provided family therapy in diverse settings such as mental health and substance abuse clinics, a family shelter, and an acute care psychiatric ward. She is currently working toward a doctorate in clinical psychology at the University of Hartford.

While I feel totally supportive of the feminist political and social agenda, I am totally committed to a systemic point of view in family therapy. It is not that he governs her; they construct each other. But I did join Margaret in commitment to the Ramirez family. I liked them, and I liked Margaret's work with them. But they would not, or could not, grow with support alone. When one is working with families with chronic problems, when we, the therapists, number ten or twenty, the arena is populated with ghosts. All the "correct" interpretations have been used, and many more that are destructive have been added. It becomes necessary to introduce novelty. The Ramirez family had been involved with the mental health system for decades. They were experts in neutralizing therapists.

The strategy I suggested was that Margaret join the husband. He had been a good father and a loyal husband, while his wife went through her two to three hospitalizations a year for drugs or schizophrenia-related psychotic episodes.

So Margaret—the helper, the supporter, the fighter for women's rights—had to join with a drunkard husband and a patriarchal supervisor in challenging Mrs. Ramirez's pattern of repeated "psychotic" episodes and multiple hospitalizations. As will be clear in Margaret's narrative, this unbalancing wasn't easy.

I don't know how Margaret felt. I continued teaching her from a position of respect for her talent, liking her spunk. I took her feminist comments to be not a provocation to me but her point of view. We rejoiced with the changes and success of the family.

Until I began considering this article, I hadn't made any connection between my choice for family therapy supervision and my own family dynamics. I always knew that the two professional choices—first the choice of the treatment modality itself and then the choice of supervisor—were tethered to my particular psychological context; I just did not know how. This account is a partial exploration of that question. It is by necessity a work in progress, as I am still unraveling my understanding of the ways supervision impacted me.

I was raised in a shifting and changing context in which family ties were downplayed as secondary to other considerations. There was a great deal of emphasis on autonomy and achievement, on intellect, knowledge, and experience. While young I was most strongly influenced by the matriarchy of grandmother and mother. Men in my family were distant providers who were uninvolved, especially during my youth. Decisions about my sister and me were made by my mother or grandmother, who were often in conflict. They agreed, however, that education is sacred, both an end in itself and the beginning of all professional growth. The value of education was a subplot within the larger story of female achievement and striving, a story in which my sister and I were expected to play a part. Like other daughters of our time, we were to overcome the docile and submissive aspects of being female that our mothers had experienced as so limiting.

I was sent to boarding schools in New England and began summer travels in Mexico and Central America. In keeping with the peculiar way in which my family habitually does things, the summer experiences of Third World poverty were supposed to offset the elitism of boarding schools and leave me marvelously well rounded. Both extremes were seen as related to the adventure of learning. Education was so unquestioningly valued that later my sister and I became very skilled at making our most outrageous requests and provocations acceptable in the eyes of our mother in the name of our need to learn, to grow, and to experience.

By the time I was thirteen, family had become something I checked in on when nothing else was happening. Adventures, new experiences, academic success, and above all independence constituted the expectations that were formative to me. These were always placed in the context of our gender. My sister and I were being raised to be strong in the hope that we would thus be inured to the kinds of hurt that were identified as female. The strength of this solidarity of gender in itself kept my father on the sidelines, a conscientious provider but emotionally suspect.

I studied anthropology in college. This choice was practical rather than intellectual, because it gave me license to travel and call it "field work." By that time I was rebelling against my family and did so in the arena that I had been taught would impact them the most powerfully—school performance. I never finished high school, took off in my second year in college, and went to live a life of adventure in Mexico. My rebellion was well engineered, if totally unconscious. I was defying the family god of learning.

Barnard College in the seventies was a good place for rebellion. Feminism and socialism were peaking in the academic climate of that time. My intellectual consciousness got the wake-up call it needed after five years of the WASP elitism that is so unconsciously and arrogantly promoted in boarding schools. The feminist position that I learned at Barnard was the lens through which I would perceive my world, a kind of basic cognitive set that both oriented and validated me.

A note about my feminism. Feminism began in my family with the garden variety men-are-beasts and women-are-their-prey rendition. Barnard gave a little sophistication and intellectual depth to this familial ideology. Society and capitalism were factored into the gender issue. Stances were taken, sisterhoods were in, positions were energized by a time and a place that gave license to feelings that were as complicated as they were tumultuous. In retrospect, I value the experience of belonging and the moral clarity that I had then. I also acknowledge the limitations, rigidities, and simplifications that went into providing that clarity and belonging.

The kind of feminism I came to in college had a lot to do with my own transition into adulthood and the reworking of family scripts that necessarily follows. The challenge in my life, of which I was not then aware, is that of coming to terms with certain emotional and familial artifacts that can easily get stored under the sheer weight of the feminist issue while not belonging there at all. Dr. Minuchin's supervision and presence helped me understand the existence of this challenge and have been instrumental in my rising to it rather than ignoring it.

My first job out of college was in foster care, for no other reason than that the unknown world of abject poverty struck me as interesting. It was just like another trip, but I got to stay home and be paid, though not much. Accidentally over the course of that job my professional self took shape. I was greatly influenced by the lack of power my clients had over their lives, which resonated with the image of the powerless female that I was brought up to fight. Ironically, although I was not aware of it, the job placed me in exactly the same position of power vis-à-vis my clients that I believed myself to be defending them from. Unfortunately, the casework position gives people an obscene amount of decision-making power over the lives of others. This power is disguised as helpfulness and even advocacy, so no one, including myself, ever has to face the fact that decisions as to whether or not a baby will ever get the chance to know its mother are routinely made by twenty-two-year-old middle-class women with no training, no children, and little awareness.

I was saved from making mistakes that could have caused me great remorse by my unshakable rebelliousness. I was hell-bent on defying a system that I recognized as inept and wrong. I became an avid family rescuer. I worked to rehabilitate mothers and fathers wilted by poverty and hopelessness. I became very adept at helping parents wiggle their way through the system without losing their children. I did this with a political mission, so I thought. I thought I could hand out empowerment to my clients like lollipops to the children. I did not question my right to do so. This glaring omission of self-questioning I now understand to be one of the predictable characteristics of power—those who have it do not need to question.

Power was not the only dynamic that propelled me through those early years. The psychological payoffs of reconnecting families motivated me, especially given my own unacknowledged needs for family connectedness.

Salvador Minuchin and his faculty arrived at my agency as part of a foundation-funded project to make foster care services more family-friendly. In his role as consultant to the teacher, Dr. Anne Brooks, he horrified me. He was the male authority figure that I felt totally committed to defying.

The anger he aroused in me was in direct relation to the power that I perceived in him. He had the ability to make me question myself, my professional role, and most important, the ways my lack of consciousness of power dynamics actually reinforced the injustice I thought I was so committed to changing. This consciousness of power—of covert power—has been the most revolutionary of the changes that have occurred in me over the course of my apprenticeship with Dr. Minuchin. It has changed my ideas not only about therapy and politics but about gender and sexism. Unapologetic about his own brand of sexism, he has been a liberating influence on the feminist in me.

It has been said that my interventions empower men at the expense of women. I don't think so. That is not how I work. I can be extremely nurturing with men, women, and children, and I can be the opposite. I can see that I sometimes join men in a comfortable male bonding and that I do not have that capacity in working with women. But my response to gender issues is from a systemic point of view. I see men as controlling and constraining women, and I see women as controlling and constraining men.

These days, too, I think my age facilitates my joining with both men and women. As an elder, I am accepted in ways that transcend gender.

My next job after leaving the foster care agency was in an outpatient drug-treatment clinic. While working at this clinic, I entered supervision with Salvador Minuchin. I spent my first year in supervision continually anxious about him. I waited for the moment when some shattering confrontation would occur; I planned defense strategies, survival skills, and safe exits. I was always on the watch for offenses not only against myself but against all of womankind. Ever ready to wage a feminist battle, I wanted to be on sure ground, in order to be safe and right.

While waiting for these anticipated battles, I watched Sal with other group members and absorbed some of his wisdom vicariously as he taught others. I think now he was more welcoming to me than I could notice then, but I did see how he extended himself to the families I brought in for consultation. I saw aspects of him that stood in stark contrast to the blustery patriarch that is his public persona. It became increasingly hard to underattend his concern and investment in me and my clients.

> *Margaret's description of the supervisory process surprised me. I knew of her feminist ideology and often elicited her opinion from a feminist perspective, but I was not aware of her distrust of me as a male. Seeing her in her agency, I was impressed by her commitment to her client families. She has an attractive energy—the ability to connect with people in a fashion that is at once respectful, concrete, and supportive. And I was impressed by her street wisdom. She has such superb command of that language that I thought she must come from a working-class background, quite probably Southern Italian. So much for my cultural competence.*

In order to learn from Minuchin, I first had to trust the things in him that I entered training most committed to fighting. I had to trust in his benign use of authority and power. But I was in a real emotional and ideological quandary about assuming that kind of vulnerability. I was aware of wanting to keep my growth intellectual and to protect the other parts of me from a supervision style that was emotionally risky. I think this is one of the points that distinguishes Dr. Minuchin's supervision. Good supervision and good therapy require not only intellectual prowess but emotional availability. It took a good deal of testing, time, and experience before I became ready for the whole package.

It was my work with the Ramirez family that gave me the opportunity to emerge from behind the defensive position that I had thought was feminist. Nina Ramirez, then in her late thirties, had had a great deal of experience with treatment systems. In fact, she had been reared to a large extent by various psychiatric establishments. Psychiatrically hospitalized repeatedly since the age of thirteen, she was averaging two to three hospitalizations a year, usually around drug induced psychosis and self-mutilation. A hospital aide had to accompany her to her intake appointment with me.

My first vague impression of Nina was that she was a typical long-term psychiatric patient, with mumbled, strangely inflected speech and a choppy, lopsided gait. She was admitted to our clinic with the diagnosis of schizophrenia, but she had received a spectrum of psychiatric labels at various times over her quarter century of patienthood. She had been given diagnoses of chronic schizophrenia, organic mood disorder, multiple substance abuse, and paranoid schizophrenia. Besides the full gamut of street drugs that Nina had used, she had also been medicated with a wide array of prescribed medications such as triaflon, prolixin, tegretol, and cogentin, none of which she took consistently or as prescribed. Her substance abuse had started with alcohol at age six and had run the gamut. Like others at the drug clinic, she considered crack the final rung of misery in her spiral down the drug ladder. During her intake interview, Nina called herself a garbage-head. This is the endearing term addicts use for those who keep their options open by doing any and all drugs they can get their hands on, rather than developing an addiction to one particular drug. Nina said she had had it with drugs and wanted to stop.

My clinic does not usually work with the mentally ill, but the clinic director, feeling that Nina's drug addiction warranted our work with her even though she was severely disturbed, made a special adjustment for her. I was not ecstatic about this decision. I had had very little experience with the mental health system and had a kind of general hands-off attitude about severe mental illness that ran along the lines of "Let doctors deal with them and their chemistry." In my mind, successful treatment was keeping these patients well medicated in other people's clinics. I was nervous and incompetent around "crazy" people.

Nina and her husband, Juan, complained of their previous treatment experiences, not coincidentally making it clear to me that they had been around the psychiatric block a time or three and could triumph over the best of my treatment intentions. I was more than willing to cede this point. I knew I was in over my head and felt sure that I would join the rest of this family's lost therapists in short order. So I thought. And so I said.

This is the way the couple looked at that time. Nina presented herself as a good, though incurable, patient. She spoke clearly and coherently about her internal states. She monitored her emotional temperature carefully and could easily and freely report on it at any given moment. She was articulate and intelligent. She had great insight. She had that dogmatic faith that one learns so well in therapeutic circles—that from the rehashing of every nuance of a feeling will come relief and cure. Even I could tell she was an exceptional patient. She could have supplied any therapist with enough angst and opportunity for juicy interpretations to be compelling, however unchanging.

Juan had not benefited from years of psychiatric attention. In fact, his presentation reflected the inattention he had experienced in his position of spouse of a very crazy person. He was ghostlike, barely discernible in the crisis that was his family. Occasionally he would snap into clear relief as he recited facts and made statements about his wife's illness. Then he would dematerialize. The couple had a dearly loved daughter, then fourteen. I chose to work with the couple alone in the hope of exploring the material that might surface when the child was not available as a detour. I also chose to work with them alone because limiting the scope also limited my sense of being overwhelmed.

The initial stage of treatment was driven by the family's usual way of operating. Focus was lost to crisis, coalitions shifted randomly, and anxiety was high, disabling family members as well as the therapist. The threat of impulses gone awry through psychiatric symptoms, drug and alcohol abuse, or violence was always present. In the first three months of treatment, Nina teetered on the edge of drug relapse, Juan floated through alcoholic stupors, and the couple threatened each other with divorce, suicide, and homicide and reported that Juanita, the daughter, was sexually active and sexually victimized. At the end of the third month, Nina was hospitalized after she slashed her wrists. I was horrified, and I was grateful for the rest.

I had survived nearly a year and a half of supervision by this point, but there had been few interactions between Sal and me. He had offered me a good many suggestions, of which I was having none. What did register with me was what I recognized as genuine interest and commitment to families. As I began to trust his warmth with them, I began to reconsider my teacher as a man capable of emotional and nurturing stances.

I brought a tape of the Ramirez family, in which Nina and Juan were having a bitter fight about Juanita. They agreed she should be punished for a recent escapade, but Nina thought Juan was being far too harsh. Sal disagreed.

MINUCHIN: He is angry, and his anger is justified. And Nina is also angry, and she denies her anger and his anger. She joins with the daughter, denying her anger at the mess the teenage daughter has made of her life and then denying him the right to his anger. I would have joined with him and challenged her lack of joining with him. Both of them are in the same boat. But she has chosen to be loyal to her daughter and deny her husband. I would have entered supporting the spouses in their pain and anger, and challenging the wife. She is a person who is unable to understand that one can be angry and loving. She has never understood ambivalence, and she goes crazy. And Margaret, you are afraid that if you push for the acceptance of love and anger at the same time, you will create psychosis. The fact is that this woman is psychotic in episodes. So she may be psychotic for half an hour instead of for a week. You cannot work in this family if you want to avoid stress. You need to be able to say, Let's do it, you'll survive and I'll survive. . . . So in this situation, I would challenge the mother. I would say to her that she is wrong because she does not accept his right to his anger and his pain. By using the word pain, you then help her with her acceptance of anger.

MARGARET: Okay, I think that is perfectly simple and to the point and actually what happens. The thing I have to learn is she's going to get psychotic anyway.

MINUCHIN: Or not.

MARGARET: But what if she does? My fear is not that I'll lose control of the session, but that she'll go crazy. I'd like you to see that point. They continue this fight, and then she can't do any more and she gets symptomatic. . . . She stops that process by having a symptom. And I get scared at this. So I go into my comforting mode, my wet blanket mode. I would have given her candy at this point if I'd had any in my office, because I was scared she would jump out the window. . . . But I wanted them to keep going, I want them to continue to have a disagreement with anger and not be blackmailed by her craziness.

MINUCHIN: She scares you, but she also angers you. At this point she needs to be challenged. There are many ways of doing it. One of the ways is if you want to talk with Juan, you talk with Juan. You know, she really is not letting you—

MARGARET: And then what would she do?

MINUCHIN: She's having a temper tantrum, and you are dignifying that by saying that her temper tantrum has meaning. What you need to say is that her temper tantrum does not have meaning. Instead, the husband becomes protective, you become protective. Both of you are saying that she has the right to childish behavior, and that is incorrect. Because you are calling childish behavior psychotic.

Minuchin's message to me was that just like the family, I needed to grow past the fear. For me, this supervision session was a breakthrough. I had been able not only to expose a piece of myself that was not acceptable to me (as I saw it as a weakness), but also to insist that Sal respond to me about it without covering it up or hiding behind the more alluring (read safer) theoretical questions raised by the work.

As my venturing out of hiding continued, I began experiencing myself as more and more centered. In supervision, I ceased instigating intellectual skirmishes, and instead I aired any skepticism that I felt in a way that involved my whole self and not just my head.

When Nina was released from the hospital, I asked the family if they would come for a consultation session with Dr. Minuchin. They could not have been better constituted to bring out the best in Minuchin, with their long list of treatment failures, their drama, and their craziness. Poor and Hispanic, they were perfect for him. For myself I felt I'd rather not have this session; they were too far gone. But Sal was interested in my description of them and suggested that we bring in the daughter as well. In other words, he began his supervision of the case by caring about my family, even when I couldn't. In terms of joining with me, this was as effective as it was simple.

> *Nina had just been discharged from one of the psychiatric hospitals where she "retired" when she obeyed the voices that ordered her to hurt herself. I had been struck by Margaret's description of Nina's high level of functioning and began by wondering about the discrepancy between her ability and her hospitalizations.*

MINUCHIN: Nina, tell me about your voices. Are they male or female?

NINA *(hesitating):* Female.

MINUCHIN: What do they tell you?

NINA *(very distressed):* You know, I really shouldn't be talking about this in front of (indicates her daughter).

MINUCHIN: Juanita, do you know about your mother's voices?

JUANITA *(looking at her mother very steadily):* Yes.

MINUCHIN: Your mother has the skill—or the misfortune—of hearing voices as if they come from outside. I hear voices, too, but they come from inside. We all hear voices. Do you hear voices, Margaret?

MARGARET: I hear voices.

MINUCHIN: Our voices tell us something about ourselves. If you feel you're shit—

NINA: Yes! Mine tell me I'm full of shit! Then they tell me to punish myself!

MINUCHIN: Your voices can be tamed. But they need other voices. Voices just as strong, to fight them. Do you hear Juan's voice? Or Juanita's?

NINA: No. Never.

MINUCHIN: Ah. Their voices are too soft.

JUAN: She doesn't tell me when the voices talk to her. Only afterward. So I don't know when they talk to her.

NINA: He doesn't mean it like that. He means you should be strong around the house.

MINUCHIN *(to Nina):* If Juan's voice were stronger, he could tame the voices you hear. The ones that tell you to punish yourself.

NINA: I'm beginning to hear my own now. It's getting stronger.

> *Nina responded to my systemic suggestion that her voices were influenced by the muted quality of Juan's and Juanita's responses in the typical "I can change alone" stance that had been drilled into her by the psychiatric establishment.*

MINUCHIN: No, your voice alone cannot be strong enough. I don't think you can do it by yourself, Nina. You need Juan's voice. You need Juanita. If they don't get stronger, the voices that tell you to hurt yourself will win.

We finished the consultation emphasizing the complementarity between the intensity of the negative voices and the weakness of Juan's. For Nina to get better, Juan had to change. The direction of treatment would be guided by the hope that Juan could heal his wife.

Everyone has struggles of conscience with unbalancing. Mine has generally been feminist as well as personal. Unbalancing requires the therapist to take sides, and it's just not fair. Basically, the therapist empowers one partner to such a degree that the complementarity of the couple is thrown so far off that the partners have to reorganize themselves. Hopefully, the new way will be healthier.

Which side do you take? That's where my idiosyncrasies lead me into a dilemma. I characteristically experience women as ready and able to do emotional work. In a way that I used to think was feminist but now have come to view as somewhat distorted, I experience men as emotionally out-to-lunch. This cognitive set causes me to violate the female solidarity that I was raised and educated to protect and uphold. Because of my firm belief in the emotional superiority of female affect, I feel I have to side with the man in unbalancing. I have to empower him. So I have to betray her, her insights and her validity, in the name of good therapy, in the name of the relationship.

So I sided with Juan. I didn't really expect much. Instead, I pretended I expected something. I am used to dismissing men, so I found little in this one. But over time, the pretending that I had so perfected led to some unforeseen consequences. As I pretended that Juan was emotionally capable, he began to come into clearer focus during our sessions. I began to wonder both personally and abstractly about the male voice, about Sal's contribution to me, and about the way I as a woman could create loneliness for myself with my certainties about males.

A pivotal session with the family showed me how surprisingly present Juan had become, how important his contribution was, and how impoverished the family was without him. Juanita had just revealed that she was pregnant. Nina was in shock, Juan in a towering rage, and Nina's mother had gone ballistic. Nina wanted to talk about her mother's reaction to Juanita's pregnancy. I asked Juan to describe their meeting.

JUAN: I was just sitting there in total shock. But then when Mama started in on Nina—I mean, of course she's upset about Juanita's getting pregnant, but the way she was blaming Nina—!

NINA: I was awfully upset. But he took care of me.

MARGARET: Wait a minute, wait. You took care of your wife? And she let you?

NINA: Yes.

MARGARET: Wait a minute, this is a first. You actually felt well cared for by him?

JUAN: I took charge.

NINA: He did.

JUAN: You know how her mother sounded to me? Like, "After all I've done for you, and you treat me like shit. And I love you but you owe me." Well, I took her on. We don't owe her a thing.

MARGARET: So how did it feel to take care of Nina?

JUAN: I felt good. I had to do it. She needed me. Pure and simple. I'm her husband. I am supposed to look after her.

NINA: I felt safe with him. He put his arm around me.

MARGARET: I think it's something about her, her letting you comfort her. You're so competent, Nina, that he's always knocking at the door asking, Hey, what can I do here? *(Though politely known as unbalancing, this was a barefaced lie.)*

NINA: I was feeling so tortured that when he put his arm around me I felt comforted and safe. Here was my husband taking care of me when I needed him.

MARGARET: But at other times when you need comforting, you get tortured, you get intense and in a lot of pain, and something happens between the two of you when you don't feel he's got the comfort for you.

JUAN: I think it's because I feel I'm being pushed and like I don't belong.

NINA: I just don't want you to get upset.

JUAN: But then I feel I'm on the outside, so I think maybe the best thing is to maintain some distance and maybe this will work itself out . . . . *(His voice trailed off, then he straightened.)* I've thought about Mama, and by now I realize that she is a very unhappy and lonely human being. In that sense, I feel sorry for her. And it's sad I feel so powerless to do anything about it. She wants so desperately to be loved. Her mother didn't even love her. She wants her mother's love like you want her love, Nina. When I think about all that anger, it's total lunacy. That's what it comes down to.

This was not a voice I had ever heard from Juan. It was as far away from out-to-lunch as it is possible to be.

So my conception of men was being deconstructed in complementary ways. In supervision, Sal was proving to be neither irrelevant nor oppressive. In sessions, Juan was becoming increasingly relevant and available. With this reworking on the one side of the gender coin, there evolved a new vision of women (myself included) that was deeper and more complex. In violating the rule of feminine solidarity that I had been raised to believe was vital to survival itself, I learned more about the ways that women, myself included, get into emotional trouble. With this expansion, I was able to see configurations of gender and personality that I had previously been blind to. Of great significance to me is that through the difficult process with this family, Nina herself came to view the unbalancing work that was occurring as helpful to her, even when it went along with challenges to her overfunctioning. It is greatly to her credit (and, I still believe, a great credit to her gender) that she was able to do this, and in so doing to show what real work women are capable of.

For myself, I am no longer sure about gender. I am neither as weak nor as strong a woman as I had previously considered myself, but I have abandoned this issue of female strength for more complicated quandaries anyway. I have a growing sense of my need to continue to discover myself—as a person, as a woman, and as a therapist. I increasingly expect and allow for such endeavors from men as well. I am certain, however, that I have more freedom to explore complicated gender issues. For me, freedom is still feminist, and good supervision liberates.

Postscript

When Juanita had her baby, she and her boyfriend moved in with Juan and Nina. This was a rather complex family arrangement, especially in a very small apartment. I was impressed with the family's resourcefulness. Nina and Juan, functioning as a team, divided the apartment, preserving the autonomy of both couples but leaving the largest possible area in common. Juan seemed to have the better sense of family boundaries, and Nina accepted his judgment.

Nina has not been hospitalized in three years.

Chapter 8

One Head, Many Hats

Hannah Levin

Hannah was the clinical director of a residential institution for children. She was trying to become a family therapist. My goal in supervision was for her to become a family therapist working in a residential institution. The difference in the two positions has to do with the way one uses authority.

Hannah's job required her participation in every conflictual situation at the institution. Her ability to look at the dynamics of the conflict, explore its roots, attend to the details, and lend her personal energy and commitment to problem solving made her good at her job. This same level of personal commitment to problem solving also characterized her therapeutic style, and therein lay the problem.

The implicit paradox in family therapy is that the family must become its own healer. That requires a therapist who is not a helper but a transformer, one who joins the family with the goal of activating its members' own alternative ways of relating. The movement from helper to transformer, from social manager to therapist, requires that we restrain our strong instinct to help. Hannah needed to incorporate uncertainty into her style—the capacity not to know, the capacity not to act. She needed to move away from solving problems and instead develop the therapeutic context in which the family struggles with conflicts, fails to resolve them, endures stress, and ultimately learns new ways. That would involve a major change. For Hannah, the ability to change was handicapped by her job. The ethos of a residential institution for disturbed adolescents is control, however benign the ideology, and that mandate organizes the staff.

In the supervision, my hope was to help Hannah discover the power of not doing. The problem was that Hannah elicited from me a tendency to

---

HANNAH LEVIN, Ph.D., is in private practice in Cranford and Maplewood, NJ. For 20 years she was a professor of psychology at Rutgers University, Albert Einstein College of Medicine, and Richmond College, CUNY. Prior to her retirement she was coordinator of mental health, Division of Juvenile Services, New Jersey Department of Corrections, and clinical director of a residential treatment center for adolescent boys.

> *micromanage her therapy. Supervision unwittingly became isomorphic with her way of working. I became a problem solver, and she responded by accepting and resisting my suggestions.*
>
> *We resolved our impasse when she began to present her second family. It was a family that always did the right thing—and was miserable.*

My father and mother were an unusual couple when they married in 1921. He, an only child, was a butcher working for his father in the wholesale meat district, having dropped out of high school at sixteen. She, one of nine children, was an honor graduate from Teachers' College of Columbia University. They shared the experience of being the children of German and Dutch Jewish immigrants and having lived in homes with numerous adult relatives—some permanent residents and some transients. This, I expect, made it seem quite normal for my mother to move into the home of my paternal grandparents. My older brother and I thus grew up in a busy home with four permanent adult residents. We were visited daily by aunts, uncles, and cousins who talked in German or Yiddish when they didn't want us to know what they were saying.

My father was a socialist. And our family was on the people's side—the Loyalists—in the Spanish Civil War. We were also on the side of justice in the cases of the Scottsboro boys and Sacco and Vanzetti. It was there, at my dinner table, that the seeds were planted for my deep and enduring identification with the underdog and my sense of responsibility. I must and always shall take part in fighting social injustice.

My mother died when I was eleven. My conscious experience of her death was unusual. I felt special because I didn't know anyone else who did not have a mother. All my friends' parents and my teachers were very solicitous of me. I was unaware at the time how an intense fear of separation would color my personal life and my professional work. This combination of tremendous freedom in my youth, which expanded with the death of my mother, identification with the underdog, sensitivity to separation, and a nurturing family led me on the circuitous path to becoming a family therapist.

The freedom of my college years filled me with intense emotions about the Second World War, but with little direction as to where I, a young woman, could play a meaningful role. My true emotional investment during college was picketing the White Castle for discriminating against blacks, and trying to join the Canadian Nurses training program so I could participate in the war.

After college, I married an aspiring writer who shared my values and was secure enough to allow me the same freedom that my father had generously granted while I was growing up. Alan and I went off to Europe in 1947 to the first World Youth Festival in Prague. In Paris that winter I taught school to young people who had stood beside their fathers and mothers as partisans. This experience deepened the political values I had absorbed from my father. When I returned to the United States I wanted to commit myself to changing America's social system.

My husband and I made a sharp left turn. With a grandiose vision and the energy of youth, we transformed ourselves into organizers and union leaders in basic industry. Our parents were uncomprehending but had the wisdom to believe it would pass. The subsequent births of our four children helped diminish our parents' anxiety about the nontraditional path we had chosen. We and our children benefited greatly from living in a crowded working class neighborhood. The children and their friends built wagons and explored used car lots without constant parental supervision, while we became familiar with the complexity and richness of life styles that differed from ours. In retrospect, I believe my political dedication and involvement saved my family from being the victims of an overresponsible mother.

After five years of this alternative life style, my husband and I each decided to make a change, Alan to journalism and I to go back to school. I entered graduate school to study psychology.

Many family therapists start as individual therapists and move gradually toward family systems. My development was different. I started working with the social system in the nonprofessional social and political worlds, then moved to being a social psychologist and university teacher. Working in the South Bronx in the late 1960s and early 1970s with concepts like "community control" and "empowerment," I was one of the early members of the new Community Psychology Division of the American Psychological Association.

For the next twenty years I was a university professor, a community activist, and a therapist seeing individuals. Then I began to work in a residential setting. When I received a foundation grant to develop a correctional program for emotionally disturbed youth, I wrote in a commitment to work with the families of the youths for the year they were in the correctional system and for a year after they left it. I asked Family Studies (Dr. Minuchin's institute in New York City) for help, and they sent a member of their faculty, Ema Genijovich, to help train me and my staff in family therapy. Then I became the clinical director of another residential treatment program, run by a well-endowed nonprofit organization. The youths in this program, referred by the state youth and family agency because of "severe emotional disturbance," were mostly from poor, multiproblem families. About 30 percent were black or Latino.

Institutional Systems versus the Family Systems Approach

I entered the beautiful grounds of the center with the hope that, as one of the three directors serving under the executive director, I would have the opportunity to develop a family-friendly environment. The executive director did not give me enthusiastic support, but she did not raise any obstacles either. Her main interest was in helping build the treatment population without increasing the size of the clinical staff.

The ideal of many residential treatment centers is the therapeutic milieu. Everyone is supposed to work together as part of the team. Unfortunately the reality is often quite different. The real goals in this institution seemed to be to keep everything cool and the beds filled. These overriding goals raised several perplexing questions for me, the clinical director. The objectives of the managers were in direct conflict with those of the clinicians. For example, in one family session the therapist challenged the parents by pointing out that they were responsible for their son's misbehavior. The parents agreed to set certain limits on the child's behavior when he visited home on the weekend. Needless to say, the child was not pleased. When he returned agitated to the cottage, he was questioned perfunctorily by the overworked child care staff: "How'd it go?" He grumbled but was quickly directed to settle down and get involved in the activity prescribed for the hour. Soon there was trouble: anger, an argument, then a fight that the staff had to break up. As far as the staff was concerned, family therapy had done it again—thrown an upset child back on their hands. Family therapy began to be viewed quite negatively by the staff. In some cases this negative feeling generalized to the families and the therapists.

I was not sure if any rapprochement was possible. But I was sure that if we increased our family therapy skills, our children would benefit. Once again I turned to Family Studies. Eventually we worked out a training group. For two years, four clinicians from the agency spent one morning a week with Ema Genijovich. I accompanied them for one year and then moved on to join Dr. Minuchin's training group.

The Minuchin Supervision Group: "Smile, You're on Camera"

I came to my first weekly supervision with Salvador Minuchin carefully dressed in a silk blouse and skirt. I didn't know I was wearing more than one hat, the ones I wear all the time. And therein lay one of the major problems I would have to confront if I were to develop as a family therapist.

In my first supervision session, Minuchin said, "Hannah is the director of an agency. She is involved, she is responsible. She is the authority. She is the teacher, the explainer. But she needs to join the family." It seemed that joining a family required listening to meanings rather than the content of conversations and observing emotional transactions rather than directing staff in some crisis situation. I turned my attention to this task.

Sal Minuchin served as the camera that pictured me in different hats. There was my responsible mother's bonnet, my activist helmet, and the somber, authoritative mortar-board that goes with my academic gown—exacting, psychokinetic hats, each with distinct demands and pressures. Gently, sometimes even harshly, but with great clarity, Sal made me aware of the burdens my different hats imposed on my therapist head and discussed them.

> *My task was to help Hannah postpone interventions, to move from the concrete toward the analogical and metaphorical, away from details and toward the exploration of patterns, away from problem solving toward the ability to endure ambiguity and discontinuity. This was no easy task for either of us. My only tactic was to poke holes in her beautiful constructs. Her response tended to be to create other constructs.*

Sal asked each supervisee that year to concentrate on one family and bring tapes of that family as we worked with them over time.

As I began to plan, I began to wonder—not for the first time—if I had any business making this commitment. I felt less au courant about the issues and ideology of contemporary family therapy than others in the group. Still, my deep engagement in the policies and practices of an agency dealing with families gave me a useful conceptual and value framework into which structural family therapy logically fit. I decided that since different families elicited different strengths and weaknesses in my therapeutic interventions, I would show tapes of at least two. I volunteered for the first session.

The Davis Family

The family consisted of the mother, Lisa; the father, Larry; Lil, nineteen; and Larry III, seventeen, a resident at our institution. Larry III had been referred to our program as an alcoholic. He had been in trouble with the law because of gun possession and petty theft and had had problems at school. He had previously been hospitalized for suicidal ideation.

Mr. and Mrs. Davis were a very dramatic, powerful, and colorful couple. They were dressed in clothes of the sixties. She wore a multicolored beaded blouse with a peasant skirt, and he had a red curly beard and wore a psychedelic tie-dyed shirt. The father was a rock musician, and the Davises had lived a counterculture life from the time they eloped in a multicolored hand-painted school bus. They had settled in a rural area, where they owned a small home on a piece of land that also held an old barn. In this building Larry practiced with his fellow musicians. Alcohol and drugs were sold, exchanged, and used. Sexual orgies accompanied their use of drugs and alcohol. With this as a model, Lil and Larry III had entered sexual activity early. Larry III had been involved in sexual relationships from the time he was six years old.

Two years ago the parents had gone into a recovery program and discovered Jesus. Mr. Davis was now a member of a group called Musicians for Christ. Larry III boasted about how cool his father used to be. He was angry that his parents, particularly his father, had given all that up and that Mr. Davis was now just an emergency room aide. His mother was just a Jesus freak, he said; she wanted him to spend all day Sunday in church.

It was clear that for the first eighteen years of their marriage, the parents had assumed very few parental responsibilities. No limits were set, and there were few controls. The children had parented themselves, doing the cooking and cleaning until they began to join the group that hung out in the barn drinking and using drugs. Now they had gone from no rules to strict rules in a way that seemed too drastic and age-inappropriate. When they were young, the children had had no rules; in adolescence and young adulthood, they had too many.

I asked Mrs. Davis how things had changed in the family when her husband got sober. Before then, she said, they were "a crazed house." Mr. Davis agreed, adding, "But as perverse as that life was, we were somebody then."

"But when Larry sobered up, Larry III went off the wall," Mrs. Davis went on. "We couldn't control him."

They were a very cohesive family. They drank and abused together, and together they all stopped. It would be my job to help the parents establish a more appropriate hierarchy, guiding the children and imposing rules by all means, but giving everybody some space and some alternatives to anger.

Minuchin made many comments after my presentation. Most were affirming: "It's a good first session. . . . Parents and the institution are working together. . . . Hannah is respectful of the family."

But he made some remarks criticizing my role as director, and these had a painful impact on me: "Hannah is talking like the director of the agency. . . . She is coaching the parents, which implies that the problem is in the child. . . . As director of the agency, can Hannah be sufficiently detached to see and hear what is happening in the family?"

I was distressed. Yes, I was the director. What was I to do about it? Thus the dilemma of the multiple hats began at our first session.

> *I saw a style of therapy that needed changing. But I first concentrated on the issue of role and the influence of institutional culture on the therapist's style. I selected a middle-distance approach, dealing in the beginning only with teaching and control as a theme of supervision.*

"This is a very difficult family," Sal said. "They take the therapist for a ride." They did, and it was an example of how my roles made entirely different demands. As a director, when parents came to see me to discuss a complaint about the institution, I listened and accepted their version of the story. They had a problem; they wanted my expert advice. Reframing, confronting, or asking them to discuss it between themselves would have been disrespectful. But in a family therapy session I had to remember that roles and expectations are different. I couldn't be the director. I had to step down, and I had to challenge the family with the understanding that everyone is part of both the problem and the solution.

Minuchin pointed out that there was relatively little interaction among the family members during the session I had presented and that I had made very little effort to get them to deal with each other. He noted again that the family was very powerful and said that I would be able to challenge them only when I created a therapeutic context where they interacted. Working then with very small elements of their behavior with each other would provide a field in which I could work. It took me a while to act on this.

One of the problems that always arose was Larry III's refusal to be videotaped. This seemed a small detail to me, so I did not challenge it. But during one session, realizing that his sitting at a distance from his parents inhibited his interaction with them, I challenged him. The parents, who were very angry at him for many reasons, joined the challenge. As they looked to me to admonish him, I said, "You are his parents. It is up to you to make him behave the way you want." With difficulty, this inexperienced parental couple initiated limit setting. They told Larry III he could not come home for weekends until he began to cooperate.

Minuchin rewarded this intervention, but he also explained that perhaps the reason I hadn't challenged Larry before was that I didn't want things to get out of control. He advised me to pay attention to how uncomfortable I felt when I was not in control. Was my director's hat protecting me like a turtleshell? Had I caught the institution's pernicious virus of control? I would have to be more vigilant and monitor myself more carefully.

Sal's comments set me thinking about which hat I was wearing. He suggested that instead of responding to a comment from the mother or son, I experience it. "Because you are caught in a field of multiple conflicting demands in a family session, you need a knowledge of yourself and your limitations. You need to know how to use yourself to create instability, so the system can grow." As I analyzed my need for control in this session I realized the powerful effect the institution was having on me. No therapist wants to hear the morning after an emotional family session that there was a riot in the cottage when Larry returned that night.

And the institutional hat was not my only chapeau. When the parents told me they would have to pay the state for Larry's stay with us, my radical social activist hat demanded that I guide them in the precise steps they should take to fight this unjust requirement. Somehow I managed to resist that impulse and simply agree that this was an unfair demand. Thus by the skin of my teeth I was successful in using myself to join the family rather than advising them.

I was less successful in a session that showed a great deal of interaction in the family. The children were criticizing the parents because the house was so filthy. They said there were piles of dirt everywhere. The parents responded defensively, and I, as the misguided responsible director, advised the parents to clean up the house. Minuchin pointed out that instead of observing what was going on and paying attention to the meaning, I was getting caught in the details. "You need to push this family to go beyond their habitual interactions," he said. "Get them to see that the dirt they are describing is their life. That is the difference between challenging and directing." Wearing my director's cap, I had moved into the comfortable role of the boss, instead of putting the parents in charge.

My goal was not to tell Hannah what she should do, but rather to get her to see metaphors instead of events, symbols instead of things. When the family was in conflict over things, I wanted her to explore not the things but the conflict. I wanted her to expand the conflict instead of offering solutions. Could I help Hannah abandon first-order change in favor of second-order?

Several months later I was able to present a session where I believed I had been able to challenge this family, instead of instructing them on what they should do. The mother was telling the official story once again, reciting all the awful things her husband had done and how she had held the family together.

MOTHER *(whining):* I hate to think of the awful things you made me do.
HANNAH: Did he ever threaten you? Did he ever hit you?
MOTHER: No.
HANNAH: Why did you stay with him?
MOTHER: The family. My religion. *(She was silent for a moment, then she looked at her husband.)* Underneath that gruff, annoying exterior, there's something wonderful I love.
FATHER *(astonished, after a moment's silence):* You never said that before.

From that moment, I told the group, the tone of their conversation had changed. Whenever one slipped back, I pointed it out, and they resumed this new, more intimate interpersonal dialogue. This, I presented proudly, was change.

"It's schmaltz," was Sal's summation. The couple were accommodating to me, the director, and had seduced me into following them. I was still concentrating on content, still being the teacher and paying attention to a solution-oriented approach. Calling it "love" didn't change that.

My first reaction was outrage: He had missed the whole point. He didn't understand the emotional intensity of what happened in the session, which admittedly is diminished when viewed on the TV screen. But after thinking about it during the week I realized that although I needed a lot more work on my therapeutic voice, it had not intervened in this case to cap the affect.

The truth is that I was caught in my focus on Hannah's style and my conflict with her. This really had been a novel family change, and I didn't recognize it. Later I told Hannah that she was right. Probably this admission had more of an impact than many of my previous challenges.

Schmaltz or not, my focus on love as a solution was completely consonant with this family's own desires. The parents talked the session over on their long ride home and decided that every day they would tell each other something they liked about the other. This went on for almost five weeks, until they ran out of new things. Then the mother told me that they were going to get married again, this time in a church, on their twenty-fifth anniversary.

The change in the family, the parents' growing closer, unbalanced them all. Larry III, who had formerly been allied with his mother against his father, reacted with great anger. He became abusive toward both me and his parents. I confronted the parents, asking what they were going to do about his behavior. They looked to me for a solution. This time I made it clear that none would be forthcoming. They were the parents, and they, together, must find new ways to deal with their son. Difficult as it was, the couple managed to set limits and make them stick. After two weeks Larry III was participating fully in family sessions, talking with both parents about his feelings, worries, and concerns, and they were all planning for his discharge. Two weeks after Larry III returned home, he gave his mother away at the wedding. The music for the wedding was arranged by the father and played by his friends. There is good schmaltz and bad, after all. This was the happy ending I favored. And it was what this family needed and wanted.

The Kraus Family

The second family I presented showed the dangers of shortcutting the process of therapy by directing people toward a pleasant ending for which they were not yet prepared.

The Kraus family wanted to please me. They played to my director role, and any novelty or imagination I possessed was stifled by their willingness to agree to be good patients. They seemed to want to talk about their life rather than enacting it, and all their frustrations in life were sugared over with the mother's smile and her never-failing "That was long ago." Everything would be all right now, she insisted, if the external problems could be solved. These included two adult children still living at home and the senile ninety-one-year-old father who also lived with them.

This was a family of overresponsible parents and underresponsible children. The father was a machine maintenance man in a large high-pressure auto assembly plant. The mother was a licensed practical nurse who took care of convalescents in their homes. They had three sons, the younger two adopted. The eldest, John, 32, had graduated from West Point but had been discharged from the Army because of asthma and lived at home on disability insurance. Ted, 26, also lived at home. He was employed part-time and was trying to overcome a long history of drug abuse. Carl, 18, was a resident at our institution. He came to our care because he and a friend liked to drop rocks on cars from a highway overpass. He had also stolen a friend's gun and brought it to school. Actually he was an extremely likable young man frustrated by learning disabilities and by parents who talked and thought for him. He said his father always screamed at him, Ted acted like a three-year-old, and his grandfather was losing it; he couldn't go back home to live.

In the first session the parents told their official story. The mother said she'd adopted two children after giving birth to one because she loved children. The father said they'd wanted to do something good for the world. They dreamed of retiring to a little house they owned in Nova Scotia. When asked why all the children were still living at home, they responded that they were being good parents. John was not well; he would leave for his own life when he got better. Ted needed help because of his addiction, and Carl wasn't capable of living alone.

I chose the third session to present to the supervision group. It showed the mother as the family switchboard. She explained what each person really meant, often cutting him off and finishing his thoughts and sentences. Their subject was Carl, who couldn't be responsible at home. I was trying hard to keep an eye open for novelty. Perhaps I could try to twist this story of the victimized, hardworking, responsible parents just a little. Trying to escape from content, I suggested that the mother join me so we could observe her husband and sons talking together. Minuchin saw this as a useful maneuver. He said, "That was right. This was a time to direct the traffic of the conversation, not take part in it."

The father and sons began to discuss the father's anger. John mentioned being hit. Carl became protective of his father, saying that he had never been hit. I was worried that John was taking too much space. I donned my director's hat and entered the conversation. Minuchin said, "Hannah responded as though that were her job. She capped the affect and didn't allow the fire to spread. She created a nice scenario, with the men talking. But then she failed to exercise self-control."

By this time in supervision Hannah had incorporated my observations. It was her job to observe herself during sessions. By now supervision was not a matter of discovering new wrinkles but instead of repeating ***directions,*** *as I had done before: "Hannah is being responsible," "Hannah is teaching."*

Therapy was getting stuck in the sweet syrup of these "good parents." I had to try something new and put them in control. I talked to them about the story they had created, the story of responsibility and self-sacrifice. Now they could write a different story.

They began to accept this frame. I was pleased. But then the phone rang in my office. It was a call to me, as director, about another resident. Although it took only a minute, I removed my therapist's hat. When I went back to the session, instead of observing their dialogue at a middle distance, I became the director, asking the parents what the biggest obstacle to their living a new story would be. Obediently, the parents described external events that would probably make the new story unrealizable. Rather than returning them to the frame of writing a new story, I allowed them to go on with an old description of how outside events were the problem.

When I viewed this tape at home before presenting it, I recognized my blunder. What I did not understand was why I had not been aware of it in the session. Sal began most helpfully, dealing with a way I might have rescued my new framing. He suggested that I might have said, à la Whitaker, "I have a crazy thought. I wonder if you two really want to be alone together." This would have jarred the narrative and shaken loose a new idea. Or I might have said to the father, "Is it impossible for your wife to think about freedom?" I might have managed a stroke-and-kick move with both of them: "I am fascinated by your self-sacrifice and your capacity to be exploited by your children. How did this happen? You're both so good! Is your goodness good?"

> *Once the exploration of a therapist's style has reached a plateau, I tend to bring my many voices to the supervisee. I ask how Peggy Papp, Jay Haley, Carl Whitaker, Murray Bowen, or I might have entered into such a situation. Or I bring up stories or plays I have read. It is time for me to share my voices and hope they will be articulated in an idiosyncratic way by my supervisees.*

Fortunately I was able to use these suggestions in future sessions. Carl kept trying to express his need not to return home when he was discharged. The mother, always the manager of family feelings, always deflected him, using content to disqualify his feelings. I wanted to empower Carl and increase the intensity in the session. The family effectively undermined my attempts by wanting to do things that pleased me. I expressed my anger and frustration in the supervisory group. "Try to be mean to them," Minuchin said. "Try to access some conflict."

"I could kick the mother," he said to the class, "because she creates the need for support and harmony. But Hannah has to learn not to be nice. She has that capacity, but she is not comfortable kicking people. She wants Walt Disney endings, not Fellini finales."

> *It had occurred to me that I was not being fair to Hannah. I had not committed myself to her change. I realized I needed to move out of complacency and create enough tension between Hannah and me to be transferred to Hannah the therapist.*

I was furious. Did he think I was such a simpleton that I couldn't appreciate complexity? At the same time, I kept mumbling to myself, "Who doesn't want happy endings?"

Once my anger subsided, I began to see how I had allowed this family, and a few others, to avoid or minimize conflict in the session. Being the director made that easier, because most families wanted to please me and I wished to please them. I believe Sal's provoking my anger led to my beginning to change. I began to gain the ability to access a family's anger, and my need to be nice diminished.

Perhaps it was stubbornness or the license to be mean, but I stuck with the Kraus family till all three boys were living away from home, Carl in a supervised independent living situation. Of course, the mother needed a lot of reassurance that she had done the right thing. Recently the parents got a cousin to take care of Grandpa while they went on their first vacation alone in thirty-one years, to Nova Scotia. They were beginning to live their new story. And I have begun to appreciate that both Fellini and Walt Disney have a place in family therapy.

Möbius Strip: The End Is Just the Beginning

Sal Minuchin did with us what he tells us to do with our families. He forced me to think in novel ways. Discomfort, loss of balance, and crazy thoughts are the new feathers on my therapeutic hat. By leaving my cortex alone and going for the thalamus, Minuchin made me experience how I must deal with families who are looking for a solution. I often left supervisory sessions troubled. I missed the happy ending, or at least the apology. But I was also stimulated, entertaining many new and crazy thoughts. The feelings came first, the thoughts and ideas later.

I believe one of the strengths I bring from my life is a very clear value system. I am not afraid to take a position. What I must develop is the ability to judge when it is useful to express my position. It is also important to know that having a strong position holds the danger of focusing one's attention on content rather than relationship.

So although I have not thrown any of my hats away, I am becoming more aware of which one sits on my head. I am also better able to control which voices I should listen to and which ones to ignore during a session. I am learning how to change filters and to shift figure and ground in a therapy session. Minuchin makes these changes and shifts with breathtaking ease; I still self-consciously crank away on manual. I miss the sense of control and comfort that went with my director's hat. But just as patients are motivated by the hope that comes with something new, I also experienced hope and excitement as I learned to innovate. I am pleased that supervision has helped me increase the range of my therapeutic voice.

Chapter 9

The Poet and the Drummer

Adam Price

Adam is a storyteller. He owns words, and it is easy to streamline them in phrases, paragraphs, and seamless content—a story. But there are two kinds of storytellers. Some see their people moving in a setting, interacting, clashing, interrupting each other, vying for the same space. Others only hear their people talking to each other. Adam gave richness to his characters by using words, but somehow his characters remained words. One of the problems with only hearing people in family therapy is the seduction of the plot and the attraction of enriching the plot by becoming part of the story. Adam tended to be central and logical, an explainer. He also believed in the reality of words. He believed in rationality.

But families are insane. How else can you explain their tenacious defense of absurd positions, their competition for worthless rewards, their fighting for ownership of inconsequential truth? One of the legacies of Whitaker's work is his enjoyment of people's absurdity and his acceptance of their humanity. I think Shakespeare's characters are so universal and ageless because they are all mad.

For a therapist to accept absurdity, tangential thoughts, and discontinuity, he needs to accept his own irrationality and the creativity of moments in which the content of the plot is interrupted, moments of uncertainty, silence, and the possibility of novelty. Cassandra and Raymond, who knew about madness, intruded on Adam's organized world, with its illusion of predictability. Poor, black, survivors of the violence and chaos that often surround the life of the oppressed, what could they get from Adam's enjoyment of complex narratives?

In therapy we are always working with people who are different from us, because everybody is. We understand them through metaphors,

---

ADAM PRICE, Ph.D. directs Outpatient Services at Newark Beth Israel Medical Center. He maintains a private practice in New York City, and in Milburn, New Jersey. His interests include psychodynamic and systems work with inner city children and their families.

analogies, and assumptions. I use the universals to join with strangers. I am a human being, a man, a spouse, a father, old, Jewish . . . I have a culture, and I am a minority. I have been poor. Now I am rich, famous, incompetent, fumbling, creative, immigrant, stranger . . . Then I make assumptions about me and them. There are ways they are different, too.

Then we build bridges, and we learn. We learn more if we accept diversity. We learn more if we accept universality. We learn more if we accept both, sequentially and at the same time. It is possible. In fact it always occurs when a family therapist joins patients.

Actually therapy works because the therapist works with differences. The difference between her and them, and between them and them. The goal is exploration of differences in the search for alternatives. For Adam to work with Cassandra and Raymond required that he give up his tight hold on the logic of content, enjoy his sense of humor, accept his fear and ignorance, and jump into the unscripted encounter. He could do it, if he could just dare to.

A wise therapist needs to present his strangeness to the family. Adam could have said something like, As you see, I am white. Sometimes I will see you right. Sometimes I will miss because I am ignorant of your ways. When I do that, if you'll correct me, I will learn.

I am Adam, a thirty-four-year-old Jewish psychologist. I am bright, verbal, and even witty. I said my first words at nine months of age. I live in language, sometimes at the expense of other forms of communication. I use language to convey a sense of knowledge and confidence. I am thoroughly at home in a world of words. This ability to link one word to the next into a coherent communication and to think on my feet has been very useful. In school it sometimes helped me to slide by, as when I had to give a presentation to my fellow fifth-graders and their parents about kamikaze pilots. As I spoke, my mother sat horrified in the audience, realizing that all I knew of the subject was her brief response to my question the evening before, "What is a kamikaze?" I spoke for ten minutes. Making things up as I go along has not been so easy as an adult. I still love, however, to demonstrate my grasp of the issues and am an avid National Public Radio fan.

I was raised in a liberal Jewish family. My father is a lawyer and my mother a psychologist. Their emphasis on learning and training as analytic thinkers no doubt contributed to their son's verbal acuity. My mother's parents were of the generation of immigrants who were active in the labor movement as well as in the socialist/Zionist movement. Pete Seeger and Eugene McCarthy were icons in my childhood home. My father devoted perhaps too much of his law practice to people who could not pay him and liked to tell of the time he drove an ice cream truck in a poor neighborhood and gave away all of the ice cream.

This environment certainly shaped my desire to help, to fix, and to rescue. It may have also led me to hospitals in the inner city where I have worked since receiving my degree. Though not a "do-gooder," nor even a social activist, I find this work meaningful. It is, however, important to note that I also grew up comfortably in an affluent community and am busy trying to provide my family with the same.

Cassandra and Raymond

Cassandra is an actress and a poet. Her works are fueled by the deep pain she endured as a child. African American and poor, living in the America of the black underclass, she was subject to all the "abuses," an antiseptic professional term that is applied to all the ways of torturing a child: physically, sexually, and emotionally. Now 42, the mother of a grown child, working day jobs to support her art, Cassandra is a true survivor, a modern Sojourner Truth, striving for recognition.

Raymond is also an artist, a jazz musician. Little is known about Raymond. He is a large African-American man who always wears sunglasses, even indoors during the winter. His shades, his stature, and certainly his demeanor make him seem threatening. What is known about Raymond is that he, like Cassandra, had a tough time of it growing up. He drinks. He believes in attacking before being attacked. Also known is that he has a history of wife abuse.

Cassandra and Raymond are struggling to survive as husband and wife. Theirs was a marriage of hope. Their love was to be a salve, easing the misery of bitterness and mistreatment. More important, they hoped to find, in marriage, salvation from the abuser/victim relationship that was so familiar to each of them. This time things would be different. Now they are involved in such a vicious power struggle that the hope is gone. The specter of victimization has returned. Raymond is more the aggressor and Cassandra more the appeaser, but each knows both sides of the conflict well.

Cassandra and Raymond are in couples therapy. I am their therapist. I am in the process of becoming a family therapist. I have been in the process for some time. In order for the therapy to be successful, something new must be learned. In the couple, in each couple member, and in the therapist, something must be awakened.

To Be Seen or Not to Be Seen

The weekly group supervision with Sal Minuchin was different from any other experience I had been involved in. I was determined to be seen as competent but fearful that my failings would be exposed. When the first trainee presented, he showed a tape of a couple session that revealed his attempt to maintain an even keel, not to rock the boat. Minuchin labeled this problem by introducing Libra, the astrological figure whose symbol is a scale. He spoke of the danger of maintaining balance and chided the therapist to enter on one side or the other in order to generate disequilibrium and create an opportunity for change. He then turned to the trainee and asked, playfully, "What is your astrological sign?" The trainee, as if reading from a script, responded "Libra." I feared my days in the class were numbered.

Several weeks later it was my turn to present a case. My first tape was of a family I had seen only once before. Worried that I would not appear competent, I responded as I had in the fifth grade: I started talking. I talked for as long as I could about as much as I could, attempting to demonstrate my knowledge of the family, their history, and dynamics. When my monologue was concluded, we watched the tape. After several minutes of viewing, Minuchin stopped the tape, which was quite uneventful, and asked, "What are you thinking at this point in the session?" I fumbled through an answer, unable to provide a coherent response. Minutes later he stopped the tape again and asked, "What are you thinking here?" And then again, moments after that, "How about here?" At this point I was quite uncomfortable. No clever words were coming to me.

Adam was a brilliant student trying to become a family therapist. To reach that goal he would need to move from understanding to empathy. Working in a clinic in the inner city, he would need to empathize with hopelessness, helplessness, violence, and despair, experiences that never were a part of his experience. He had to learn how some people can transform the capacity to survive dehumanizing poverty and racism—not a short trek.

When Adam presented his first family, he was what he wanted to be: a brilliant student, knowledgeable, witty, thoughtful. But when he watched the tape his fluency disappeared whenever I asked him what he had been thinking about in a part of the session.

When in a session family members talk with each other and the therapist is silent, I usually ask, "What are you thinking now?" My purpose is to help the supervisee recognize any tangential thoughts. Frequently therapists intervene without articulating the mental map of the family that is prompting their intervention. Another purpose of my inquiry is to highlight the information from the family traveling along the auditory and visual channels. The auditory carries mostly meaning and the visual mostly affect and relationship messages. Most of my supervisees have been well trained in listening and responding to content, but they seem unable to articulate the meaning of visual data.

If they remain myopic to the transactions reflected in nonverbal behavior, they may find themselves caught unprepared by the emotionality of the sessions or simply blind to events that modify significantly the stories that family members tell. Adam's lack of responses to my simple queries organized my mode of supervising him. I felt his reliance on content had the effect of narrowing his understanding of and contact with family members. This style would need to expand. I didn't know how or where.

Minuchin asked the members of the supervision group to respond to what they had seen in the tape, and they did so with greater clarity and insight than I had mustered. I had failed in my first mission to win the acceptance and praise of my supervisor and peers. I felt I was being told, You think you know, and you need to know, but you do not know. This experience greatly unsettled me. Where I had hoped to be seen as capable, I felt incompetent.

I did not expect to feel so confused during the first supervisory session of the year. I expected Minuchin to be warm, encouraging, even complimentary in the first go around. I know that I tried to elicit such a response through my warmth and humor, but it was not forthcoming. Instead I was made to feel very unsure of myself. I was challenged, chided, and even negatively compared with my peers. Later in the year, when I kidded that I would save myself embarrassment if I did not have to present a recent session, Minuchin responded, "No, you should not save yourself the embarrassment. It is important that you feel embarrassed." I knew he was right.

As a supervisor I knew that I could not applaud Adam whenever he was brilliant. I was going to have to be distant, stingy with approval, and demanding, in the hope that he could experience, in the stress of supervision, some element he could transform into empathy for people facing impossible odds.

I learned to be comfortable with uncertainty from Carl Whitaker. From Borges I learned to take both roads at a crossing. I try to impart to my supervisees this openness to multiple realities. They need to accept that at any point their view of family reality is partial; therefore almost any intervention is correct, but only the beginning of possibilities. This acceptance is necessary for the ability to dare, to suggest a possibility and not be embarrassed if it doesn't fit. I felt that Adam's need to be correct and to be appreciated as correct simply had to be challenged.

In order to expand as a therapist I would have to take risks. I would have to leave the shell of the intellect and allow myself to become vulnerable. I would also have to allow tender parts of myself to be seen:

the unsure, the tentative, and the unknowing. Some fundamental aspects of who I was as a therapist were being called into question. I was asked to change, but I was unsure exactly what to change or how to change it. I received some help from Raymond and Cassandra Jackson, who, in their quest to render each other harmless and controllable, created what I feared most, an incompetent therapist.

The Poet and the Drummer

Cassandra initially called the clinic, located in an economically depressed, predominantly African-American community, for help with marital problems. She had been in treatment previously at another clinic, where she received individual therapy. She apparently terminated treatment when the therapist urged her to leave her husband. Clinical records from this therapist indicated that Raymond was an alcoholic who became angry and violent when drunk. At one time, the record read, he assaulted Cassandra to the point where "blood was all over the walls." He was also reported to be extremely jealous and to restrict most of Cassandra's social movements.

Cassandra's history was tragic. At age two-and-a-half she was abandoned by her mother, and she was raised in foster homes until the age of eight, when she and her mother were reunited. Cassandra had one son, who was born when she was fifteen. Raymond and Cassandra moved in together after knowing each other only a few months. They were married the following year. Cassandra had completed two years of college and attended acting school.

Raymond grew up with similar disadvantages. His parents were separated, though his father remained in contact with him. Raymond's mother was reported to have been explosive and physically abusive. Once she broke Raymond's arm. Raymond was also exposed to his mother's frequent sexual encounters. He described the household as chaotic. Raymond became heavily involved with drugs as an older teen and young adult. He gave up drugs when he joined the Nation of Islam, while it was under the leadership of Elijah ben Mohammed and Malcolm X. He later left the Nation of Islam but is still a practicing Muslim. Raymond has two children in their late thirties, the product of his first marriage. He also has two children in their early teens, the product of a second marriage. Cassandra reports that Raymond was physically abusive toward his second wife, who died when the children were young. The talk in the community is that Raymond was to blame for her death, perhaps not directly but through repeated abuse. Cassandra sticks by her husband on this matter.

When I first spoke to Cassandra by phone, she told me that many people were intimidated by her husband. She worried that I too might fear him. She recognized that in order to be helpful, I must not be afraid. I reassured her that I had worked with a variety of people and felt confident I could handle myself.

> *Adam had been raised in a comfortable middle-class family, enjoying security, love, and protection. Such an upbringing makes understanding stories like Cassandra's and Raymond's very difficult. What kind of human skills, flexibility, and endurance does it take to overcome a childhood of blight? Did Adam really have the tools to help? Or was he lying more or less convincingly to himself: I can handle myself.*

Upon meeting Raymond, I was struck by his sunglasses, which he kept on during the entire session, and by the smell of alcohol on his breath. During the first session, I asked Raymond and Cassandra about their history of violence and referred to the report of blood on the walls. Raymond responded that this comment was exaggerated and acknowledged only one violent incident, when they first met some years back. Cassandra confirmed this statement.

Cassandra spoke of Raymond's jealousy and protectiveness. He denied these accusations, noted that he was always being accused, and retorted that she was controlling. I sensed what Cassandra was referring to in her initial phone call to me. Raymond was a large man; I experienced his presence as intimidating. It was during this first session that I began to realize that Raymond's agenda was for Cassandra to receive individual counseling in his presence. The goal of this treatment would be to help Cassandra deal with her history of sexual abuse. Raymond was present ostensibly to "help," but according to Cassandra, he could not tolerate her being seen alone. I suspected that Cassandra hoped to use the sessions for couples work, and I proceeded in this fashion.

Part of my response to Raymond during that first session and later had to do with his size and his manner. It is also clear to me, however, that part of my response had to do with race. Raymond's preferred style of presenting himself made it easy to see in him an incarnation of the stereotype of "the angry black man."

I like to think of myself as a therapist who is sensitive to issues of race and ethnicity. Certainly, having been raised in a family that prided itself on its social consciousness predisposes me to think in this way. I have learned the value of openly acknowledging my ignorance with patients who are different from me racially or ethnically. I appreciate that, given how widespread and insidious racism is in our society, the African American needs to evaluate the potential for discrimination in any interaction with white America, therapy being no exception.

So, when I detected in my response to Raymond the presence of a racial stereotype, I endeavored to move beyond it. I thought I had succeeded. In looking back now, I wonder if my sense of cultural competence betrayed me. Perhaps my ability to detect my stereotypical thinking fooled me into overestimating the ease with which I could get beyond it. For while I thought I was successful in purging my response to Raymond of its racial component, I continued to experience him as angry and threatening. As will become clear, it was precisely this framing of Raymond as menacing that had to change before I could intervene effectively with him.

My first several sessions with Raymond and Cassandra went nowhere. I was able to recognize how much Raymond dominated Cassandra, how he talked over her and cut her off. I also saw how she fell prey to his verbal traps and how she tried unsuccessfully to make him realize that he was domineering. Despite these observations, my interventions were sparse and ineffectual. What follows is an excerpt of a session I presented in supervision. Cassandra began by observing that her husband seemed tense that day. She thought that it was due to his anticipation of the session.

RAYMOND: It wasn't like, Oh, gee, I hate going to this place. Now the stress that you felt about coming here today, then you have to express that. You know, speak for you.

CASSANDRA: I didn't really feel *(looking down)*—

RAYMOND: And it would be nice if you wouldn't try to—

CASSANDRA: Speak for you?

RAYMOND: Speak for me.

CASSANDRA: I was just trying to account for why today it seemed like every little thing I said, you took it the wrong way.

RAYMOND: Oh, yeah, for instance?

CASSANDRA: It doesn't matter. I don't have to pick out—

RAYMOND: Do you remember?

CASSANDRA: Yeah, but I am not going to speak on it.

RAYMOND: Oh, you are not going to speak on it. Then I don't know what you are talking about.

CASSANDRA: I just felt that we were kind of at odds with each other all afternoon and I just attributed it to the fact of coming here this afternoon.

RAYMOND: Oh, yeah, that's what you attributed it to? I asked what you wanted for dinner. Did I ask you that?

CASSANDRA: Yeah.

RAYMOND: And we talked about what we might want for dinner. We agreed on some shrimp or something like that.

In this interaction, Raymond defeated Cassandra's attempt to discuss her concerns by denying their validity, asking her to focus on specifics and sidetracking to details. He also dominated the conversation by frequently interrupting her. She responded only to the content and was thus controlled by him. The session continued in much the same way. Later Raymond upped the ante, suggesting that if Cassandra was so unhappy she should file for a divorce or otherwise stop complaining. I felt myself silently siding with her as the victim and wishing she would leave Raymond. Yet I was aware that she did not want to leave him. I was also aware that I was observing the Jacksons behave in only one way. It was perhaps the only dance they knew, but there was the possibility that in another context a different style of interaction could emerge.

In this session, I was mostly silent. I had no clue how to help them change the context. The truth is that I was afraid of Raymond and had no words to counter his combative stance. I made one rather lame attempt to point out the complementarity of their situation: that Cassandra wanted her husband to become less intimidating, while he wanted her to be less afraid. My intellectual approach was as effective as attempting to get a ten-year-old boy to put down his baseball glove to come in and play the piano. My words and ideas had little relevance to the couple's emotionality and anger. Like Cassandra, I was immobilized. It's not that I didn't know better. But I was under stress, as a result of seeing Raymond as threatening. And under stress, I reverted to my strong suit, my ability to use language. In the session, I was a prisoner of my preferred therapeutic style. And to the extent that my facility with language reflected my Jewish background, I was a prisoner of my own ethnicity.

I was also under stress when I presented the session for supervision, apprehensive about how Sal would respond to my immobility during the session. After watching the tape for several minutes and asking at key moments why I was silent and did not intervene, he asked, "Does he play in a band?"

> *Adam had been tracking Cassandra and Raymond's dialogue and making comments about the nature of their relationship. His interventions were nicely constructed but bland, so that they disappeared in the emotionality of this couple. I thought that he needed to* be *there, not to comment. I also knew that when Adam talked he embarked on a seamless narrative that*

didn't leave space for questions or doubt. I had observed him for ten or fifteen minutes of the session unable to raise his voice above the intense interpersonal field of the session, and then I had listened to him rationalize his ineffectiveness in a coherent narrative in supervision. I needed to help him discover where he had been, how he felt, how he could create a pause, how to increase intensity, how to be discontinuous, how to survive the couple's emotionality and anger and be helpful.

I started with "Does he play in a band?" knowing only that what I wanted was for Adam to experience that he had been controlled by and made ineffective by his fear of Raymond.

ADAM: Yes, I think he plays in a variety of bands.

MINUCHIN: And he is the conductor?

ADAM: He's the drummer.

MINUCHIN: He's not the conductor? Did it occur to you that he is the conductor?

ADAM: It occurs to me that the percussion controls the rhythm. But the conductor, no. It also occurred to me that playing the drums is very angry.

MINUCHIN: Yes, but you see if you think of anger, you will be intimidated, but . . . if you think of an orchestra and he is the conductor, but he doesn't let you play whatever instrument you play, even if your instrument is a cymbal, you know he will not have a good orchestra. I would have moved to some type of metaphor that talks about the silences and the melody. Can you have an orchestra that is only percussion? At this point I would say, "You know, in this session I feel silenced. You are not only the drummer but you are also the therapist." Something that says, "Give me space." Something that says, "Give me a voice."

Mimicking Adam's style of playing with words, I offered him a metaphor that used the content of the session but moved away from it, to a more generalizable level. Perhaps he would be able to peg the issues of interpersonal context, mutuality, and autonomy in the field of music, joining Raymond while challenging him.

ADAM: I felt intimidated by his anger.

MINUCHIN: That's not anger, just control. You felt intimidated by his control. You felt uncomfortable because he didn't let you talk. But you should have searched for something to bring back your sense of competence. Get up, do something.

ADAM: You mean change my posture? Stand up?

MINUCHIN: If you challenge him directly, he will best you. There is no danger. He will just best you. You are more comfortable in a position when you can say something and it has meaning and he will take what you said and play with it.

ADAM: Yes, I know he's stronger than me. I know I can't win.

MINUCHIN: So what can you do?

ADAM: I don't know.

MINUCHIN: But you need to know, because you are there.

At this point, Minuchin engaged me in a role play, in which he took the role of the patient. At times he addressed me and at times he spoke to the class, but his comments were all within the context of the role play, where he attempted to defeat my effectiveness as a therapist, much as Raymond had done.

> *I knew I had not been helpful. In a strange dynamic twist, we were reenacting the session in supervision, and Adam, feeling controlled by me, was rendered speechless.*
>
> *The isomorphism between supervision and therapy offered me at this point the experience of how Adam responds when he cannot use language and meaning freely. But I doubted that Adam understood this. Therefore I engaged him in a role play, a technique I rarely use, hoping to push him to use other aspects of his repertoire when in similar situations.*

MINUCHIN *(changes seat):* So say something. I am Raymond. And I said to Adam whatever Raymond said to Adam. *(As Raymond)* I am saying something straight and you twist it.

ADAM: Umm, well, I . . .

MINUCHIN *(interrupting):* Wait a moment. You do know. Because that's exactly what you did. And we came, we even paid money, but—

ADAM: I think that—

MINUCHIN *(interrupting):* No! You see—

ADAM: You're not letting me play my instrument! That's a difficult thing!

MINUCHIN: What kind of instrument do you play, Adam?

ADAM: I play the instrument of being a therapist.

MINUCHIN: Well, what instrument is that?

ADAM: You see—

MINUCHIN: You see what you are doing?

ADAM: You take my melody away from me! You put me on the defensive. I can't help you. I can't talk if I am up against the wall. You are very good at that.

MINUCHIN: What are you doing now?

ADAM: I think you know what I'm talking about.

MINUCHIN: You are playing a game. Melodies, instruments. Why don't you talk straight? I think you have something in mind, but you are not saying what it is. You are playing games.

MINUCHIN *(as supervisor now):* You need to do something that does not create a power operation. Raymond is not dangerous. He's controlling and paranoid, but he's no danger to you. Except that for the moment he has paralyzed you. He is threatening your standing as a competent therapist. Look what he's doing to you here. He's shaming you in the presence of this excellent audience. At this point he is beating you at your own game. It's not his game. Raymond is telling Cassandra how to think and how to feel. And you are silent.

> *I wanted Adam to feel the class's presence the next time he met Cassandra and Raymond. So I ended the supervision at a peak of intensity. I hoped that Adam, feeling observed by us, would have to move beyond his preferred style and expand into doing something different. Anything different.*

Although I was being told that it was my lack of presence in the session and not me that was lousy, I felt lousy. I had attempted in the role play to incorporate the metaphor and style of the supervisor indiscriminately in the interaction. Eventually I recognized that neither my supervisor's style nor his approval would make me a better therapist. I had to go beyond my perceived limits and be different before my patients could act differently. The supervision helped me to recognize my fear of Raymond. It also helped me see how I had been induced into playing a role that Raymond and Cassandra needed me to play.

The irony is that I did indeed need to become incompetent. I had to experience the discomfort of not knowing how to intervene and of seeing my first line of defense fail, in order to discover other resources.

This next segment, from the session that followed, illustrates how the emotional struggle I experienced after feeling incompetent both in front of the couple and in supervision allowed me to find a different voice. The supervision helped me to move beyond my reliance on language. With Sal as my foe I was ineffective, because I merely hurled words at him, and my words failed me. I recognized that my position toward Raymond had to be different. I had to challenge Raymond on a different, more emotional level in order to create a space for myself. I chose to interrupt Raymond until he had to listen to me. It was not what I had to say that made the difference; it was the fact that I required him to listen.

In this session, Cassandra began by asking to end the couple's treatment and to begin individual therapy. She also requested a female therapist. Raymond believed she was uncomfortable seeing a man, but Cassandra insisted the gender of the therapist was irrelevant to her.

CASSANDRA: I am saying, if Adam were my counselor—let's say you and I weren't married and I needed a counselor and they picked him as he was my counselor, he'd be sitting in that chair, and I'd tell him exactly how I feel, and this is no reflection on you, Raymond, I wouldn't care as long as I have a rapport.

RAYMOND: You would reveal all your past history to him?

CASSANDRA: I wouldn't care. I don't care what Adam would think about that.

RAYMOND: So you would and you wouldn't—

CASSANDRA: I wouldn't care, other than to help me.

ADAM: Raymond, let me ask you a question.

RAYMOND: So you wouldn't have a problem with that.

CASSANDRA: I wouldn't care. Cause I know it's you, it's not me that has trouble with it.

RAYMOND: You think I am uncomfortable with it?

CASSANDRA: Of course you are uncomfortable with it.

ADAM: Raymond.

RAYMOND: So why don't I just sit here while you reveal your thing?

ADAM: Raymond, I'd like to ask you a question.

RAYMOND: Why don't I just sit here while you reveal your past?

ADAM: Raymond.

RAYMOND: I can't get an answer.

ADAM: Raymond.

CASSANDRA: Especially when you look so angry.

RAYMOND: Oh, so now I look angry. She's accusing me of looking angry.

ADAM: Raymond, it's hard to get your attention.

RAYMOND: No, I want to get an answer to this question.

ADAM: No, I am telling you that it is hard to get your attention. What I wanted to say was that you are a musician. You're a drummer. I am interested in jazz, but I don't know a lot about it. When you are drumming, who leads the group?

RAYMOND: Whoever is in charge. Could be the keyboardist. Could be whoever is on horn.

ADAM: And is it ever the drummer?

RAYMOND: Sometimes.

ADAM: And when you are drumming, do you listen to what other people are—

RAYMOND: You be right in the pocket of the rhythm! You be right in there, you know, in sync with what is happening. You be grooving together, and you keep that going. Like a syncopated clock. You constantly do that, you constantly keep the rhythm going. And whatever, the horns, the piano that's playing. You know where the changes are, because you come back to the bridge of the song. Make your changes and come back. Make your changes and come back. And take it all down.

ADAM: What's happening here in this duet is that you are doing all the drumming. You are leading the, what would you call it, the duo? And I don't think that Cassandra's instrument is really being heard.

RAYMOND: Okay, so according to what she just said, she don't have no problem being in a session with you, or anybody else, in just a one-on-one situation with you and her. Is that correct?

CASSANDRA: Yes.

RAYMOND: So I might as well leave.

CASSANDRA: Why would you want to leave?

ADAM: You see, there are different melodies in an orchestra.

RAYMOND: How can I be—

ADAM: Raymond, I am talking.

RAYMOND: How—

ADAM: Raymond! *(Raymond sighs.)* Raymond, there are different melodies in an orchestra, in a duet, in a quartet. There are different melodies. You have the dominant melody.

RAYMOND: Here, only because I am under the protection of this forum, yourself. At home I don't deal with that.

ADAM: I am dealing with what's here.

RAYMOND: At home she orchestrates everything.

ADAM: Her voice is not getting played out. Just like in a jazz quartet, you have to make space for the bass, because if you do not make space for the bass, it will not be heard.

Although the metaphor of a conductor and orchestra introduced by Minuchin was useful, what made the difference was my persistence in making Raymond listen to me. The challenge to his dominance was crucial in helping the couple move out of their dominant/submissive roles. Ultimately Cassandra would need to feel empowered enough to take Raymond on herself.

Later in the session, I challenged Raymond more directly.

ADAM: You are not letting me have a voice. You are taking my voice away.

RAYMOND: Speak, I'm not taking anyone's voice away.

ADAM: No, no, with the looks that you make.

RAYMOND: I was looking at my wife.

CASSANDRA: But I try to tell him what that does to me.

ADAM: Cassandra, I am talking to Raymond. You are a dynamic man. I am sure that you are a talented man in what you do. But what I notice when I watch the tape of the last session—

(Raymond starts to interrupt me and Cassandra touches his leg. Raymond laughs.)

RAYMOND: See what she did to me? She gave me a "Be quiet" gesture.

ADAM: What I am saying is that when I saw the tape last week, I did not say anything. What I found was that you were crowding me out.

RAYMOND: Last week?

ADAM: And today. That might be what you need to do, and that's fine, but then I can't be a therapist to you.

RAYMOND: So what would you suggest I do?

ADAM: I don't have a suggestion for you—

RAYMOND: But what are you saying—

ADAM: in terms of what you should do. I want to see if you can understand Cassandra, and I want you to understand where I am coming from.

RAYMOND: Okay. If I tell you where she is coming from and I am right, would that tell you that I understand her?

ADAM: She has to tell you that she feels understood. Maybe you can figure it out. I do not know if you will be able to or not.

I then asked Cassandra to explain to Raymond why she had felt bruised by him during the last session. At this point, there was a perceptible change in her. For the first time, she abandoned her resigned posture and sat forward in her chair. Her voice became louder and more animated. She was ready to take her husband on rather than engaging in a senseless argument. I remained silent, and Cassandra fought for her right to speak, in much the same way that she had observed me doing moments before. When Raymond attempted to pin her down to details, she resisted. She told Raymond that his reactions to her comments silenced her.

Toward the end of the session, Raymond interrupted Cassandra, who responded with a laugh. I asked why she laughed when at this particular moment she meant to cry. She acknowledged that her true feelings were not being revealed. I suggested that this type of response made Raymond's job of understanding her more difficult. I then asked how, in her poetry, she communicated sadness. Cassandra recited a very sad and beautiful poem she had written, and she began to cry. She then addressed her husband in a direct, straightforward manner about the problems in the marriage. She continued this more empowered stance in the next session. Unfortunately for me, this session was to be the last. Cassandra got a new job and said she was unable to continue in treatment.

A year later, separate follow-up calls to Cassandra and Raymond yielded interesting findings. Approximately two months before the call, Raymond came home one evening to find that Cassandra had left the apartment. After he had dropped her off at work that morning, she had returned with a friend, taken her clothes, television, and even the pictures on the wall and moved to a new apartment. Raymond was devastated and could not eat or sleep for several days. He also admitted breaking down in tears. Although he knew where Cassandra worked and had access to her new phone number, he did not pursue her. Three weeks later Cassandra contacted Raymond, and they reconciled, but with the condition that Raymond get a day job. Raymond reported that things had improved and that Cassandra's departure had caused him to re-examine his role in the relationship. He was shocked by how much he had fallen apart when she left, and he now took her more seriously.

Cassandra called the reconciliation conditional, although she acknowledged she had not made that point clear to Raymond. She insisted that he keep his own apartment and was not prepared to have him move in with her until he found work and things in the relationship improved. She acknowledged that he had ceased being sarcastic and verbally abusive and that he allowed her to socialize without him. She felt additional changes were necessary, however, and believed the couple would need therapy to make further progress. Both Raymond and Cassandra reported that no violence had occurred since termination of therapy with me.

Raymond felt that aspects of the therapy were beneficial. He thought my presence had helped him state his feelings without being seen by Cassandra as a monster. He also felt he had recognized that he could beat Cassandra in argument on technical grounds alone, regardless of who was right. He acknowledged that this fact impeded their communication considerably.

Cassandra also thought the therapy had been helpful. She said that I was the first therapist who was not afraid of her husband, or at least kept any fear I had hidden. She felt this lack of fear helped me to work with the couple and also allowed her to witness someone who was not afraid of Raymond.

Most helpful was the understanding she gained about her lack of voice in the relationship. A week before she moved out, she had reviewed one of the session tapes I had copied for her. She felt this tape was instrumental in her decision to leave.

For me, these one-year follow-up calls were extremely interesting and full of surprises. I was surprised to hear that it was Cassandra who had ended the therapy, though she did so under pressure from Raymond. I was impressed that they had each taken something concrete and substantial from the sessions, and even more impressed that Cassandra's viewing of a taped session had stirred her to make a move. No doubt much more work lay ahead for this couple. But they had moved forward, stepped into the unknown, and begun to change. Cassandra had tried on a new voice and played a new instrument, and I think Raymond may have retuned his drum.

In reviewing my work with the Jacksons, I realize that I too had made some changes. Through supervision, I recognized that I had to interact differently with Raymond in order to gain space for myself as a therapist. To challenge him I had to leave the safe distance of a calm, objective demeanor and depart my castle of words. I had to put on boxing gloves and enter the ring. Since that time I have noticed a change in myself as a therapist. I see what I say and how I say it as an intervention rather than as a communication. As a result, my language reflects more the background of the family and is more metaphorical. For example, with one family whose father served in the military and is now in the security field, I used phrases such as "divide and conquer" or "line of defense." In approaching a mother whose boyfriend had sexually abused her children, I asked, "Whose soul was most hurt by these events?" I did not ask her how each of her children had reacted and who worried her most.

I also feel more willing to take risks, and I think I have more fun. In a recent example, a couple had come to me to help resolve their marital conflicts. One focus of conflict involved the husband's difficulty maintaining an erection during sex with his wife. The couple were professional, Jewish, and their highly verbal, intellectualized style was entirely familiar to me. Their fights often began over some abstract quality of the relationship. Any detail could become central in a moment. Then the couple would meander through meaningless discussions that effectively avoided conflict.

At the beginning of treatment I tended to join them in their overreliance on words. As soon as I understood field and background, my interventions became more complex. In one session, the wife tried to convince her husband that since he knew he would not be able to sustain an erection, there was no reason for him to worry about whether or not he would be able to. I observed the backhanded criticism, but rather than commenting, I wrote two notes, crumpled the two pieces of paper and tossed one to the wife and the other to the husband.

The incompetence I had experienced at the hands of the Jacksons, in coordination with the challenge I had experienced from Sal, had created tension and discomfort in me. The solution I found was to discover a new area of competence, one familiar to me in other areas of my life but unfamiliar to me as a therapist.

In the end, what I found through the course of supervision were new voices within myself. In the language of the metaphor I used with Raymond, although in supervision I was playing in Minuchin's orchestra, it was still my interpretation of the material that mattered.

I am reminded of the story of Leo Smitt, the pianist well known for his association with the composer Aaron Copeland. Early in his career, Smitt had the opportunity to perform a new work of Copeland's for the composer. He approached the date with trepidation. After all, what would happen if his interpretation of the piece did not please its creator? When the date for the performance arrived, he was surprised to find Copeland stretched out on a couch as if—Smitt said—he were anticipating a pleasurable event. After the performance, Copeland praised him. Smitt asked him if the performance was in line with the composer's original intentions. Copeland responded that he didn't care. What fascinated him was the variety with which his works were interpreted.

Similarly, as hard as I strove to emulate Minuchin's style, my success lay in me. While some things change, some things do stay the same. I am not a devoté of classical music. I heard the Smitt/Copeland story on National Public Radio.

Chapter 10

"The Oedipal Son" Revisited

Gil Tunnell

The truth is, I don't remember Gil's first two years of supervision clearly. Very early on I identified his style of learning as one of keeping distant and assimilating knowledge without risking personal involvement. I accepted that style, but it coopted me. I gave feedback that was almost exclusively theoretical and didactic.

Then Gil began to work with the Hurwitz family. They were a nice, middle-class Jewish family who genuinely cared for their children. David, the youngest, had been hospitalized in a psychiatric ward because of poking his finger in his eye so hard that it threatened to blind him.

David was asymptomatic in the hospital. His symptom reappeared whenever he went home. In a wiser world everyone would realize that his symptoms must be related to his family. But psychiatric staffs are blinded (no pun intended) by their ideological zeroing in on the internal world of the individual patient.

Gil worked in that world, too. He viewed David as an individual patient when he started family therapy. Gil had brought from his own family a capacity for distance that saved him from the Hurwitz family. He created a therapy of parallel journeys. Family and therapist traveled alongside each other without touching.

But to change psychotic families you need a therapy of passion. Gil could have learned a lot from Carl Whitaker, who enjoyed the absurd intricacies of irrationality and conveyed to his students the creativity lying at its sources. My style of irrationality is different. I tilt at windmills. But Gil could not follow me into direct challenge.

GIL TUNNELL, Ph.D., is the director of the Family Studies Program in the Department of Psychiatry at Beth Israel Medical Center in New York City and is also in private practice. He teaches family therapy at New York University and The New School for Social Research. He is a founding member and former chair of the Task Force on AIDS for the New York State Psychological Association.

Still, there are many ways to challenge, and many of them are gentle. There is a difference between challenge and confrontation. My style is frequently confrontative—in fact, that is my signature. But therapists also need to know how to intervene in a family at different levels of intensity. They need to have a whole repertoire of ways of challenging family patterns.

In a violent family, courtesy can be a challenge. Support, open emotions, and caring can bring hesitation and discomfort. "Crazy thoughts" à la Whitaker may introduce discontinuity to a proper and logical family. As for intensity, I remember a session in which Charles Fishman asked a patient, "Why don't you leave your parents' house today?" His voice was gentle and soft, but he repeated the question twenty times during the session. A very gentle therapist can be an extremely effective challenger without ever raising his voice.

But the Hurwitz family needed more. Gil carried generations of courtesy; it was in his genes. But with this family he would have to jump out of the grooves of his detached, intellectual style. He was going to have to create an intensity that wouldn't always be so polite.

Supervision on the treatment case described here began during my third year of training with Salvador Minuchin, which followed several years of graduate-level training in family therapy. Prior to this case, systems thinking had been mostly a cognitive exercise for me. I enjoyed teaching comparisons of the various schools of family therapy and developing interesting interventions in my clinical work, but I see in retrospect that I wasn't emotionally engaged in my work with families. I rarely felt their pain, nor did I participate actively with them in their struggles. My distant "don't get too involved" therapeutic style was a consequence of several factors. I am a Southern WASP, cautious about getting too close to people either in real life or in therapy. My initial training as a research psychologist had taught me skepticism about the possibility of change through psychotherapy. And my earliest training in family therapy was from a strategic (Haley/Erickson) model.

When I left the South and was exposed to other ways of being, I began to appreciate how dominant a determinant of my personality being raised as a Southern WASP had become. But I was many years into training before I realized the extent to which my background had influenced my therapeutic style as well. In my family, feelings were anathema. They clouded the mind and hampered objectivity. One might have feelings from time to time, of course, but one should somehow get rid of them and generally keep them to oneself. Emotions most certainly did not serve to connect people to one another. Even when it was clear that a family member was upset or troubled, I learned as a youngster the WASP code that it was impolite to notice. Family members cared about one another, but individual boundaries were more highly regarded than emotional connections.

Although great importance was placed on family life in my small rural community, far more importance was placed on appearing as a family unit to the community than on feeling connected with one's relatives. The extended family on my father's side almost never missed a weekly Sunday afternoon visit to my grandparents. Part of it was like a family tribunal, where the younger members of the family were called to account and the elders disbursed advice. The emphasis, it seemed to me as a young child, was on amassing achievements about which the family could feel pride. Anything more emotionally complex was downplayed. Good marks in school were praised, but a relative's drinking was only whispered about. In the view of my family, people could be pretty messy, and one should try as much as possible to avoid the mess. My family photo album has many photographs of holiday tables elegantly set with wonderfully prepared Southern food. But these photos have no people in them; they were taken before the family sat down. Children, who were regarded as "little adults," were expected to be seen but not heard. Physical nurturance almost never occurred beyond a very young age, especially for boys.

The positive part of being raised this way was that children were taught to be autonomous and independent, to take responsibility for themselves and solve their own problems without bothering others. But reaching out to family members on an emotional level was discouraged and was rarely gratifying. When one chanced to confide in someone, the feedback was usually of the "pull yourself up, get yourself together" variety. The essential message was that life is foremost about accepting responsibility for oneself. Too much involvement with others would get you sidetracked.

For as long as I can remember, I had been curious about human behavior, although I was routinely criticized by my family for asking too many questions of that kind. Only my paternal grandmother and an aunt indulged me. When it came time to choose a career, I didn't pursue clinical psychology. I got a doctoral degree in social and personality psychology research, a choice that again reflects an attitude of keeping distant and being objective, taking great pains not to get involved. I did research and was happy teaching psychology and statistics courses to undergraduates, until one summer I began supervising social work students on their master's theses. I found myself less interested in their research designs than in the clinical matters they were writing about.

Several years later I returned to graduate school for respecialization in clinical psychology. I did not pursue the traditional psychologist's interest in individual psychodynamics, however, but instead opted for training in family therapy. Systems thinking seemed far more objective and less mysterious than the unconscious. Still a social psychologist at heart, I thought that the phenomena of interest—families—could be more readily observed (especially from behind a one-way mirror), and that therefore potentially more "objective" interventions could be constructed.

In my seminars in family therapy, I read Minuchin's classic texts on structural family therapy, but my earliest clinical work followed a strategic model. From strategic supervisors, I learned to give lots of homework tasks and to tell metaphorical stories, using the sessions to sow ideas and expecting change to occur between sessions. This model allowed me to maintain a proper scientific attitude. If the family changed between sessions, it showed that the intervention had been effective.

In the strategic model, the therapist is viewed as the expert who knows the solution to the family's problem. The therapist just has to be clever enough to design an intervention that will change the family before they return for the next session. (This model now seems vaguely reminiscent of my family's Sunday afternoon tribunal, with my grandfather giving his weekly advice to each individual but generally not getting too involved.)

For me, the strategic work was very exciting, but essentially it was an intellectual endeavor. I was getting somewhat more involved with people, but my clinical work was decidedly conducted from a distance.

During my first two years of training with Sal Minuchin, I quickly learned that structural family therapy attempted to create change within the session—and that these sessions were often intense. I saw Sal create change in many families, and strategic therapy began to seem tame by comparison. But I couldn't see myself acting so forcefully. It demanded far too much personal involvement in the clinical process. So I continued working at some distance and managed not to present my family cases very often. Sal must have sensed my reluctance to show my work, but he didn't address it. I learned passively, by observing Sal work with the other trainees.

I was relieved that he didn't challenge me, yet I knew I was missing out. Sal works with trainees by challenging their therapeutic style, much as he works with families by challenging their family process. Just as he chooses which family member to challenge and does not work with everyone with equal intensity, Sal does not work with every trainee with equal intensity. I wondered privately whether he saw me as not strong enough to take his intense style of training, or whether he believed my clinical skills were so undeveloped that I didn't really have a "style." For whatever reason, not much change occurred for me in those first two years. I think now that the most fundamental reason nothing major happened was that I was so withholding as a person and with my clinical work that I didn't give Sal much to work with. I was not ready.

I think in the beginning both Gil and I were satisfied with our tacit arrangement. But I began to match his avoidance too much. I don't think he learned much the second year, at least not from me. Perhaps I felt he couldn't change or wouldn't, so my interest in his development as a practitioner waned. I don't know why he enrolled for a third year, or why I accepted him, but I'm glad we did.

Ready or not, the situation changed dramatically in the third year of training. Minuchin began challenging me with the first supervision of the year. I did have a therapeutic style, but it was very soft. I knew then that the year was going to be different, perhaps because of the nature of the case being supervised, perhaps because Sal had finally had enough of my reticence, perhaps because I was more ready.

Now, years later, I can put this experience in some perspective. It was a year of transformation for me—of personal disruption but also of personal growth—and it has had lasting effects on me. For the first time as a family therapist, and probably in my life, I experimented with being confrontational, being discontinuous, and also being more authentic. At no time in that year did I ever confront my client family very effectively, but the seed did take root and now I can confront other families effectively. Confrontation is still not my preferred style, but I am less afraid of it and have found ways to do it that match my basic personality. While my voice remains soft, something I suppose I am stuck with, soft is no longer the first word observers use to describe my style. More fundamental than any change in voice or style, however, is the change in the way I think. Whatever I am doing or saying to a family, I am always thinking structurally about the family and about what interventions might have a chance of helping the family change its structure. Beyond everything else, Sal taught me how to think.

I think it is important to repeat here that there are different ways to create change. Confrontation is one of them. But challenge and confrontation are different animals. You can challenge a pattern by being soft and

> *supportive. In a violent family, being soft and polite is a challenge. So is being concrete in a family fond of intellectual abstractions, or being courteous in a rude family. My particular skill of amplifying differences and encouraging conflicts has been called confrontation. I think it is more complex than that.*

I believe Sal thinks the primary thing he taught me is to be more confrontational and challenging. He certainly did that. But he also taught me how to join emotionally with a family. I don't think he thinks of his own style in that way. In his training, he emphasizes unbalancing and confrontation, not the importance of joining and connection. Yet in his work, he is as skillful in the latter as in the former. Sal taught me how to go back and forth, sometimes working close and sometimes being distant. He would call this "zooming in and out." I can use that technique now. I can also both be empathic and sensitive with a family and be provocative. Most important, when affect emerges in the session, I am not afraid of it. Sometimes I find myself crying along with them, and that's okay.

> *A therapist has to know a family experientially. He has to be buffeted by the family members' needs. If the therapist always travels at middle distance, he will miss that experience. So the supervisory task is to teach the supervisee how family members push and pull each other, through his own responses to them. I had to find the way to shove Gil into this experience.*

THE HURWITZ FAMILY

David Hurwitz, twenty-two, was hospitalized for inflicting injuries to his right eye. He would stab the eye with his finger, stopping only when someone in the family discovered what he was doing or the eye began to bleed. Hospitalized, he was treated with a combination of anti-anxiety medication and behavioral therapy. The eye gouging extinguished fairly quickly, but the staff observed that whenever David went home on weekends, or his family visited him in the hospital, the symptom reappeared.

> *It is amazing that over a hospitalization of eighteen months for a symptom that reappeared whenever he rejoined his family, David remained the official identified patient.*

David was the youngest son in a family of five adult children who all still lived with their parents. David and the eldest son, Herb, thirty-five, worked in the parents' business. Mary, thirty-two, was employed and lived in a small apartment she had renovated for herself in the basement. The younger daughters, Shelly, twenty-eight, and Rebecca, twenty-four, were working part-time and going to college. Mary, Rebecca, and Shelly, with no roles in the family business and with ongoing dating relationships, were less central to the tight coalition of David, Herb, and the parents.

In what appeared to be a traditional marriage, Herbert ran the business and Stella ran the home. Stella had been fired from several jobs because of interpersonal conflicts. She wanted to work, but Herbert said she had caused such trouble that he preferred her to stay home, run the house, and do the bookkeeping for his business. Their family dream was that all the children would eventually join the business. Stella said the children would, of course, marry, but she hoped they'd never live more than a block from home. Stella said she was very anxious when any of the children were away from her, particularly David, who'd been sickly as a child. Herbert was also anxious. He was a recovering gambler who now regularly attended Gamblers Anonymous. That was his primary social outlet.

The first session occurred in the hospital with the entire family present. I watched Stella embrace David. He was wearing a hospital gown. Stella ran to him, threw her arms around him, then stood, hugging him, playing with his chest hair. Stunned by this, I asked them to sit down and tried to concentrate on getting a family history. Today, as I write about the scene, I cannot imagine myself not being more active then and there.

Each family member focused on David. They said he was the only family problem and complained that his behavior was disrupting all their lives. Trying to get a fuller picture of the family, one that did not center around David, I asked them to tell me about their family before David got sick. They told me about their usual routine after dinner: Father would go to Gamblers Anonymous or stay downstairs, while Mother and the children watched the best TV in the house—in the parents' bedroom. David often sat beside his mother on the bed, and often remained when the other children went to bed.

Still managing to ignore the obvious, I tried to get the family to elaborate more on who they were. I asked them what themes a television producer might pick to make a TV movie of them. They were, it seemed, a "together" family, a family that was "all for one and one for all." I ended the consultation formulating a treatment contract that attempted to reframe their enmeshment. I told them they seemed to me like a set of Christmas tree lights wired in series; if one bulb went out, they all did. If they wanted to work with me, my job would be to wire them in parallel, so that each bulb, still connected to all the others, could be independent. The family's response was indulgent. "That's a nice way of looking at it, Dr. Tunnell, and we will work with you. Just remember that we are Jewish."

Beginning Supervision

At that time Minuchin was supervising by having each trainee select three members of the group to serve as a team of peer supervisors. His role was to supervise the teams.

> *I like to be central and get involved in dyadic transactions with my supervisees. But sometimes I feel that this interferes with the participation and learning of all the trainees, or I may feel burnt out. So I may ask the trainees to work in supervisory groups and move myself to a more distant position of teaching the supervisory process. I think alternating between the two organizations during the year brings excitement and new learning dimensions to groups of advanced trainees.*

Sal couldn't stay out of my team's attempts to supervise the Hurwitz case. Everyone was as caught up as I was in the fascinating individual Oedipal element. Sal was critical and direct, though not harsh. He said my attempt to reframe with the metaphor of the Christmas lights was inappropriate, a Christian metaphor. He said it reflected my WASP-ish equanimity. This comment brought the Jewish/Protestant theme that had begun in therapy into supervision. Sal was also skeptical about any attempt to use stories. The narrative approach was just becoming popular in the family field, and many of us were experimenting with it. But he thought it would fail in this case. With the Hurwitz family, I would have to do more to create a change-producing crisis.

> *I was very worried about the evident mismatch between this family's needs and Gil's style. Here was a family with intense demands for closeness and loyalty. Extremely emotional, not self-aware, undifferentiated in internal structure but strongly defended against the outside, they would be able to adapt almost anything to their togetherness. Against this Jewish phalanx, Gil was trying to offer intelligent comments. His pronouncements didn't have a prayer of being effective. The family were behaving like good patients, requesting advice. But I had worked with this kind of family, and I knew that such families simply absorb reason, sometimes reflecting it back but never allowing it to affect their experience.*

I was glad Gil had to work with the Hurwitz family. They would be good for him. Now, how could I help Gil be good for them?

I tried first to get Gil to experience the family as his adversary. It was their fault that he looked incompetent. They were creating the situation that was showing his ineptitude to me and the entire class. I hoped very much that Gil would develop a self-defensive anger that he would take with him to the next session. With me and the entire class at the forefront of his mind, he might not so automatically use his logical responses, and instead let his uncertainty lead him into a more active search for something new.

Sal said this family was making mashed potatoes out of me. He demanded that I do something to induce structural change, because this was a very serious symptom in a serious case. Determined to create intensity, I decided to play on the Oedipal theme. In the next session I told the family that David "unconsciously" was curious about the parents' sexual relationship. I linked his curiosity to his eye-gouging: David was sticking things where they didn't belong.

I don't think psychoanalytically, and I didn't believe this hypothesis. I used it to take a risk and to get the family's reaction. Their response was to ask David whether it was true. To my surprise, he said that, Well, yes, he had been curious and began to ask them detailed questions about their sexual relationship. I was even more surprised when Herbert began to answer his son's questions in detail, until Stella finally asked, "David, what does all this have to do with you?"

Watching the session on videotape, Sal was less amazed by the family's conversation than by my inaction. I had allowed, if not encouraged, an inappropriate conversation between the parents and their adult son about their sexual relationship. He attacked my exploration of the Oedipal theme as overly rational and said that my conversational style with the family was entirely too polite and too patient. I had let the session run away from me. Sal was visibly angry. He stood up and pretended to pour coffee over my head, shaming me before the other trainees.

I was dumbfounded. Hadn't I done what he told me to do? I had intensified the therapy. I had brought taboo topics into the session. The proper WASP had asked a family to discuss sex. What did Sal want from me?

I wanted this logical thinker to experience a Joycean grammar, more like the family's. Gil's "novelty" had been in the direction of more of the same. He had kept David as the identified patient, increased the parents'

> *curiosity about David's ways of thinking and being, and, by exploring it, increased the family's proximity. All the while he had remained the curious but detached intellectual therapist.*
>
> *I was frustrated. Turning my empty coffee cup over his head was simulated annoyance, but I was becoming genuinely angry at Gil. I had spent two years trying to teach him. He was bright and competent. So why was he so damn stuck? Part of me was working strategically, creating intensity and hierarchy between us. But I was also aware that I had really blown my cool.*

I know firsthand now how a family must feel when its structure is challenged. One's sense of organization is totally disrupted. Regrouping in the old structure is impossible, but there's nothing yet to take its place. Instead, there is intense anxiety.

The hours after that supervision were agony for me. The other trainees urged me to come have lunch and talk about it. I thanked them and declined; I was due back at the hospital. Instead I walked the streets around Sal's office, feeling dazed, anxious, confused, and helpless. This case had made me feel helpless from the start, but what I felt that afternoon was far more extreme. Sal had finally succeeded in jarring me out of my rut. But what was I going to do now?

At the time I couldn't appreciate the parallel between what Sal had done to me and what I had to do with the family. I only knew that I had to do something that was not soft. But what if I made a mess of it, and David got worse? What if he actually blinded himself?

I don't know how it happened. But somehow my distress—and my anxiety that David might blind himself—became the new focus of therapy. In the next session I made some very simple structural interventions. I seated the parents on the sofa, and had David sit in his own chair. Whenever the parents spoke for David, or when they interjected themselves in a conversation with David, I stopped them. I encouraged the parents to talk and stopped David from interrupting. All this is rather basic structural family therapy technique. But I had never been so active in a session.

Sal said these structural techniques wouldn't be enough to provide either quick symptomatic relief or enduring structural change. But he did recognize what a major shift this was for me. He maintained his usual critical role, urging me to be less soft and more active, but he acknowledged the change. Interestingly, he noted that this change in style was actually rooted in who I am as a WASP, ever conscious of boundaries and appropriate distance. Maybe my heritage could be utilized as a resource instead of seen as a deficit. Here again, this was like his therapy. Sal finds a small step within a family's dysfunctional dance that can be built on. Now he had found a resource within me that could be tapped effectively with this family.

The videotape of the supervision shows that Sal is sitting closer to me. He is friendlier, particularly as he watches my new maneuvers with the family. He continues to criticize me, but he is also very supporting. That sense of support would allow me to take greater risks in becoming adversarial with the family.

> *Gil was changing. It wasn't only that he was working with structural boundary definition. He was daring to take risks. His interpretations were more than intellectual. His body posture showed participation. He moved forward when he directed or interrupted a family member.*
>
> *I was happy that he was clearly feeling my friendliness. I had been concerned about my reactions in the previous supervisory session, so I was glad that he felt comfortable with me.*

Minuchin's Consultation with the Family

I began to try to shift the label of identified patient from David to Stella. I developed the theme that Mother was depressed and lonely because Father neglected her, and that was why she turned to her son David. Yet these ideas lacked punch. And I never said directly to the parents that their behavior, if unchecked, would finish in blinding their son. Sal did just that in a very intense consultation. In fact, in my four years of watching him work, I never saw Sal challenge a family more intensely.

Early in the session Sal called David's gouging his eyes a private show, done for his parents' benefit. His behavior was linked to them, not to anything within him. "I am Jewish," Sal said, "and I understand these things. David is a good son, sacrificing himself for his mother. This is a Greek tragedy with Jewish actors."

These were merely ideas, but Sal began to unbalance the power structure by deliberately ignoring the intrusive Stella. When she insisted on speaking he interrupted her. When she asked whether David's compulsive behavior might be due to his eating massive doses of carbohydrates, Sal said that was crazy. David wasn't crazy. The family was. He left the room at that point.

The parents began to fight. Herbert called Stella a stupid woman nobody wants to deal with. David was quiet but leaning forward, tracking his parent's arguments. Sal returned and dramatically punctuated what everyone had just witnessed: a wife emotionally demeaned, neglected by her husband, turning for solace to a child who had to blind himself as a way of remaining loyal to her. At that moment the understanding of David's symptom became fully systemic. By blinding himself, he would give his mother a new role in life, one that would take her off his father's hands. Stella would always be there to help the disabled David. In a final flourish, Sal said there was no way out. David was going to blind himself as a sacrifice to his parents, and Stella would become his seeing-eye mother. That was that. And he walked out.

In the supervisory debriefing that followed the consultation, I discussed my satisfaction at finally arriving at the true systemic explanation for David's symptom. It all made sense to me now. True to form, Sal was discontinuous. He said he didn't care whether the idea was correct or not. What mattered was whether the ideas were sufficiently novel to shake up the family structure. Therapy is an imaginative process that engages families to think and behave differently. Whether something is true or not, we can never know. I was uncomfortable all over again. At the same time, this freed me to find new ways of challenging the family.

In the consultation, I experienced the difficulties I always have in reaching highly enmeshed families. They are cooperative, request instructions, and seem willing to follow directions that in fact they completely deflect. I had to make an impact on both the family and the therapist with my interventions.

Gil was changing. But he still believed in the power of words. Like the Almighty, if he spoke the word, there would be light.

A consultation is an ideal format for high emotional intensity. A consultant can be like a hit-and-run driver. He can create strong impact without the need to join and comfort. So I asked David why he was in the hospital. He said he was getting better. I said that was wrong. They treated him as if he were crazy, but it was his family that was crazy. Stella defended him by recounting his bizarre symptoms. I said he was protecting her. When Herbert attacked Stella I said he was cruel, forcing her to seek David's protection. Every element was interpreted as pushing or pulling some member of the family. Nothing was unconnected, nothing was autonomous. The "truth" of that interpretation is inconsequential. What matters is that in an emotionally charged session, it all seemed to make sense. By the end of the consultation everything was tied into David's eye gouging. As in all tragedies, everything was leading to the inevitable self-destructive fall. David was going to blind himself for his family's sake. Gil was able to use that prediction as a tool for family individuation.

In the sessions that followed I repeated the prophesy, again and again. Sadly, but inexorably, I told the family that eventually David would blind himself for Stella's sake. There was no way out.

Seeking to distract me from their sad fate and to reject the interactional framing of David's symptom, the parents countered that their drama was less tragic than the problems of other families with dysfunctional children. I shook my head at that. Their tragedy was far greater, because their son was purposely disabling himself for his mother. I was polite and quiet. But the parents became very uncomfortable.

As we moved toward the Christmas holidays, the parents bought me a beautiful leather wallet. I thought it might be a bribe for me to back off. So I thanked them and gave it back. I did say that if by the end of my work with them David had managed not to blind himself, I would accept their gift.

My training team were shocked that I refused the gift. But Sal backed me up, which was very important to me that day. He explained that accepting gifts is often appropriate, but in this instance I had done the right thing. I think his support was more than approval of how I had handled a technical issue. I think he was privately pleased that I could be impolite. I was capable of being discontinuous, and by responding in a way that the family could not have anticipated, I had punctuated the seriousness of their circumstances.

Sal also seemed to enjoy a subsequent session in which I compared my Protestant family to the Hurwitzes. The family was in the middle of their usual patterns, interrupting each other, everybody attending to each other's business. I said, "Are all Jewish families like this? I tell you, you're different from mine." The family began discussing Protestant families. How sedate we are. We remain poised under the most difficult conditions, but we never show our feelings for one another.

"You're right," I said. "We have different ways of handling adversity, and also of viewing the world. What strikes me about you is, you're close, but you've taught David that the world is such an unsafe place that he'll never be able to make his way in it. He'll never be able to leave you. And to a WASP, that's a very sad thing. My family isn't so close, but at least my brothers and I were able to leave home."

Slowly over the next nine months, the family began to change. The parents stopped putting David under their microscope. They continued to fight with each other, but David learned to stay out. He stopped meddling in his parents' business, and he stopped gouging his eye. After eighteen months of hospitalization, he was discharged back home.

When it became clear that David's behavior had changed, the older son, Herb, took over as intermediary for the parents. In the continuing family sessions, Herb was coached to stay out of his parents' relationship and to spend more time with his brother instead. Different coalitions were formed, and different, flexible boundaries were drawn. David stayed symptom-free. Eventually he got a part-time job and began to develop his own friends.

A year after Sal had met with the family, he invited us all back for a consultation. While Sal remained behind the one-way mirror, the family explained, to the invisible viewers as much as to me, how much they had changed. I expressed my doubts that these changes were real. But the family overruled me. All the children now refused to be seduced into their parents' problems. Shelly was engaged to be married. Herb and Rebecca had moved out, and Mary was looking for her own apartment. Sal entered the room and said that the family had indeed changed. Why was I so puzzled, he asked. Clearly I had been effective with this family.

Stella spoke of that first meeting with Sal, and how he had called her crazy, and how furious she had been. She said she understood now what he had been trying to do, and she thanked him. I feel the same way about my supervision.

Chapter 11

Into the Crucible

Israela Meyerstein

In Isaac Bashevis Singer's Yentl, *which Barbra Streisand adapted to the movies, a young girl disguised herself as a boy to satisfy her thirst for knowledge, since women were not allowed to be scholars in Jewish orthodoxy. Israela had that thirst for knowledge.*

I had known her for a number of years. We had met at many professional meetings, and she had organized a workshop for me at Sheppard Pratt, the hospital where she directed the family therapy program. So my first question when she asked me for supervision was "Why?" It was clear she didn't need more training. She had made pilgrimages through nearly all the schools of family therapy: Peggy Papp, Goolishian, Weakland, the Milan school, brief therapy, narrative, structural, and some I don't remember.

And therein lay the problem. She carried all of them with her, intact. Her knowledge was encyclopedic. Her Milan school prescription at the end of a session carried every essential component. It was neutral, it included all family members, positive connotation, the consequences of change, and the paradoxical direction not to change. Her narrative approach never failed to explore the exceptions as a pathway for re-storying. In brief therapy, she was always positive. Equally conversant with the structural school, she would create enactments, unbalance, and so on. But unfortunately Israela's style resembled the state of the field of family therapy: There was little integration.

I think Israela had never abandoned the exploration of any new approach until she mastered it. But then, always finding that there were

---

Israela Meyerstein is a social worker in private practice in Baltimore, MD, where she directs the Family and Marriage Therapy Program at Sheppard Pratt Hospital. An AAMFT Approved Supervisor, Israela Meyerstein has taught therapists for over twenty years, and has published articles and book chapters in the field of family therapy.

gaps, she started a new search. I think seeking supervision with me marked such a new beginning.

To me, her style seemed Talmudic. She attended to details among family members to construct elegant narratives. Since she joined comfortably with people, worked well in proximity, and was a good explainer, families liked her and improved with her. So my task was somewhat complicated.

I think that without being aware of it, I joined and challenged Israela within the Jewish tradition. While she was a guarded intellectual, I responded by emphasizing spontaneity and feeling—the Hasidic versus the Talmudic, the mystery of healing versus the exploration of meaning. This required Israela to abandon her intellectual centrality and put her knowledge aside in favor of increased attention to her personal responses to a family dance. I assumed that her knowledge would then reappear, integrated.

In the spirit of Talmudic tradition, I have commentary to offer on Sal's commentary. While Sal correctly captured both my thirst for knowledge and my search, I don't know whether he realized that my seeking him as a supervisor was to end my searching. I wasn't looking to study yet another current family therapy approach or method. Rather, I knew Sal would deal with me, my therapeutic style, and my use of self. I regarded Sal not so much as a "structural" family therapist but as someone who, by virtue of his vast experience and clinical wisdom, had an integrative knowledge of the entire field that transcended method.

> *Crucible:* A refractory (capable of enduring high temperature) vessel in which a transfigurative process occurs through heat, pressure, or some other catalyst altering the shape, strength, and nature of substances. The crucible maintains structural integrity and nonreactivity while containing these transformative processes. (Schnarch, 1991, 158–159)

Taking the risk of entering the crucible of training by becoming a student after twenty years as a therapist and teacher seemed like a worthy midlife adventure. For a while I had been feeling a growing discomfort that my intellectual knowledge of family therapy practices had grown disproportionate to my experiential abilities. I began to question whether my theoretical/clinical choices in recent years were more than just esthetic preference and instead were masking areas of underdeveloped self.

As a therapist I wanted to feel more comfortable dealing with passion at the interior of families, not letting anger or strong emotions create anxiety and skew my responses into protecting certain members or avoiding challenging others. I wanted to restore my vision, my ability to observe process—a capacity that I think had been blunted by a growing focus on beliefs, content, and language—so I could better apprehend the dramas underlying the stories that were told. As a supervisor, I wanted to fine-tune my ability to assess trainees' idiosyncratic styles and help them broaden their repertories of available responses. In therapy and supervision I wanted to develop more focus and intensity in my sessions. So I would have to do some stretching of self.

The qualities I sought in a supervisor were clinical artistry and wisdom, openness to wrestling with new developments in the field at a theoretical and practical level, an integrative bent, and interest in expanding the self of the therapist. Moreover, the supervisor, who would be a kind of sculptor into whose hands I was placing myself, needed to have personal qualities of trustworthiness, respect, and interest in my growth.

I was born in 1948 in New York City. My parents were first-generation Jewish immigrants from Poland. They met in the United States and married before the Second World War. After the war ended, my father, returning from the service, learned that his parents, brother, and sister had been killed in concentration camps. In 1947 my parents lost their only child, a three-and-a-half-year-old daughter, after an emergency appendectomy. In 1948 the state of Israel was born, after which I am named.

I must have represented a new start for my parents as they tried to put their shattered lives back together. They were determined to shield me from the pains they had experienced. Having found security in each other, they devoted themselves to creating a long, happy childhood for their children, perhaps to compensate for the aborted childhoods each had had.

My mother was an ever-patient, nurturing caretaker, upbeat and optimistic. Intelligent and wise in common sense, she was full of enthusiasm about our lives and exerted a good deal of control in guiding us. My father was a kind, soft-spoken man, with a sensitive temperament. As an ophthalmologist, he genuinely cared about his patients and students. He was learned and intelligent, spoke several languages, and wrote several books. A man of science, he seemed to have answers to all the "why" questions a young child could ask.

I am the eldest of three girls; my sisters are six and eight years younger than me. My closeness to my mother and father made me serious, responsible, and overly sensitive to parental expectations and approval. Education was a supreme value in my family. All three daughters were encouraged to pursue professional education but also to become mothers and raise children. My parents were always supportive of my accomplishments but rarely encouraged risk-taking or imposed tough challenges.

My family was quiet and reserved. My parents rarely fought. When tensions did arise, my mother would soothe ruffled feathers. As I was growing up, I always saw my mother as the strong one and my father as weak. Only in retrospect did I understand how he more than held his own. My mother had difficulty tolerating his melancholy, so she would try to boost him up. In later years, my father's cardiac illness organized family life and dominated my parents' lives. My mother protected him in every possible way, including from our teenage storms. She progressively overfunctioned for two people. We all grew up with the dread that my father would die, so it was a shock when my mother took ill and died of pancreatic cancer at sixty-five. My father survived. After her death he turned to poetry and lived until almost eighty.

I think I was a challenging but good child who always bought the family line. Perhaps I became a family therapist better to understand the complex interior of families.

I attended college in New York, where I met my husband, who introduced travel, adventure, and more risk taking into my life. He wrested me out of my comfortable family niche to live as students in Israel, where we established lives separate from both our families. Over the course of twenty-five years we have raised three beautiful boys, all different in appearance and personality. Our eldest son is leaving home now, so a new part of the family cycle is beginning.

Searching Through All the Schools

I first encountered family therapy in Israel in 1971 as a volunteer social worker at Hadassah hospital, observing families in treatment through a one-way mirror. My limited grasp of the language led me to use my eyes to observe nonverbal communication, the invisible rules that organize family interaction. Working with several poor families taught me the relativism of norms in different cultures and showed me that emotional conditions are rarely separable from socioeconomic contexts.

In Israel I read everything about family therapy that I could put my hands on. Having learned that what I was watching was called Structural Family Therapy, as practiced by Avner Barcai, I returned to the United States determined to absorb more. I eagerly presented cases when Harry Aponte came to consult at my field placement agency. My first position after completing my master's degree in social work was in Galveston, Texas, where a small, enthusiastic group of family therapists had invented Multiple Impact Therapy in the fifties. Galveston proved to be an exciting, creative learning environment where family therapy blossomed with anti-establishment zeal. I worked with Harry

Goolishian, a mentor, for several years in cotherapy, which was the preferred model used in training and therapy. After my fellowship year I was asked to set up a family therapy training program for paraprofessionals in a community mental health center.

In Galveston new ideas were welcomed in the search for workable models in treating families. In 1975, John Weakland came to teach the new and popular brief therapy approach. That was the first time I experienced the seduction of language; it was unfamiliar turf, where hearing and words counted more than vision. Suddenly, therapists were taking notes at a polite distance during sessions, treating parsimonious parts of families, and delivering cleverly crafted interventions. There was little interest in integrating models; once a new wave came ashore it swept other ideas away.

In 1977, we moved back east to Allentown. I attended the Extern Program at the Philadelphia Child Guidance Clinic, studying with Peggy Papp because I wanted to integrate her work on "resistance" with the structural approach. I became interested in the Milan team: their use of positive connotation, the team approach, and the more elaborate cognitive style. The team approach seemed a natural extension of cotherapy. It reminded me of the Multiple Impact Theory of Galveston. It added multiple perspectives and the security of the therapist as part of a "group mind." I found the team collaboration a wonderful learning tool when I conducted group supervision in a free-standing training program that I codirected.

In Allentown, I also became interested in families with medical illness, resulting from a growing awareness of my own family's patterns during the ordeal of my mother's illness and death. I had finally discovered an area that grabbed me intellectually and emotionally, and I began to seek out professional experiences that would teach me more about it. I collaborated with a family physician in his office and consulted with Ed Friedman to learn a Bowenian perspective on family functioning around illness.

In the mid-eighties we moved to Baltimore, where I renewed a private practice and started a family therapy training program at Sheppard Pratt psychiatric hospital. With the advent of the solution-focused approaches, I found myself embracing the positive, benign approach to families; it was all so ego-syntonic. Yet as I followed the new waves of problem-determined, constructivist, collaborative language, then narrative ideas, I began to feel a loss of mooring when the emphasis on narrative and conversation overshadowed family interaction process. I wanted to be clearer on the relationship between family stories and process: how to integrate the spoken narratives with the invisible dramas played out within families and how to respond when the two were in conflict. I felt the need to clarify for myself what was fundamental and worth holding onto.

For me essential realities include developmental imperatives, cultural context, and gender. Biological "facts" of our lives—that time introduces physical changes in the direction of greater size, complexity, aging, and death—influence people as individuals and as they construct relationships with others. I sought a family therapy that wasn't about to lose these essences, so I began my training adventure with Salvador Minuchin.

Entering the Crucible

Becoming a student again felt liberating and terrifying all at once. It was a risk fraught with self-exposure, the danger of finally being found out, and feeling like a failure.

I first presented a couple with whom I had had a good relationship in therapy for a number of months. Edward was a faculty member at a local university. He was bright and articulate. Kathy was a part-time nursery school teacher. She was pleasant, witty, and deferential. Edward and Kathy had been married fourteen years and had two children. There was humor and affection in their rather traditional complementary relationship, but these were often overshadowed by anger, deprecation, and despair when Edward scolded Kathy. The couple's pattern of his self-righteous responsibility and her irresponsible rebellion, particularly in money matters, characterized many of their transactions.

The presenting problem was Edward's request for guidance in dealing with his wife's bipolar illness after she was hospitalized. My efforts included broadening the problem definition beyond her diagnosis to their daily life and helping them negotiate issues such as work, finances, and home responsibilities. The first segment I showed illustrated my encouraging Edward to appeal to his wife emotionally as a peer instead of acting like her overresponsible parent. I was trying to convince Edward to stop overfunctioning by explaining that this increased Kathy's irresponsibility.

> *The segment showed an intelligent, highly verbal husband, talking like an academician. He was eager to learn and very interested in Israela's explanation. The wife seemed pleasant and pliable. She participated when encouraged but preferred a smiling passivity. Israela was engaging the husband well with the lure of reason, but their dialogue was excluding the wife.*

Sal stopped the tape and asked the group's opinions. They thought I was too central, that I was talking too much as the expert and not facilitating interaction between the couple. Sal said, "You are capping the affect. You are working from the head up. It's too cognitive. Too much explaining." And in a more challenging tone, he asked, "Where did you learn this?"

I felt as though I had just been thrown into a freezing pool. I received no validation whatsoever from the group or the supervisor. I had to say to myself, "Keep swimming, you'll warm up eventually. You have overcome the fear of exposure and survived."

> *I really don't recognize myself in these pronouncements. I thought I was being controlled and gentle, following my decision that my supervision of Israela would accommodate to her cognitive style out of respect for her level of experience. That I was experienced as so crushing an authority was probably due to Israela's feeling of exposure in the face of the group and her own need for excellence.*

In the next session with the couple I made a strong effort to introduce more symmetry by encouraging Kathy to speak up more. Internally I felt a shift to focusing on the couple as a unit, trying to get them to interact more. But when I presented the tape, I saw little of this shift. I was disconcerted to notice that even as I was boosting Kathy, Edward was nodding, seconding my words. Sal said, "You are too reasonable. Your privileging of reason and language is perpetuating a coalition with the husband that disempowers the wife."

I wondered if it took a process-oriented therapist to notice this. Would a focus just on language have kept the process invisible? What effect would that have had on therapy?

> *Israela had responded to my supervisory input by increasing her joining with the wife, focusing on her needs and encouraging her participation. But since her own style remained intellectual and explanatory, very similar to the husband's, the effect was once again a dialogue with the husband that left the wife incompetent.*

We continued showing the tape for a few more minutes, including a segment where I was attempting to encourage Kathy to negotiate with Edward about finances. "This is not about money," Sal reminded me. "It's about relationship."

How could I change something as fundamental to me as being reasonable? "It's in my genes!" I protested. Sal replied that a personality change was not necessary—just a context-specific shift. I wrestled with the challenge. Did I need to become unreasonable? Or could the opposite of reason be simply emotion? I realized I had to find some way to break through the thinking and the language that were trapping me.

In the next session, I decided to create a sculpture that might make Edward feel the absurd extremity of his position and Kathy experience the discomfort of hers. I had Edward stand up on the couch, pointing his finger at Kathy while he lectured her on the sin of financial irresponsibility. I asked Kathy to kneel on the floor, grasping her wallet with a partly penitent, partly rebellious attitude, and I used the mirror on my wall to reflect their invisible patterns back to them.

The sculpture was powerful for the couple. The group members liked it, and Sal called it "very nice," asking if it was novel for me and whether I was familiar with Peggy Papp's work.

> *Israela had indeed produced a very nice sculpture in response to my suggesting movement away from intellectual exploration. Privately I considered this a problem of being too good a student. Being both creative and highly knowledgeable about all the schools of family therapy, Israela could access any number of correct techniques and use them appropriately without changing her style. This was technique shifting, not change.*

At last I had the sense that accomplishment would be rewarded, particularly if it represented novelty in therapeutic style. Happily I showed a later segment of the same session, in which I reframed Kathy's extremes of behavior, particularly her irresponsibility, as "ultraresponsible" in the service of boosting Edward and making a nice childhood for his children. Sal doubted that the elaborate cognitive reframing would effect change.

My well-worn style was being challenged and run into the ground. Sal conveyed that he was on my side despite his challenge, but he made it clear that he expected me to solve this problem. I was going to have to search through unused alternatives. But challenge wasn't the only mechanism. If I had been merely blocked, I would have felt stuck. Sal's joining and challenging included comments like "You are good at explaining," quickly followed by "but it traps you." "You use too many words." "Be more direct." "Use more metaphorical language." It felt as though someone were shining a flashlight in a new direction without specific instructions. I sensed that my cognitive repertoire was not useless, but I was going to have to expand beyond it.

In the next session, I spent more time encouraging Kathy to speak up, challenging Edward's patronizing comments and blocking his lecturing. Kathy resisted the invitation to be more competent and assertive, saying it was hopeless to try to change Edward. I had them repeat the sculpture as an ordeal, asking Kathy to recast their positions to create greater parity. I then left them with the dilemma of remaining in their strange arrangement.

In the next session it appeared that my unbalancing efforts had pushed the system beyond its limits. Kathy was more directly assertive, and Edward suggested that this be the last session. Kathy was protesting Edward's being a "clamp." Edward was ready to dump financial obligations on his wife.

Viewing the tape, Sal pointed out the need to rejoin Edward. He also suggested that I encourage Kathy to teach Edward to relax and have fun.

Sal continued to chip away at my staying too close to their language: "Use more startling metaphors. What you do, you do well, but you should take more leaps and risks." Just as the couple had moved past the range of their thermostat, I must move past mine. My next challenge would be how to leap. I found inspiration in one of my father's poems, realizing, as my father's daughter, that a poetic streak must also exist in me.

Poet's Leap

A poet has to take a leap
of imagination, abandon
horizonality of prose

that deals with sequences
of action in one plane.
Get acquainted with quantum

physics to perceive a world
of four dimensions, where
space-time goes to the heart

of Creation. If you want to
imitate the Creator, his sparse
words that made things happen

in the universe, make your
images relevant, leaping
to hide between the lines.

Be aware you are stepping
on high ground, where air is thin.
There is risk of falling into
world of the mundane.

—George Gorin (1990)

A Stuck Case, or On Facing Fear of Failure

Sal felt that Edward and Kathy had a limited range of emotional expression. He questioned how I would fare with a family with more emotionality. I summoned the courage to present a stuck case of a couple whose interaction made me feel helpless. Doing so meant encountering my fear of failure, but I accepted the risk.

Jerry and Susan, a couple in their late fifties, had come to me after rejecting two other therapists. Jerry was an engineer, Susan a librarian. She had recently undergone surgery following a car accident. She was enraged at Jerry for not "understanding" her needs and not offering enough support and compliments. While Jerry accompanied Susan on all her medical appointments, he made rather meager efforts to communicate. Except for a period of two months, when Susan openly showed her neediness and Jerry responded with closeness, their interactions were characterized by hostile attacks from Susan and Jerry's defending himself. Susan's verbal battering was quite visible to me; Jerry's defensiveness and withdrawal, which left Susan feeling judged and abandoned, were not.

The couple had been married for thirty years and had one young adult son. For most of their marriage Jerry had been the main patient, suffering from a variety of illnesses. Susan had been the caretaker who managed everything in the home. Now for the first time she was somewhat dependent on Jerry, and they were deadlocked. I felt stymied by Susan's angry, whiny attacks and sympathized with Jerry.

> *This was an extremely difficult couple in which the wife disqualified any and every one of the husband's comments and then criticized his silence. As Israela tried to intervene in the patterns of escalating anger, the wife experienced her intervention as joining with the husband, and she challenged Israela.*

In presenting the case I summarized the interventions that had failed, from solution focus to externalizing the "handicap's" demands as a common threat, to defining Jerry as a novice who needed practice, to describing their anger as protecting against vulnerability.

> *Again I was impressed not only by the number of voices Israela had at her disposal but by the way she could carry them in her healer's pouch, available for her use as separate patterns. But the ostrich feather she had selected for use with this couple was an unfortunate choice among her riches.*

The first segment I selected showed my interrupting their repeated pattern of accusation and defense by taking a large pillow and putting a symbolic barrier between them. I described how they were in "warring trenches," caught in a pattern of the wife's firing missiles to grab her husband's attention and the husband's running for cover because the wife was attacking. Sal liked the concrete sculpture. He said, "You are very creative." This touched a deep spring of valued competence within me. Sal was amused by the couple's absurd pattern and my trying to be fair to each: "You need to be more absurd." Going from reasonable to absurd was quite a leap indeed. But Sal had created a major perturbation and blocked all the old pathways. I was under great pressure to try a novel way to expand.

I was trying to introduce distance in a therapeutic system where the wife, in the despair of her trauma, demanded support from everybody and lashed out at anybody who supplied it. I thought a Whitaker-like capacity to see the absurdity of life's dilemmas might introduce quiet in the couple's complexity and give the therapist some respite.

Mulling over the directive to be more absurd, I came up with two different interventions, one cognitive and distant and one more action-oriented and proximal. I created an elaborate Milan-style letter from the team, with positive connotation, direct and embedded suggestions, split opinions, restraint of change, and an absurd laugh criticizing the therapist for even trying to change the couple's patterns. But delivering the intervention seemed to have little effect on this couple; they merely resumed their arguments. I experienced firsthand the insufficient leverage of this remote and largely cognitive intervention with such an emotionally charged couple.

As a Milan intervention, Israela's creation was perfect. But introduced at a time when the couple could not respond to its intellectual content, it couldn't work.

Sal pounced on my continuing reliance on cognitive means: "Your frontal lobe is too active; I want you to go limbic." I tried to create absurdity. I offered the couple bataka bats, since they were already beating each other up emotionally. I organized a target game, which they played reluctantly. Afterwards Susan left a message that she would not return, because I hadn't listened to her feelings. I called back to apologize and was able to convince them to come in again. In the next session I focused carefully on listening to Susan's pain, fears, and hurt. But rejoining her was tricky, because any effort at all to connect with

Jerry was viewed as taking his side. I explored history to alter the interaction in the present, but Susan could not tolerate any interpretive scrutiny of her past. She was satisfied only when I portrayed Jerry's power over her punitively, and at these times he felt blamed. I knew I had succeeded in rejoining Susan, but it was not clear whether Jerry would return. I felt bullied by Susan but didn't know how to extricate myself constructively. And along with all this, I was supposed to be working on "going limbic"?

I had experienced firsthand that I go cognitive under pressure, perhaps to create a safer distance. That was in all likelihood a native tendency that had been reinforced over my years as the "neutral" therapist, confidential social worker, and relatively private person. Was I being too reasonable? Or was I afraid of what might happen if I dipped into more emotional intensity?

I also wondered about the learning of such leaps. Do some people learn better through support and coaching, while others do better through challenge and confusion? If I tended to go cognitive under anxiety, how would anxiety-producing supervision help me let go? I understood that I needed to be more present emotionally, use my feelings, and challenge while being connected. What helped me absorb this lesson was Sal's challenge followed by a clear direction ("GO LIMBIC") and a demonstration of how to do it and his "being there."

Re-evolution in the Brain, or On Going Limbic

In subsequent sessions, I consistently did more checks on my gut. How does this make me feel? What does this remind me of? I decided to focus on feelings and use them, hoping that it would be only a matter of time and practice. I began to freely associate before, during, and after sessions and to volunteer personal stories and reactions in sessions rather impulsively. I began to understand what "being discontinuous" meant, and for this first time, I appreciated Whitaker. I was amazed at the deep and powerful impact this shift had. Opening a Pandora's box, I had found instead a treasure chest and discovered a new and powerful cotherapist resource: myself.

For the next supervision I presented Edward and Kathy again. They were doing a little better. I evoked a fantasy of Kathy, children, and dog huddled together on the bed in warmth and comfort, as if in an exclusive club, with Edward knocking at the door wishing he could come in. I wanted to contaminate Kathy's blissful picture of mother and children alone together so she could turn toward her husband. I wondered aloud whether their young daughters would know how to turn to their husbands when they married or would remain turned only to their mother.

Minuchin gave very positive feedback about the session: "I like you and think you are a very good therapist. I enjoy watching your work because it is complex, like a story in the *New Yorker.* Then, "But your language is too New York for this couple, especially the wife." Sal is so good at segueing from joining to challenging that the hook is in before you see him cast the line.

Sal liked the discontinuous "club" fantasy, which validated my efforts to "go limbic." Going limbic had helped me access different channels, and metaphors were flowing freely from me now. I understood why I had been unable to "think" of metaphors with my cognitive filter screening everything.

It was exciting to explore this new territory. I found myself creating idiosyncratic "sculptural metaphors" by concretizing idioms of speech. I had used a pillow to make "warring trenches" to illustrate blocked communication. Props like darts and targets dramatized hostile interaction. A tied rope described my feeling that hands were tied. Expressing and externalizing a metaphorical description of a relationship in concrete sculptural form seemed to have the potential for tapping into deeper experience.

In the next session with Susan and Jerry, I was determined not to let Susan bully me. I insisted that each of them talk to me to lessen their nonproductive arguments with each other. This way Jerry had to listen to Susan's fears and pain without defending himself, and Susan had to keep quiet while he spoke. They each spoke about what seemed lost in the relationship and their wish for courtship and romance. I presented the tragedy of each paralyzing the other and remaining alone. I challenged Jerry to take the initiative and Susan to open the door a crack. In supervision Sal felt this approach to decreasing their reactivity was useful.

In the next session, Jerry reported inviting Susan on several dates. I supported and congratulated him for beginning to court his wife despite her resistance. I reframed her self-described "spewing venom" as protecting them both from dealing with fears and awkward vulnerabilities with each other. I likened Susan's evasiveness to the squid who squirts an inky cloud to darken the waters and keep perceived enemies confused.

Later I showed a segment of the session where I interrupted Susan in mid-harangue and had her tie a strap around my hands. I described my dilemma of wanting to help her yet feeling helpless because she had tied my hands. Sal liked my use of discontinuous action, suggesting I increase the intensity through duration and repetition. He felt that

Susan's attachment to her victimization cemented and justified her rage. Amplifying my helplessness was a form of challenging that she might not be able to batter down.

Susan called to cancel the next session, reporting that Jerry had taken ill. It sounded as though Jerry had become the patient once again and Susan had returned to being the caretaker. Susan expressed interest in returning to therapy, but my sense was that the equilibrium of their previous relationship had been restored.

Sal musingly described my style in the last session with Jerry and Susan: "You are like a hummingbird who picks at the small details of language around the edges; instead you should learn to be a condor." That hit home, for I have often felt my sessions lacked concentrated intensity.

From Hummingbird to Condor: On Flying with Intensity

As usual the challenge seemed huge. I was being asked to do exactly what I couldn't easily do—walk toward the storm. Hummingbirds are small and dainty, flapping their wings seventy times a second to produce a humming sound. Condors are powerful, graceful fliers who glide long distances, rarely moving their wings. Sal's condor image struck me as aggressive in male fashion and left me confused as to how to implement it as a woman, in my own style.

Going from hummingbird to condor also meant economy—less is more. I began to say less and to encourage family members to talk to each other. I found that if I managed my anxiety and held back on overresponsibility I did have the patience to sit it out, making minimal interventions and letting family members do more of the work. My role became less central. I was more of a catalyst, intensifying transactions by prolonging their duration, repeating, or not responding. I felt more effective; I was working less, and more was happening. I was developing a new confidence in my ability to guide my flight. It was a feeling very different from my careful, anxious, cognitive planning of sessions. I was exerting leadership through spontaneous use of self.

Toward Therapeutic Leadership: On Imaginative Construction

Sal's final feedback to me was "You get hooked when you listen too closely to language. To maintain leadership you have to become centered in your experience of the family." Listening to my inner self helped me discover and define internal reactions and use them as springboards. I was beginning to realize that inspiration from my imagination could help transport me to a different plane, transcending the family's problem-saturated language, mood, reality, and trance. Collaboration with the family was essential, but imagination was the key inner resource that could strengthen my therapeutic influence, especially when translated into movement for the family.

I felt sad as the training year approached its end. I realized that expanding self is not a simple nor a brief task. Like the conductor of an orchestra, I needed to use all my instrumental resources. The training confirmed what I had known about therapy, supervision, and change. It's about saltology—the study of leaps. For me the greatest growth steps followed sessions where strong challenge was balanced with concern and being there. Once the flashlight was pointed in a direction and I understood what I needed to change, I could grapple with the challenge and move forward.

Just as therapists are never invisible to families, supervisors are never invisible to students. Sal Minuchin teaches directly and indirectly. He creates a kind of double bind for a trainee: "You are expert at doing this, and you are stuck because you are so good at it." He positively connotes behavior, then bankrupts its usefulness. Old channels are blocked as he challenges one to risk new behavior, creating intense motivation fueled by the positive power of the relationship. As soon as alternatives appear, Sal stabilizes them, then moves on to the next challenge.

My training experience was unquestionably a transformative process on many levels: therapist technique, style, personality tendencies, and family-of-origin programming. Heat and stress were required for the process. The outcome was a stronger, more authentic and resilient therapist, with a restored belief in myself. In reflecting with gratitude on my experience in the crucible, I am strongly impressed with Minuchin's personal engagement with his families and students, his deep faith in people's abilities to continue to grow and expand their potential. What is further remarkable about Sal's intense style of supervision is that when you leave the crucible, you can look back and credit yourself for doing the work that allowed the transformation to occur.

Chapter 12

Confronting the Gorilla

Dorothy G. Leicht

Dorothy was a seasoned individual therapist who knew how to be silent while she gave her patients space to develop their stories. She was also an Ericksonian therapist and was therefore trained to think strategically. So it was surprising that as a family therapist she acted spontaneously rather than according to a plan.

For Dorothy, spontaneity translated into a practice in which she would follow the family members' story lines. She was responsive to their queries and always had a number of solutions available. Since she was a good joiner and was skillfully supportive, families liked her. But while they stayed in therapy and were satisfied, they didn't change.

I challenged Dorothy's attention to detail and urged her to see family patterns. Dorothy's response would be some variation of a disqualifier: "Now that you point it out, I see it, but I didn't see it before." As we played out these scenarios over and over, the intensity of my challenges was matched by the intensity of her variations of "I didn't see it." It was a standoff that exhausted both of us.

Dorothy's style is common among individual therapists and among family therapists in transition. It is usually accompanied by a belief system that relies on empathy, and a practice that encourages disclosure on the part of the patient and availability on the part of the therapist. The stance I try to teach the therapist, however, is one of middle-range exploration of family patterns and strategic use of self in helping family members develop alternate ways of relating. My aim is to develop a therapist who is both strategic and self-aware.

For Dorothy, that meant adapting her repertoire to include planning, focus, and commitment of her therapeutic goals. She first needed to

DOROTHY G. LEICHT is a therapist and supervisor at Echo Hills Counseling Center–Phelps Memorial Hospital in Hastings-on-Hudson, New York. She lectures and gives workshops on stress management and has a private practice in Mamaroneck, New York.

> *acknowledge that in therapy she was trapped rather than spontaneous. I began to point out to her some of her nonverbal behavior; the moments in which she was responding to an event in the session but her response was invisible because she didn't articulate it. We began to pay attention to her tangential thoughts at such moments, and consider how they could be used to develop and implement therapeutic strategies.*
>
> *We engaged in a peculiar dialogue, in which I would say, "You know," and she would reply, "I don't." This became modified to "I know only when you tell me," and, as I refused to be the Seeing-Eye supervisor, Dorothy began to recognize and own up to her knowledge.*

Clinical social work is my second career. I look back on my first career with pride and pleasure: a continuing partnership with my husband, two fine sons, a daughter-in-law who has become part of the family, and another one in the wings. Becoming a wife and mother was not a conscious choice; I was a product of the forties and fifties when the predominant message to women was to marry, have a family, and live happily ever after.

I come from a middle class family. My father ran his own successful business and my mother stayed home and raised the children. We lived in a New York City suburb and spent summers on Cape Cod close to my father's large, warm, close-knit family. My life was ordered and comfortable until I was fifteen, when one summer day, my father died.

Suddenly what had been ordered and comfortable became chaotic and frightening. Life went on, we weren't forced to move, we didn't go hungry, but mother was never able to deal with the loss of her husband. Old animosities between my father's family and my mother resurfaced, and where supports had been, tensions developed. My mother did her best, but she was lonely and lost, and couldn't provide the guidance and support that my sister and I needed. That fall, when my sister returned to college, I was left with my mother. As we both tried to cope with our loss, I became the parent, she the child.

After high school, I went to college for two years, but my mother's loneliness and my lack of interest in school brought me home again to resume my role as caretaker and problem solver.

I worked in New York City and lived at home for a year, until I met my husband, moved to the suburbs, had my children, and worked at my job as wife, mother, and community volunteer.

It was the influence of the sixties and the woman's movement that made me begin to think that I could do more, that as one career was slowing down I could have another. My interest in people, my own therapy, and my experience as a problem solver—both at home and as a volunteer—led naturally to my becoming a clinical social worker. I returned to school to finish my undergraduate degree and then went on to get my master's in social work.

After graduation, I began work at an outpatient mental health clinic in Westchester. I was fortunate to find a position where training was valued and promoted. My supervisor and two other members of the staff had trained at the Ackerman Institute. The orientation of the clinic was a systems approach to working with families. At weekly team meetings staff presented live and videotaped cases. The live meetings used a two-way mirror, reflecting team, and delivered written and verbal messages to families in the style of the Milan group. The major influences were Haley's strategic work and Milton Erickson. Erickson's work appealed to me, and I spent two years at the Erickson Institute learning Ericksonian psychotherapy and hypnosis.

Although I was seeing families, and believed I had a systems perspective, my focus was becoming more and more on individuals. I wanted to do family work, but didn't feel grounded or comfortable with it. I knew that I needed to get more training.

My decision to apply for supervision with Salvador Minuchin was several years in the making. I knew Minuchin's work in family therapy through his books and conferences, and more directly through my experience with two colleagues whose work had changed dramatically during their two-year supervisions. Their descriptions of supervision were both exciting and daunting. My colleagues were bright, mature, experienced clinicians, who were used to live and videotaped supervision, but their experience with Salvador Minuchin was clearly difficult. They described him as brilliant, but tough, the most significant supervision they had ever had, but the hardest on their egos and sense of competency. What they were doing sounded wonderful, what they were feeling sounded terrible, and so I postponed and delayed. For several years I talked about applying but would miss the application period, and put it off to the next year.

It would be this difficulty in committing myself to what I wanted, and the accompanying lack of self-confidence, that would be a central theme in my work with Sal Minuchin. This was a problem that inhibited my work as a psychotherapist, and as a person, and most certainly was at the root of my self-description as a late bloomer. But time is not on the side of late bloomers. Finally I applied to the Institute and was accepted.

At our first supervisory meeting, we introduced ourselves and gave a description of our background in family therapy. After hearing the others, I realized that although I had been practicing longer than most of them, they all had more experience with structural family therapy. During my admission interview with Sal he told me that he had a difficult time supervising my Clinic colleagues because of their individual orientation. And now at this first supervisory meeting he again commented that since the orientation of my colleagues and the context within which I was working was essentially a concentration on individual psychology, he didn't think I would change. I felt like the youngest child of the family, who goes to school and has to live down the family reputation. I told Sal that I didn't agree that I wouldn't change, and he said, "Well, prove me wrong." For the next two years I tried to do that.

My task during the first year was to change the lens through which I viewed behavior. When I looked at a family, I saw individuals. My way of doing family therapy was to work with each family member. I did not see patterns of behavior, the interactions between people, or how people created other people's behavior. I knew complementarity intellectually, but not operationally. My eye was trained on the individual.

Retraining my eye was like being able to bring up the image of computer stereo designs or gestalt field and ground—easy when you can relax and let the new picture appear, but almost impossible when you stay with what you expect to see. Sal would describe the process of relaxing as taking a middle-distant position, watching from the top corner of the room, and not getting caught in the content of what was happening. This was the exact opposite of what I had been doing. My Ericksonian work had trained me to listen to the story and to the words, and I didn't realize what a shift I was going to have to make and how hard it would be.

The first case I presented for supervision was a couple who had suffered fifteen years of a bad marriage. The husband was passive, and the wife's efforts to activate him were making her a shrew and him more passive-aggressive. They fought continually, and the children were the battleground on which the war was fought. The parents resisted my efforts to involve the children. Add to this a therapist who is trying to change the way she works, and you have a scary picture. Yet the family changed when I gave up problem solving and allowed them to work it out on their own.

My next case was a couple. They had an eight-year-old child, but I didn't include her in the therapy. It took me the first year to understand the importance of children as a valuable therapeutic resource in the family system, and one that I had consistently underutilized. In this case, the child was the place where the parents could come together, let go of their need to be right, and be natural, playful, loving, and cooperative.

This was the second time they had come for couple therapy. I had seen them the year before and had also seen the wife individually. I had clearly defined what therapy was: an internal search that went on between the therapist and the individual.

Sal would repeatedly tell us family therapy wasn't that, it wasn't a story we were writing, it was a play we were directing, and that we needed to get the actors to play the parts they needed to play. Gradually I began to understand that enactment was the play, the play was the thing, and change consisted of those moments when people were not allowed to remain in their habitual grooves of behavior. It was our job, by whatever means we thought of, to create those moments. Supervision was a mirror of that process and Sal was pushing me to do things differently. But my grooves were deep.

By the second year, I understood what structural family therapy was about, but from theory to operation was a long hard road. One major change that had taken place was that I began to work with whole families, and not just with couples.

The first family I worked with during my second year was a stepparent family. Helen, the mother, and her second husband, Joe, both in their middle thirties, had been together for five years. Helen sought therapy for the family because her children from her first marriage—Jim, thirteen, and Mary, ten—were continually in conflict with their stepfather.

Joe, a recovering alcoholic, had settled into an acquiescent style within the household. When tension in the family finally exceeded his level of tolerance, he would lash out; however, these episodes were infrequent. Helen, a firm, take-charge type of person, found his elusiveness intolerable and berated him for not taking more responsibility for disciplining the children. When Joe relented and made attempts to assume a parental position, the children resisted his authority, and he became enraged. His efforts to gain their compliance were rendered ineffective by his wife's critical coaching, which helped him to see how he was doing it all wrong. Joe would then retreat in a state of helpless exasperation, leaving him further and further out of the parenting loop.

I knew that the key issue here, as in all stepfamilies, was family reorganization. The mother and her children had been a tight unit, and the addition of a stepfather necessitated an adjustment to the system that allowed for phasing in a new member. For this adjustment to be achieved, the stepfather needed help from the mother. Ultimately, he would be able to participate in the executive functioning of the family if the mother gave her blessing and made room for him. My goal was to activate and empower the stepfather. My major concern was that I would lose focus and be pulled back into the content of the family.

I introduced the videotape of my session with the family by emphasizing that this was a stepfamily and that the mother, Helen, carried the dominant voice and was very central in the family process, as she had been in her first marriage. Therefore, I had been working to allow Joe to have more of a voice and become more central in the process.

DOROTHY: So, how have you been doing in school, Jim?

JIM: It's never good enough for him. *(to stepfather)* All you ever do is complain about my school work! Why can't you give it a rest?

JOE: First thing I said was, school work is your job, from now until June—

MOTHER: Do you understand what we are saying? If we are satisfied with your school work, you won't have to ask for privileges, because they will naturally be given to you.

DOROTHY: So how is he doing?

Sal immediately stopped the tape and turned to the class. "I want you to pay attention to the small movements among family members as an indicator of patterns," he said. "Then you can decide what you want to do. The father is talking, and since he is the stepfather, his talking is an important behavior that you want to foster. The mother's interruption states that anything that has to do with the children comes through her.

"Now here is something that goes against your goal of the therapy: creating a unified family in which the father shares in executive functioning. You can decide to observe and not do anything. But you need to observe what is happening at this level of minutiae, because it is at this level that the patterns are created and maintained. You need to train yourself to see."

Sal replayed the segment and continued his commentary. "Joe says something. Mother amplifies what he says. But what she is actually saying to the stepfather is, My children are my territory. You stay out. And what I want you to observe, Dorothy, is that this happening is a nonhappening unless you make it an event. In effect it is invisible. And since you tend to listen instead of watching, these things for the most part remain invisible. Put it this way. She says, 'Blah, blah, blah,' and he says, 'Bleet, bleet, bleet.' That will help you think think patterns instead of listening to content.

"Content has a tremendous power to unify all the trends and make a story, and you tend not to see who is contributing to the story. I want you to transcend the details and to pay attention to patterns."

Sal was pointing out that I didn't see the patterns of behavior. But what began to emerge was something even more basic than not seeing the patterns: my difficulty in using what I saw, taking a position, and holding to it. This became the central theme of my next supervision session.

Again I showed a videotape of my work with this same stepparent family. During the session, I had reached a point where I was working to promote a discussion of some parenting issue between the mother and stepfather.

DOROTHY *(to the parents):* I know you talked about this before, but talk about it again.

MOTHER: We did talk about it, and we just talked about this yesterday. You increase the demand—

FATHER: I know—

MOTHER: And it is inappropriate.

FATHER: I know. And I sometimes just don't know what to do. It is like the coat thing.

MOTHER: We almost didn't find anything to fit him *(referring to the son).* So should we buy him an inappropriate coat?

FATHER: I know.

BOY *(to Mother):* That's what I said the first time we were out.

FATHER: I know. That's why I suggested we go to a store in New Jersey.

On the tape, one could see Dorothy looking at the boy, tensing her body as if in preparation to speak, then sitting back in her chair.

Sal stopped the tape and, looking at the floor in front of him, said, "You were going to do something, and the boy interrupted you. What stopped you from going ahead with what you wanted to do?"

My voice was low and intense. I avoided looking at Dorothy, conveying deep disappointment at her performance. I had decided that only high emotional intensity between us could stop her automatic responses.

DOROTHY: When I looked at the tape I could see that.

MINUCHIN: No, don't tell me that you didn't see it then. Something happened that disrupted what you wanted to do. What handicapped you from maintaining the focus?

DOROTHY: I don't know, but I don't think I have a focus.

MINUCHIN: Isn't that strange? We all know the direction in which you are going. We even agree with the direction you are going. Why don't you go in the direction you want to go? The boy reactivates a previous pattern. It is a moment for you as a person to be committed to your movement. Why don't you commit yourself? I am not talking about thinking of very fancy strategies. I am talking about the fact that you want to do that. And this is the second time the boy interferes with what you want to do. What did you feel then?

DOROTHY: I think that is the point I get pulled into the minutiae, into what's going on.

Dorothy's anger was directed at me. She was visibly upset and wanted to escape from our stressful transaction. But I felt that to lower the intensity of the encounter would be isomorphic with her way of doing therapy. Furthermore, I thought she was an intelligent person but an underfunctioning therapist. Leaving her where she was would have been to betray her. I became relentless.

MINUCHIN: It is wrong, and it is repetitive. I am sure you saw that, and I am sure you know that is not what you want to do. The question is, What handicaps you in using your own authority? What handicaps you from saying to the boy, Hey, wait a minute, that is between your Dad and your Mother?

DOROTHY: I don't know, I don't know. Yes, I am not strongly enough committed to what I am doing. I don't know, because it starts all over again and I lose it.

I didn't allow Dorothy this escape hatch. My goal was to make it impossible for Dorothy to meet with this family again without feeling my presence in the room.

MINUCHIN: That is strange that you don't know, because you clearly do know. Besides, it's not even a question of lack of knowledge. It is a question of commitment to your position in the process.

Sal flipped on the videotape again.

MOTHER: When we bought it, it was over, but Jim doesn't know what he wants. *(to husband)* I am not putting you down in any way.

DOROTHY *(to mother):* Could he have gone with Joe to buy the coat?

MOTHER: Not at all.

FATHER: That is why we went last night, the four of us.

DOROTHY: The four of you?

FATHER: Yes, all together to a mall. It is a big mall. I thought we would have a better shot at finding something there.

DOROTHY *(to mother):* What would happen if the two of them went shopping?

Sal again stopped the tape and turned to me.

> *At this point I was determined to signal every moment that Dorothy failed to follow her own therapeutic goal.*

MINUCHIN: To whom did you ask that question?

DOROTHY: To the mother.

MINUCHIN: Why?

DOROTHY: I wanted to see what's possible in terms of her not being so central and controlling everything.

MINUCHIN: What you did is the opposite of what you want. You interrupted the father while he was talking and activated the mother. Why do you want to activate her? I thought you wanted him to talk?

> *My language was repetitive. What do you want? Why don't you do what you want? She needed to see herself as a framer of the therapeutic process.*

DOROTHY: That is interesting. I guess I am thinking it is only going to happen with her permission.

MINUCHIN: No, it happened with your permission. You are permitting her to be central. That is not what you want.

DOROTHY: But Joe is only going to be able to have a role if she permits it.

MINUCHIN: No, if you permit it. *(Sal turned to the class.)* I cannot accept that she doesn't know. I think that Dorothy needs to be respectful of herself. I think if she doesn't respect herself she will not commit herself to the way in which she wants to work. *(He turned back to me.)* For you it is a commitment to your own ideas. You don't respect your ideas. You are an experienced therapist. You have years of experience. You know how to think but you don't respect that.

He was like a gorilla in my path. I couldn't cajole or distract him. He was becoming more and more impatient, and I was becoming more and more discouraged. Each time I had to present a session, it was an ordeal. I was living up to the family reputation—difficult to teach, maybe impossible. It was a predicament. I couldn't go back, I couldn't go forward. This was the moment when I had to let go of the handrail of content, jump into uncertainty, and trust that something would come if I knew where I wanted to go, believed in myself, and was willing to take a stand.

The family I presented at my next supervisory session was a single-parent family with three children: two sons, aged twenty and sixteen, and a daughter, fourteen. They had been referred by the school because both the sixteen- and fourteen-year-old were failing. The mother, Jennifer, in her early forties, had been divorced by the children's father two years ago. Since the divorce he had had no contact with them. The divorce resulted in the family's moving to a new community and mother's returning to full-time employment. The elder son, Matthew, had been living outside the home at the time but returned immediately to fill the gap created by his father's exit.

Matthew, neatly dressed in a sport coat and slacks, was the first to respond to my questions. He clearly was the spokesperson for the family. The mother, who appeared distraught and defeated by the situation, accommodated to her son's narrative. She was, however, genuinely concerned about her sixteen-year-old son, Jason, who had been hospitalized for suicidal ideation within the past year and who was currently under psychiatric care. He was failing in school, and there was some suspicion of substance abuse. Jason appeared sad and disheveled and offered mumbled responses to any questions I directed to him. Jane, an attractive fourteen-year-old, had some spunk to her. She too was of concern to the mother, not only because of her school performance but also because of her noncompliant behavior. Matthew reminded his mother that she was running with the wrong group of friends.

During the first session, Matthew talked with authority while his brother and sister sniped back at his attempts to direct them. The mother's attempt to support Matthew revealed that she dealt with her children as a sibling-parent. Jennifer fell into escalating arguments with her youngest children that ended with her retreating in helpless frustration.

This family was adrift with no hierarchical structure. The mother and daughter had in effect abandoned ship—the mother out of the house working and dating, and the daughter running with her friends. The sons presided over the wreck, angry and blaming. The mother needed to be helped to take charge of her family and to set her elder son free. I needed to take charge of the therapy.

I showed a section of tape in which the family was arguing about the messiness of the house. They went around and around about whose responsibility it was to do what. I found myself intervening in an effort to help them organize a plan to clean the place up. Sal pointed out that again I had been captured by the content and had fallen into a problem-solving mode. "See, what I am concerned about here," he said, "is your ability to move from the concrete to the metaphoric to capture meaning in such a way that it changes the experience. They could live in a dirty house. The question is, Can you begin to look at a set of disparate facts and move to a higher level of generalizability, so that they begin to look at themselves as part of a system? I think you are tied to the concreteness of the family."

> *Dorothy had begun to change, and the language of my supervision was changing as well. I was more didactic and less personal. I was exploring concepts instead of concrete maneuvers. But Dorothy didn't see that I was changing as she changed.*

Sal continued to push me, and after one supervision I was so angry with him that I asked to see him after class. We were unable to meet that day but made an appointment for the next week. That day it snowed, and I didn't come to class. But the fact is, I was backing away from confronting Sal. Sal wouldn't let that happen, and another appointment was made. We talked, but what we talked about wasn't as important as the fact that we talked. I had taken a stand on my own behalf, and that was a change. I think this was a turning point for me in supervision. I was determined that I would prove this man wrong and that I would change.

> *As I remember, we talked for an hour about many issues, some having to do with supervision, some simply about life. But there was no hierarchy—we were talking as colleagues.*

Before the next supervision, I went back to all my taped supervisions. I watched them and then watched them again. I knew that I wanted to focus on the elder son's recent announcement that he was moving out. For all the problems I was having, the family was changing. The mother had begun to take charge, and the son could now leave.

MATTHEW: I am moving out, so I want something to happen.

DOROTHY: So that is a change in the family.

MOTHER: Yes, it had to happen eventually, and actually I feel that from Matthew it is a vote of confidence in me that you *(to Matthew)* don't feel obligated to the family.

JASON: I want to do that, too.

DOROTHY: That's a normal feeling for a sixteen-year-old. To want to feel that way and to be independent.

MATTHEW: I guess that creates a role for him. As I move out, he becomes the man of the house.

DOROTHY: Jason, will you get Matthew's room, or how will that work?

Sal stopped the tape and addressed the class. "Let's talk about maps. There is now a significant event going on in the family. They are moving from being four to being three. And since Matthew is a dominant member, I would work with them to frame the options of being three as a positive experience. See what I am talking about, Dorothy? Here is a mind-set."

I was determined to show Sal that I could develop a frame, a mind-set, and then a focus. The next session I had with the family was the first time I kept my focus, sat back clear of the content, and took charge. Change was occurring; the son was moving out, and I was moving also. So as I introduced the tape of this family at the next supervision, I indicated that my framework had been that something was happening in this family and things would be different, and that that was my only focus.

> *Dorothy's presentation was clear and was given like a challenge to the class. Here was a different therapist. She wanted us to know that she knew where she was going. I wanted the group to acknowledge her change.*

Sal asked the class to respond to my introductory presentation. They remarked that it was decidedly different. I had not presented details, but rather a framework with a focus. He simply added that he agreed and asked me to start the tape.

The session began with the family members kidding one another about a variety of insignificant issues. Jason began bantering with Matthew about a phone card, and I intervened.

DOROTHY: So you think, Matthew, that Jason doesn't want to talk about your leaving? And this is the second time you are leaving?

MATTHEW *(laughs):* Yes, every three years or so I leave.

DOROTHY *(to the family):* How do you get him to come back?

JASON *(laughs):* He kind of imposes himself upon us.

DOROTHY *(to Matthew):* You had kind of the father role in the family.

MATTHEW: Well, you could say that.

DOROTHY *(to Jason):* You don't think so, Jason?

JASON: Yes, he had the father role, or maybe he just thinks he has. Maybe you think so a little.

MATTHEW *(to Jason):* Do you think I try to replace a father or be an older brother?

JASON: You take some of the responsibility of the father's role.

MATTHEW: Like what?

JANE: You try to ground us, and it doesn't work.

DOROTHY: You are a good brother and a good sister, so you give him a lot of things to be concerned about.

JASON: I didn't say that.

DOROTHY: No, I'm saying that.

JASON: Don't say that.

DOROTHY: Well, I am saying that. So, he can be fatherly then?

JASON: That is way too abstract for me.

MOTHER: When Matthew first moved back in, there were a lot of problems. I think you *(to Matthew)* try to do too much. It seems you felt all the responsibility to take care of everybody, and you were having a lot of trouble. I think that happened in the beginning, and I think now Matthew has a different attitude. He is much more able to distance himself now and say, This is my brother and sister rather than, This is my responsibility.

MATTHEW: Well, you see, it is not that I don't care; it is just that sometimes you get tired. It depends, like Jane the other night wanted to go out for the weekend, and she was punished. So Mom and I had a talk.

DOROTHY *(to the family):* So, you think he will do this by mail, or will he come home to do it?

MATTHEW *(laughs):* Oh, I will probably come home to do it.

Sal stopped the tape and said, "So what happens to the family in this session is that they become observers of their own phenomenon. I think that is very good. You created the frame in which they transact. You have introduced one theme—he is leaving—and you kept to that." He started the tape again.

JASON *(to mother):* Right after Dad was gone you said there would be no problems, but there were. And now with Matthew going you say there is going to be a small problem? From no problems with our Dad to a small problem, what's going to be happening?

MOTHER *(to Jason):* So what can you do? What would be the choice, for Matthew not to move out?
(Matthew tries to interrupt and I stop him).

DOROTHY *(to mother):* You know, you always talk to Matthew. Now with Matthew moving out, will you start talking to Jason?

Sal stopped the tape and asked for comments from the class. They enthusiastically stated that this was clearly different, that I had clearly committed myself to a direction that was interactional, and I was not allowing Matthew to interfere with where I wanted to go. I wished I could end the supervisory session there, but Sal started the tape again.

DOROTHY *(to Jason):* Will you be able to talk with your mother this way when Matthew is gone?

Sal immediately stopped the tape.

MINUCHIN: I'm interested in your thinking.

DOROTHY: My thinking is that this is the next oldest and that he will be a help to his mother. He is very much a baby in this family. So my thinking is to have him begin to take a role in the family.

MINUCHIN *(to class):* That is intervention at the middle distance. She is looking at process, and her intervention does not follow content. That was one of the biggest problems that Dorothy had. Here we see she is listening to the content and is following the process and intervenes at the level of relationships. She is very much centered in a particular exploration. So *(he turned to me)* you are successful. So maybe you can tell us a little about how it came about?

I said that I thought that it had to do with his challenge. He smiled and responded that since he is known to be difficult, he wasn't sure that he really needed more encouragement in that area. I countered that his challenge was based on a belief that I could expand as a therapist. He had done with me what he was pushing me to do with the family. He had a focus, stayed with it, and was committed to my changing.

I do therapy differently now. When I feel that I'm being drawn into content, I go to the top corner of the room where I can observe process, untrapped by content and free to act. When I'm fearful of confronting, I remember the gorilla who would not let me go down my usual path.

Chapter 13

Men and Dependency

The Treatment of a Same-Sex Couple

David E. Greenan

In our first interview, David wanted me to know that he is gay. I think he told me even before he described his training in family therapy. I didn't know what he wanted me to do with that knowledge, though it was clearly something he didn't want to leave in the closet. But of course this definition of himself also defined me—as hetero. It created a world in which we had to meet from different continents, defined by our sexual orientation. He also told me that he had been an actor and director for ten years. I told him that one of my unrealized ambitions in life was to be a playwright. That bridged the continents for me, though I don't think it had any effect on him. This issue of self-definition became the focus of our dialogue in supervision.

One of the problems that postmodernism has introduced into family therapy is its focus on diversity. The challenge to the imperialism of the dominant culture may produce a world of small turfs, where we are protected against the Other.

David was working with a homosexual couple who had selected him because, among other things, they believed that because he was homosexual, he would understand them and their context. When David decided to bring this case for supervision with me, he crossed over the boundary of narrow cultural niches, trusting that I could respect the idiosyncrasies of the couple and of the therapist and join them in my understanding of the

David E. Greenan is a psychologist and family therapist in private practice in New York City. He recently joined the faculty of The Minuchin Center for the Family and consults for them to hospital-based perinatal programs, collaborating with program staff to provide treatment to women who are chemically dependent. Dr. Greenan is also on the faculty of New York University Medical Center, where he teaches and supervises psychology interns.

universal aspects of couples. I welcomed his decision, since, like Harry Stack Sullivan, I believe that "anyone and everyone is more human than otherwise." That belief doesn't deny differences or oppose diversity, but it incorporates the idiosyncrasies of our complex humanity.

As will be clear in what follows, the process was complicated. Neither David nor I was comfortable. In the beginning, David felt that as a representative of the gay community he had to defend "gayness" against the prejudices of myself and the other supervisors. I in turn felt that to join David I needed to tread softly, be cautious in my supervisory responses, and mute my challenges. As therapy and supervision proceeded, we learned to trust each other's perspective. David's therapy became more complex as he became just a family therapist who is gay, and his clients became less the representatives of a social group and more idiosyncratic in their couple's dance.

I was born just as my father's mounted infantry company arrived in North Africa to prepare for the invasion of Italy, during the final stages of the Second World War. Nearly three years later, when my father returned to our home in northern New England, I reportedly cried out from my crib, "Who's dat man?" Whether the story is accurate or not, it has symbolic meaning for me. How to connect with my father—or with male mentors and friends—has been a lifelong challenge. In my experience, I'm not unique in that respect. In my family, men knew how to compete with one another or collaborate on some task, but we had difficulty expressing our feelings, acknowledging our need for one another.

After returning from overseas, my father buried himself in work, building a practice as a small-town physician. Like his father, he was a good provider for the family. I was the youngest of three children. My older sister died in infancy. My brother is four years older, developmentally always ahead of me. I could never quite catch up to him. As I entered junior high, he was thinking about college. And as I began attending high school, he went off to college. My brother and I had specific roles in our family system. My role was to be the stand-in for my father in his absence. When he was present, I was pulled in to be the peacemaker for the family. My brother lucked out, getting to play the rebel, a role I always coveted. The pull to take up the role of peacemaker has been a difficult one for me to cast off, and it influenced how I initially worked with families as a therapist. For me, challenging families was equated with conflict, and conflict, especially between men, was to be avoided.

The patriarchal hierarchy of the Catholic Church played a central role in my family of Celtic origins, paralleling the emotional dynamics of my family. Nuns taught me my catechism and tried to drill subservience into me, attempting to tame my desire to be the class rebel. The priest remained the ultimate and aloof authority figure in this system. The problem was that he also remained elusive, hidden behind the screen of the confessional. My father's parents, both working-class immigrants who died before I was born, adhered to their cultural norm that a priest or doctor was the most esteemed citizen of a town. Reportedly they gave my father those two career choices—he could be either a priest or a doctor. Fortunately for me, he chose to become a physician. As a second-generation Irish American, he felt a strong pull to assimilate and succeed. An Irish brogue was never heard in our house.

Besides my mother, the women in the family consisted of a maternal grandmother and her three sisters. They doted on me and my brother. Women got to express affection in my family. The only time men could be excused for showing feelings was when they were under the influence of alcohol, and then their eruption of feelings could be attributed to "the whiskey talkin'." This norm was reinforced for me along with the other cultural taboo against same-sex erotic feelings. As an adult, I've had to struggle at times with feelings of shame and weakness that emerge when I need support or nurturance from a man. The unspoken message that I internalized as a child equated my needs for male nurturance with weakness or defect. I don't think these feelings are unique to me as a gay man. The shame I can experience when negotiating intimacy needs with a man is a recurring theme that I observe when I work with both heterosexual and gay men.

Family of origin and culture contributed to making me into a future family therapist. Another major influence that shaped my professional identity as a family therapist was my earlier career in the theater. For ten years before returning to graduate school to become a psychologist, I trained and worked as an actor. Much of my training was with Uta Hagen and Herbert Berghof, who emphasized that the essence of theater is the illumination of human behavior as the author assumes the imaginary "as if" of the character in the circumstances of the play. Self-observation and the use of oneself to explore the universal experiences that we share as human beings formed the basis of the essential truth and art of the theatrical experience. It wasn't bad training for a therapist either. Given my family of origin, it's not surprising that I was attracted to an art form that encourages the expression of feelings. However, the life of an actor is often one of chronic unemployment, incompatible with my family value always to be industrious and self-sufficient.

In 1986, responding to the many losses that I had experienced from the AIDS epidemic, I began to do volunteer work with individuals and families coping with AIDS. I found the work challenging and rewarding, so much so that I decided to go back to school to study the impact of catastrophic illness on families. During graduate school, I also worked intensively studying group dynamics. Of particular interest to me, and expanding upon my earlier training as an actor, were the concepts of parallel process and projective identification. I learned that if I could understand feelings and behaviors induced by the group, I would have insights into the psychological process of the group-as-a-whole. Although I didn't know it at the time, this training would also serve as a springboard in the expansion of my roles to that of a family therapist under Salvador Minuchin's supervision.

Once in clinical internship, I began to work with families for the first time since I had been a volunteer during my early graduate school years. As interns, we were taught a strategic model for working with families, with coaching and solution-focused homework assignments given at the end of each session. The supervision was live from behind a one-way mirror. It was a relatively cool medium; conflict was minimized in the sessions. The family was expected to do much of its work between sessions. Sessions were often used as a check-up period to ascertain families' goals and monitor their progress on homework assignments. The concept of using my feelings as a diagnostic tool to make hypotheses about the family's dynamics, or encouraging enactments in the treatment room to observe how the family coconstructed one another, was not yet part of my repertoire as a family therapist.

As I ended my doctoral research year, I began supervision with Minuchin. I was also working under a federal grant to develop systems interventions for inner-city perinatal women who were chemically addicted. Many of the interventions that we developed for these homeless women focused on the belief that if they could take up their roles as responsible women and mothers, they would be motivated to lead drug-free lives. Developing interventions that enabled them to reunite their families challenged the traditional norm of the therapeutic community that posits that self-healing is the necessary ingredient for being drug-free. Simultaneously, I was working with more traditional families, and I continued to see male couples, an interest that I had developed while doing my doctoral research. As I began supervision with Sal Minuchin, the first family that I chose to present was a middle-class Asian family. It would be several months before I would work up the courage to bring in a male couple for supervision. In retrospect, I realize that my defenses against feeling vulnerable with men were already mobilized as I began supervision. Old feelings, fears of being exposed as incompetent, an imposter, reared their ugly heads. Although I think all men share these feelings, they are particularly toxic for gay men, as we are frequently encouraged by society to present the "false self," to conform to the heterosexual majority culture.

The Male Couple and Treatment Issues

Somehow in the middle of a very long winter I mustered up the courage to bring in a male couple for supervision. I had disclosed my sexual orientation to Sal during my initial interview, but I felt I was coming out to him all over again. Furthermore, I wasn't sure how my colleagues in supervision would respond. Most disconcerting of all was my fear that the couple, and by inference all gay men, would be pathologized.

> *This need for solidarity did not bode well for the therapeutic task that demands an exploration of the individual couple with its idiosyncrasies rather than its universalities.*

The couple consisted of Robert, a thirty-year-old artist, and Samuel, a thirty-seven-year-old finance executive. They had been living together for two years. Robert had not "come out" until his mid-twenties, and this was his first commitment to a relationship. Samuel, who reported that he had known that he was gay since childhood, had been in several long-term relationships.

When I first met the couple, Robert bounced into the room dressed in a baseball cap, athletic shirt, jeans, and running shoes. He looked much younger than thirty. He was easy to engage and readily offered details about his life. Samuel, in tweedy business attire, seemed guarded. He reported working long hours on Wall Street and often feeling overwhelmed with his job. He looked exhausted and much older than his age.

In the first session, the couple identified their major problem as difficulty with communication. They had participated in a commitment ceremony the year before, but like many same-sex couples, they had yet to develop rituals that identified them as a family. In spite of Robert's gregariousness and their Western charm, they seemed guarded. I had difficulty eliciting specific problems that they were experiencing. Playing it safe, I initially focused on them as individuals rather than on them as a couple. I chose to do a genogram that pulled the focus away from the couple and explored their individual histories.

Both men had grown up in the West. Samuel reported being raised in an aristocratic family, surrounded with antiques and fine china. His family had great difficulty expressing feelings. Emotions were expressed primarily through intellectual word sparring. His role in his family of origin was to be his mother's confidant and to "fix her" whenever she became upset. I was aware of feeling scrutinized by him, and when I ventured an intervention intended to challenge them as a couple, I felt he dismissed me.

Robert reported being raised by stepparents. He grew up in a highly volatile working-class family where boundaries were nonexistent and emotional chaos overwhelmed him. He spoke angrily about not having been able to acknowledge being gay until his mid-twenties. He did not appear psychologically fragile, but he reported a history of emotional instability. In college, he had been treated for depression, but he had not experienced any symptoms since graduating. Both men reported histories of individual therapy and had the facility with psychological jargon to prove it.

The one stresser that the couple mutually experienced was the strain of financial difficulties. Robert was strapped, not having sold any of his artwork in several months. He had done some odd jobs, but nothing that could alleviate the couple's financial pressures. For all practical purposes, Samuel's salary was the couple's source of income, and he appeared to run their household as well. With the surfacing of this material, I felt that we had plenty to work with. We contracted for eight sessions.

Avoidance of Conflict

During the third session, Robert said that he was anxious about the approaching Christmas holidays. Last year had been difficult for them. Robert reported that he had had a brief affair with another man for the second time since they had been together as a couple.

The previous week they had gone to a holiday party, where Samuel got drunk, stirring up Robert's old fears that their relationship was unstable. Samuel said he was using alcohol to relieve the tension that he felt from his work. He agreed to limit his alcohol intake to two drinks at any one time. I was also concerned about their use of a third person to relieve tension in their relationship. They agreed to have no extramarital affairs for the duration of treatment.

At the point when I brought this couple in for supervision, I was frustrated with my own growing sense of impotency and ineffectiveness with them. I had ended the last two sessions trying to patch up their differences while the session ran over, fearing they might split up before the next session. In retrospect, I was caught in an old belief that interpersonal conflicts always lead to distancing.

The good news was that they reported getting through the holidays without a major incident. For the first time, they had spent Christmas and New Year's together as a couple, socializing with other couples rather than returning separately to their families of origin. I supported these new behaviors by normalizing the need for couples to find their own rituals and traditions as they created their adult family. But the blow-ups at the end of each session were continuing, possibly indicating that they needed to do some work that I wasn't permitting.

> *David assumed two tasks, only one of which was therapeutic. The therapeutic task was his relationship with Robert and Samuel. But he also saw himself as a standard bearer of a group. He was afraid that if he failed therapeutically, he would be blamed as a gay man for the failure of a gay couple.*
>
> *While I had seen him working with other families, when he was a family therapist who was gay, here he saw himself as a gay family therapist.*

Although I was unaware of it, a parallel process was already occurring in my supervision group. I was as anxious about letting Minuchin see me as a family therapist as the couple had been about letting me into their relationship. My supervision colleagues told me that I had described the men very clearly as individuals but I had given no sense of the men as a couple. I was surprised as I watched the tape to see how calm I appeared, knowing how anxious I felt that the couple would be pathologized and I would be perceived as incompetent. I was also surprised to see how closely my calm presentation in supervision mirrored Samuel's laid-back manner in the session, a further clue to the parallel process that was happening.

I maintained a professional demeanor to hide my anxieties and fears of incompetence. But Sal quieted my fears with his first comments, "I don't know a lot of male couples, and I'm not sure that the group has a lot of experience with them. You will have to educate us."

> *I had been concerned about this supervision. I knew of David's reluctance to present a same-sex couple, and I was determined that no homophobia from me or the group would embarrass him or interfere with his progress as a therapist. So I started supervision by assigning him the task of teaching us and braked my impulse to comment on the couple's patterns of interaction, and the fact that most of David's interventions were directed toward individual insights.*
>
> *Of course, by avoiding a direct challenge I was curtailing my supervisory freedom and unwittingly joining David's avoidance.*

Sal's comments, besides empowering me to take up my role, helped me focus on dynamics that may be characteristic of male couples, as well as the dynamics they share with heterosexual couples. I thought about the developmental theory of gay identity formation and the exaggerated need gay men frequently experience to maintain their independence. In general, men are acculturated to be independent. For gay men, however, dependency needs in an intimate relationship with another man may stir up fears of prior shameful labels; that is, as adults in intimate male relationships, gay men may reexperience many shameful childhood incidents, recalling memories of being ostracized by peers and father figures for being "queer." So when a gay man in an intimate relationship with another man experiences the need to be held and comforted, he may dismiss the need because he confuses the feeling with the internalized homophobic label that he's a "queer," defective. Additionally, as in any couple, dependency needs may stir up fear of fusion and enmeshment.

I wondered if my interventions had been leading them away from their needs as a couple. Sal confirmed my fear. "I don't see them as a couple. There is denial of their complementarity as a couple. Your emphasis is on working with the individual. But I think dependency in a couple is a good thing." Later he said, "I'm interested in how they are as a couple. But I would move to concreteness with them, because this is a family that talks about talking. They talk in generalities, so I would move to details. Your use of intellectual metaphors is lost, because with an intellectual like Samuel, they are not a novelty."

I left the supervision session wondering if I too was caught in a similar dynamic, overintellectualizing feelings to defend against fear of dependency with my supervisor. My own need for approval and acceptance was keeping me from taking risks to be more creative in the treatment and keeping me defended against exposing my sense of vulnerability for not having the answers. As I continued to work with Minuchin and this couple, I became clearer about my own "blind spots" against dependency needs.

One of the complexities of supervising a therapist's style is that while I am focusing on the therapeutic system and expansion of the therapist's repertoire, I may unwittingly be touching aspects of the supervisee's individual life. I think this phenomenon characterizes most human encounters, and while I am aware of my supervisory intentions, I do not know how my intervention may be reverberating for the individual. This is another way therapy and supervision are isomorphic. The supervisor must be respectful because he is responsible for the effects of his interventions.

The next supervision session with this couple occurred about a month later. In the interim, they had been in for three sessions. This time Robert reported feeling very depressed and anxious about recurring adolescent thoughts of hurting himself and Samuel appeared lethargic and depressed. Their moods contrasted with those of the prior session, when they had come in ebullient and affectionate toward one another. This time, they reported having "tricked" with a third man over the weekend. They had gone to a dance club, where the other man had indicated a sexual interest in Samuel. They had brought him home, and he had spent the night with them.

I immediately was caught up in the dynamic of the threesome and felt that it could be a destabilizing influence on the couple. I focused the session on the incident and reframed the event as Samuel's way of taking care of the relationship—an intervention that didn't graft with the couple. My understanding of the couple's dance had been that Samuel's introducing a third party who was explicitly interested in him allowed him to moderate intimacy in their relationship. The third party temporarily saved Samuel from having to deal with Robert's feelings of emotional emptiness. The dynamic may also have served to dampen both men's fears of fusion and enmeshment within the relationship as possibilities for deeper intimacy increased in the session.

Minuchin introduced another possible course the session could have taken. "When a heterosexual couple comes to me and talks only about sex, I move them to talk about who washes the dishes. The same dynamics will be seen in all their transactions." Later in the session, using the terminology of the Rorschach, he said, "I'm interested in dd's, not W's. Go from the generalities to the specifics."

> *At this point, I was convinced that David's ideology was handicapping his treatment. He was seeing a same-sex couple. I was seeing a couple who, like all couples, transacted issues of power and intimacy in the small details of daily events.*

What confused me was that in the session when they reported participating in the threesome, Samuel and Robert were communicating in ways I had not seen before. It seemed they could hear each other for the first time. Samuel spoke about his fear that he needed to "fix" Robert when his feelings of failure as an artist overwhelmed him. Robert had been able to tell Samuel that he didn't need fixing, if only Samuel would listen. Robert also spoke about his sense of lost adolescence, in not having dated any men until he was in his mid-twenties. They spoke to each other, tentatively, about their fears of fusion and absorption in the relationship. I had stayed focused on the dynamic of the introduction of a third party in the relationship, missing an opportunity to highlight their increased ability to hear each other.

Sal focused primarily on my proximity to the couple. "You have created novelty in the relationship, and that is good, but what you are seeing is danger. You're too close to them. Your response to novelty should be supportive. Instead you kept your clinical language. They are discovering complementarity, experiencing themselves as individuals within a couple. Use the language of constructionism. 'Samuel, you are creating a Robert you can trust. Robert, you are creating a mate who is not a father.' You should tell them they are doing very good work. It is important to underline commitment, the genuine discovery of being a couple, and to reinforce that behavior. If I see a good moment I want to emphasize, I screen out bad moments. Otherwise you diffuse the effect of the novel behavior that the couple has achieved."

I hadn't supported the new behavior that I had observed in that session. This was a blind spot in my own understanding of constructing relationships.

Several weeks and sessions passed before my next presentation. The couple again experimented with a threesome. I created a narrative that focused on Robert's need to up the ante in the relationship and awaken Samuel emotionally by engaging a third person. Knowing that many gay couples report successfully negotiating an open relationship, I also questioned my stance that extramarital affairs don't work for most couples.

In the session I presented, Robert had become highly emotional and Samuel had closed down, saying that he was too tired to work.

> *As I saw the couple's dynamics, Robert was a bright, rather demanding and childish young man to whom Samuel responded with studied caution. When Robert was angry at Samuel, Samuel slowed his tempo and became pedantic, assuming a posture of detachment that stirred Robert to search for closeness.*

I was aware of feeling annoyed with Samuel and what I perceived to be his withholding position. I offered him two choices. "We can either end the session, or you can go get some coffee to wake you up!" Although aware of my frustration with Samuel, I didn't have enough distance from the couple to understand and use my feelings.

Minuchin responded to the tape, "Samuel makes you angry as you try to get him involved in the session. That's what he does to Robert. What does that tell you? That is the couple's dynamic. Feel what's happening, and use it."

I began to wonder if I was once again capping affect, taking up the familiar role of peacemaker, echoing my family of origin. Samuel was angry at Robert. I stepped between them and deflected the anger. As Sal pointed out, even my language focused on affect as an impersonal object. Robert said that he was afraid when he and Samuel brought another man home. I said "of what," instead of "of whom?" The effect was to disembody his feeling.

Parallel process was not a new concept for me, but for some reason I wasn't using my awareness of my feelings to understand how the couple danced together. I wasn't yet free to hear and interpret the subtext of their communications. Like many men, I feared that heightening the conflict between them would lead to disengagement rather than an opportunity for greater intimacy.

Earlier in the session, Samuel had complained of fatigue. He also mentioned the weight of their financial burdens. He was not only the primary source of income for the couple but also the one who maintained their home, doing all the cooking and bookkeeping. Sal suggested that if I hadn't been overly close to the couple, I might have seen that Samuel's repressed anger addressed real inequities in the relationship. He was carrying the lion's share of the load, but no one was hearing that.

> *Any therapist working with a heterosexual couple would probably tune in if either spouse was carrying so much of the burden. The situation would be quite visible, and the inequity of the relationship would be explored. Why was Samuel's position as the exploited member of this couple not part of the therapeutic story? It seems an interesting result of the couple's being seen as a homosexual couple, as opposed to a couple. Issues of complementarity that are natural in a couple tended to be obscured.*

Sal's comments gave me some distance, so I could see the dynamic from an intermediate distance. "Same-sex couples are in uncharted territories. This couple is working as if they are of equal power. They are not. But where a heterosexual couple can talk about roles and role reversal, for homosexual couples there are not such clear roles to reverse."

As spring approached, the couple indicated a desire to terminate. By the time the couple's sessions ended, Robert had secured a lucrative part-time job that helped alleviate their financial difficulties. They had also negotiated a division of household chores that distributed tasks more evenly. Both men reported more stability in the relationship. As termination approached, we reviewed what they had achieved during the course of therapy, and I assured them they could come back for a check-up if they ever experienced the need.

Crisis: Opportunity for Insight and Intimacy

During the following summer, Robert's stepfather died suddenly. Robert called and said he would like to schedule a few sessions to deal with this sudden loss. One-on-one sessions focused on his grief. Robert's stepfather had known that his son was gay, although he had rarely acknowledged Robert's spousal relationship with Samuel. Pursuing a theme that I often hear from gay men, Robert grieved for the lost opportunities for closeness to his stepfather. Robert felt that his stepfather sensed that he was different from other boys as a child, but they had never been able to talk about their ensuing alienation. Robert had felt close to his stepfather as an adult. He experienced mixed feelings at the funeral when many of his stepfather's friends told stories about his boasting to them about his son. Though he was sad that they had never had that conversation, he felt accepted by his stepfather as he dealt with this first major loss in his life.

Concurrently, Robert was able to gain insight into the distancing effect that his anger often had on other people, and how he tended to isolate himself, a repetition pattern that reenacted the dynamics of his family of origin. This effect became clearer to both of us when he became angry at me in a session for not providing him with a quick answer to a question I believed was too complicated to answer in that manner. As I endeavored to explain the roller coaster of feelings that frequently accompanies a major loss, he withdrew and appeared dejected. As we explored his feelings, Robert once again experienced the grief of his stepfather's death and his anger at me for not being able to make it go away. As he recognized how his withdrawal precluded the possibility of my helping him, we explored the parallel meaning it might have in his relationship with Samuel.

Robert's response to his grief—his initial withdrawal and then anger—is a reaction that I have experienced myself and often see in other men as a defense against the intolerable feelings of abandonment that we experience on the death of a loved one. My willingness to witness his anger and not retreat, to explore its meaning and the effect it might have on other people, helped Robert through this stage of grieving as he ended therapy. I didn't know then how important this work would become as the couple resumed therapy and we explored the coconstruction of their relationship at a new level.

Couples Therapy Resumes: Conflict Leads to Growth

Some time in the late fall, when I had not seen them as a couple in several months, Robert called and requested a couples session. I was concerned that because I had been seeing Robert individually, Samuel might feel that I was more joined with his partner. But Minuchin thought that continued couples treatment would be possible as long as I was careful to join with Samuel when they returned. He recommended that to facilitate the rejoining, it would be good for Robert to review with Samuel the insights that he had gained during the bereavement work.

It was clear that the couple was under considerable stress. Samuel had recently started a new, highly paid job on Wall Street that required long hours. He appeared exhausted and confirmed that he was, reporting feeling overwhelmed not only by his work but by the emotional demands that Robert was exerting. Robert countered that he felt Samuel had abandoned him since starting his new job. This was confirmed, he said, at a recent holiday party in Samuel's new company. Even though it was a gay affirmative firm, Samuel had introduced Robert to his colleagues as a friend.

As Robert railed at Samuel for this perceived trivialization of their relationship, I observed Samuel withdraw. His eyes seemed to glaze over. I waffled between their two positions. I supported Robert with a metaphor that there was "a party going on, and he felt excluded." Possibly in a flight to intellectualization as a defense against the strong feelings they were expressing, I chose to normalize Samuel's behavior with an explanation. Though "out" at work, Samuel might have experienced a resurgence of old homophobia at this office event. I also talked about how it is not uncommon for gay men to feel that their self-esteem is threatened whenever they "come out," particularly in a dominant culture setting. My intervention did not calm the emotional storm building in the session. Samuel complained that Robert didn't understand him and bolted out of the session, saying he was too exhausted to engage in this type of emotional interaction. Though I had felt empathy for Samuel in his struggle to be comfortable as an openly gay man, I realized that by the end of the session, I had emotionally joined with Robert in his position as "the victim."

In supervision, Sal commented on my middle distance with the couple. He wondered why I had not joined with Samuel in his ability to respond to Robert's flood of emotions. Overwhelmed by Robert's emotions, Samuel had closed down, exacerbating Robert's fear of abandonment. Could I work more proximally with the couple and not fear that I would lose my hierarchy in the session? This question not only helped me understand my feelings with the couple but simultaneously gave me insight into my relationship with Minuchin and the supervision group. During this second year of supervision, as I presented other families, I had begun to experience myself as becoming more trusting with Sal. Although I still wanted his approval, I was more willing to engage in a dialogue and could still feel supported by him. It would be interesting to see how this more complex relationship would transfer to the treatment of the couple.

Just before Christmas, the couple canceled their session because of their work and holiday schedules. A couple of days before Christmas, however, Robert called to say that he was feeling suicidal and requested an individual session. I said I felt it would be more helpful to see them as a couple, but he insisted that we meet alone. During the individual session, he disclosed that he had been having a sexual affair with a fellow sculptor over the past couple of months. Recently, as this man's career had taken off, he'd felt that he was doomed to be a failure. He worried that if Samuel found out about the affair, their relationship would be destroyed.

After ascertaining that he did not have a suicide plan and assessing that he was not acutely suicidal, I made a contract with Robert that we would speak on the phone over the holiday. Much to my consternation, he did not call at the agreed-on time. I called him at home. He was surprised to hear from me and told me that he was feeling better. He and Samuel had enjoyed their Christmas, and he had simply forgotten to call at the scheduled time. I scheduled an appointment for them the following week.

In the meantime, I had a session with Minuchin. My main question was what to do with my own feelings of frustration and anger. I had been left worrying over Christmas while Robert had been enjoying his holiday. We had made a contract, and he hadn't honored it. Sal reflected, "Robert insists on seeing himself as a victim. He doesn't take responsibility for his behavior. You reach out to help him, and he slaps your hand. That's what he does to Samuel." I then explored with Sal what I should do with the secret of the extramarital affair. We both felt that revealing the affair at this time would be destructive and could only support Robert's self-selected role as "the victim." We agreed that the affair was not much of a threat to their relationship.

When I went into the next session, I felt I had sufficient insight into the meaning of my own feelings that I could use them to help the couple explore the possible parallels in their dynamics. But sessions never go as planned. Robert came alone, reporting that Samuel was in bed with a severe case of the flu. I decided to use the session to focus on our dyadic relationship, similar to the way I had worked with him in the summer. During the session, he was able to identify his sense of anger and resentment at feeling overwhelmed emotionally and to realize that he was engaging in a sexual affair to soothe these feelings. In reaching out to me for help and then rejecting my assistance, he had only increased his feelings of helplessness and isolation. This dynamic evoked childhood memories of being part of an enmeshed family that didn't allow space for his emotional needs. In rejecting my offer of help, he had recreated the familiar dynamic of the abused and the abuser. What wasn't clear to either of us, as Sal observed in my next supervision, was how much power Robert obtained with Samuel in this role of "the victim."

The next session began with the couple relating an argument they had had when two other couples were coming over for dinner. Robert had agreed to clean the apartment while Samuel prepared dinner. As the dinner hour approached, Samuel got mad at Robert because he had not done the cleaning. During the session, Robert began to lecture Samuel about how he liked to do things at his own pace. It was no big deal if the apartment didn't get cleaned for the party. Once again I observed Samuel's eyes glaze over as he distanced himself from Robert.

I got up, walked over to the couple, and asked Samuel to get down on his knees. Robert was to stand up and continue talking. This simple move had a powerful effect, as it made explicit to both men the dynamic that they were coconstructing. Samuel was delighted at first. Then he became self-conscious as Robert let me know how angry my behavior made him. I said I thought he was lecturing Samuel and had lost his audience. If that was the impact he wanted to have on Samuel, he should continue; otherwise, he might want to explore a different way of communicating with him.

Robert then refused to talk and became withdrawn. Both men appeared uneasy, as if an explosion were about to occur. I decided not to avoid the conflict, trusting Sal's advice that opportunities for change frequently arise when the therapist is willing to unbalance the system. Using my experience of the session, I reflected my feelings to Robert. I said I felt I had hurt him, and that I was now aware of feeling a need to be careful with him. I also observed how quickly he had become the patient in the session, and how that appeared to isolate him. As our time was up, I ended the session by asking the couple to think about how they had created these roles for each other.

This session marked a drastic change in behavior for me as a family therapist. Instead of talking about affect and avoiding conflict, I had used the "here-and-now" re-enactment of the couple's dynamics to intervene and unbalance the system. Rather than talk about feelings, I had intensified them in the session through physically moving the couple. Robert was able to experience his power in the "victim role" with Samuel. Samuel understood viscerally how he withheld from Robert in response to the perceived inequity of power. It took a great deal of self-monitoring for me, but I even managed not to try to rebalance the system as they departed.

The next session had an entirely different feel to it. Samuel began the session, a novelty, by talking about feeling burned out and about the difficulty he had with allowing himself to be consoled. He related it to his childhood and the norms that had existed in his WASP family—a family that considered it a character flaw to need comforting. Men were expected to keep a stiff upper lip.

I had never heard Samuel talk so openly. At one point, he began to weep over the many friends he has lost since the onset of the AIDS epidemic. This was new behavior for him. But Robert continued to respond in the pattern familiar to the couple. He began a monologue, offering Samuel suggestions, talking about how helpful he found it to ask for what he wants.

After a minute or two I was aware that Samuel was withdrawing. I interrupted Robert and asked Samuel what he was feeling. He said, "I feel I'm in school being lectured at." I asked him how Robert might talk so he didn't feel he was being lectured. Samuel responded, "I think different words would help. It all starts with 'I want.'" I asked Samuel why that made him angry. At that point, Samuel shifted from a coconstruction dialogue of their relationship to an introspective monologue. The rest of the session focused on Samuel's lack of comfort with letting Robert support him. I framed this as a challenge to the couple. Could Samuel give up his role as caretaker and allow Robert to take care of him?

The supervision that followed raised many questions, and Sal didn't make me comfortable by providing any answers. "The session is good, but I would always push for complexity. Robert is talking only from Robert's perspective. Samuel says he doesn't trust people to hear him. When he said to Robert 'You always say I, never we,' why didn't you move to support him?"

I answered that perhaps I didn't trust what I was seeing. "You saw Samuel changing. Don't you trust that Samuel will accept you if you join him? They are working at a different level, responding in new ways. Now they are in therapy."

Minuchin's challenge continued to reverberate within me long after the supervision, and I didn't find any quick answer. I've discovered that some of the answer may lie in my becoming more comfortable with a dynamic form of therapy that activates families emotionally to discover new ways of relating. This is a style of therapy that requires me to use my total being in the encounter. It's driven by theory, but it's not only talk therapy; it's an active form of treatment. It's live theater with a full cast of characters—the human drama being acted out in the therapy hour in all its complexity.

Another part of the answer has to do with trust. I need to be more willing to trust what I'm asking the couple to do—take a leap of faith into an unscripted encounter. I need to trust the sacredness of the therapeutic hour to uncover some of the universal truths that we collectively share in our experience as human beings. That requires not only use of self but belief in the human potential for growth and trust in the collective wisdom of "we." I also have had to learn to trust that I'm not responsible for the answers. My role is to unbalance the system, to start the questions.

The rest of the answer has to do with me as a man and how I've learned about how men negotiate power and intimacy and recognize dependency needs. Men, gay or heterosexual, are acculturated to be strong and invincible; how do we then deal with the inevitable feelings of weakness and vulnerability? Is it safer to identify with the role of the victim rather than to risk being challenged for being strong? How do we tolerate feelings of strength and weakness simultaneously, needs for independence and dependence? Do these feelings, which seem so dichotomous, exist on a continuum? And how do men in an intimate relationship resolve these conflicts together?

I can't end this chapter with any pretense that I have found all the answers. But I can report that Robert and Samuel found a new way of relating. They are less afraid of fusion and enmeshment as they appear more versatile in their roles with each other. They have become more accepting of their complementarity. Samuel loves his new work. Robert likes to tinker with his hobbies while he pursues his sculpting, and that's okay. They are much more tolerant of each other's idiosyncracies and simultaneously much more supportive of each other. Their basic personalities and the way they relate to the world haven't changed, but they appear more comfortable with disagreeing and less threatened by tending to each other's needs. They have a much greater sense of being a couple, and I experienced them that way too as they ended therapy. I felt much freer to enter and challenge the system, even though my role was often to act more as a witness to their family process, perhaps like an older brother who supports their growth.

Sal modeled that behavior by providing a safe place to explore human relationships, free of the induction that occurs in treatment with a family. In the course of that supervision, I gained greater trust and belief in the strength of relationships to foster growth. The acceptance and insights provided by the supervision detoxified my fear of feeling incompetent and shamed as a new family therapist. Simultaneously, Sal normalized the dynamics of a male couple, honoring the unique features of gay men in an intimate relationship while placing their dynamics within the context of the struggles inherent to all couples. Expressing belief in me as a therapist, he challenged and encouraged me to think more complexly. My fear that challenge creates distance had the paradoxical and therapeutic effect of creating closeness, in both supervision and treatment.

The fear that I experienced before beginning supervision with Minuchin was mirrored in the initial mistrust of the couple in treatment. The impact of marginalization of gay men by the majority culture has ramifications for gay couples as they experience the reality of isolation and society's pathologizing. The treatment focused on normalizing their needs for nurture and dependency and expanding on the complementarity of their roles. When they left treatment, I experienced them as less hierarchical in relationship to one another and to me. Simultaneously, there was less need to pathologize each other and more acceptance of their status as a young couple negotiating the early stages of their relationship. Paralleling the treatment was the dynamic I experienced in supervision—a senior male mentor, respectful yet challenging me to grow, patient with me as I stumbled, coaching me to develop new strengths. As therapy and supervision ended, I experienced myself in a similar trusting and respectful relationship with the male couple.

Chapter 14

The Shit-Painter

Wai-Yung Lee

With Wai-Yung, the supervisory dance was more complex than with any of the other supervisees. It started with a hierarchical relationship in which I saw myself as interested, but at a distance—my preferred supervisorial stance. Wai-Yung, seeking a mutual commitment to her quest for learning, insisted that I accept the proximity she associated with a teacher/student trek.

She demonstrated the seriousness of her engagement by flying in weekly from Toronto, a journey that started at dawn and kept her in the office, watching tapes, well into the evening before she caught a plane back home. In the group, she was curious, seemingly unafraid of exposure, always ready to engage me and the other supervisees in exploratory dialogues.

As a teacher I was strongly attracted to the poetic bent of her interventions and a certain off-the-wall quality in her responses. She was unconventional in ways that invited curiosity about the nature of her thinking. I liked it when she asked an orthodox Jewish patient if his God was mischievous. Something in her style allowed her to ask off-limits questions without eliciting suspicion. To my Western understanding, here was an intelligent, adult Chinese woman who often behaved with the undefended openness of a child.

She was always asking questions. She expected answers, too, and as I supplied them, I began to become her Teacher.

Being the teacher Wai-Yung wanted demanded an expansion of my style. Wai-Yung demanded proximity and mutual respect along with knowledge. Somehow we managed to establish a hierarchical yet collegial

---

WAI-YUNG LEE is a faculty member of the Minuchin Center for the Family in New York, and director of Family Studies in Hong Kong. With extensive experience in the field of mental deficiency, she has worked and provided training in Toronto, New York, and London and is currently a regular visiting lecturer at the Graduate School of Social Work and Social Administration at the University of Hong Kong. She has studied and worked with Salvador Minuchin for over six years.

> *relationship that facilitated her learning. Somehow I learned to complement her exploration. When she was baroque, I was simple. When she was concrete, I was creative. If she went off on a tangent, I centralized. I know I grew as a teacher, because she demanded so strongly to be taught.*

When Minuchin first interviewed me as a candidate for his supervision group, he asked me: "Do you consider yourself an American Chinese, or a Chinese living in America?" I have lived most of my adult life in North America, mostly in Canada. But my answer to Minuchin's question came without thinking, "I am a Chinese living in America." It was a long way for me to find myself in New York studying family therapy with Salvador Minuchin.

I came from what one might call a totally dysfunctional family from a complex and dying subculture of Chinese origin. My father had three wives all at the same time. My own mother was the second wife. She left for another man when I was about three years old. In my photo album, I cut out the only picture I had of her and replaced it with a picture of my father's third wife, simply because she was the most beautiful one of them all. When my new mother also left for another man, I told everybody that she had been killed in a bizarre accident. I did that not because I was angry with her but just because it did not reflect well on my father that two of his wives had left him for other men. As a child, I felt I had the magic to adopt and disown people at will. My bonding to women was mostly through my nannies, and I had three of them at different times as I was growing up.

I have only one brother, twenty years my senior. He has never taken a job in his life, and after marrying, he still lives in my father's house. But the house was always full of people, particularly at dinnertime. It was after the war, so relatives who came with their families for a few nights' refuge ended up staying forever. Widowed servants who came to work with their children, and strangers who just appeared in the house, stayed on. My home was only a backdrop for many of the everyday life dramas to take place, except that some of the players who took center stage in my house were total strangers.

Therefore, I do not know if one should put my family in the category of the enmeshed or the disengaged. It was enmeshed because people never seemed to leave the house (except my two mothers); it was disengaged because there was a great deal of mental space amongst all of us while the physical space kept on shrinking. It was such a different way of living and relating, yet to me it was a well-coordinated household and all relationships were transacted in an orderly manner.

Since there were no clear values or firm restrictions that I had to follow, I never learned to reason. I learned that there are no absolute rules in people, except the rules of life. As a young girl, I spent late nights in the opium room where my father entertained his friends, listening to all the adult conversation and stories amid the smoke and piping sound made by the opium "gun." Father was a man of very few words, and the only times I remember that he expressed his feelings were when he was singing fragments from some popular Chinese opera in his bath. From him, I learned that things are understood without need of explanation. People can feel very close in silence.

My gender role was also blurred. I never paid much attention to gender differences until I went to the university. When I was ten years old, my father gave me a gun that shot lead bullets. I went around shooting birds and neighbors' windows. One day I threw a stone at a neighbor's son, and there was blood flowing out from his forehead. I was so afraid that he would die that I hid. When I finally got home, I remember my father standing in the courtyard admiring his large tank of exotic goldfish. With his eyes fixed on the gracefully swimming creatures he said to me softly, "Why did you do that? What kind of a woman are you growing up to be?"

From my father I realized that life is mostly full of questions and there is no need for answers. Therefore, there was very little concern for excessive planning or goal setting and certainly no point in making a fuss of any emotional display. There was many a time when my father left to go on a trip and then reappeared shortly because he had missed the train or the plane. But that was perfectly all right as long as there were goldfish swimming in the tank, or other amusements in life that drew our attention.

When my father eventually took the trip of no return, I never quite believed it. I still have recurring dreams of his coming home and saying that he had missed his flight again. In my repertoire of cognitive constructs there was no such thing as finality.

My childhood taught me that the world is only a stage backdrop. There was a theatre in the house, and there was also a theatre from my bedroom window, where I witnessed all the absurdities of everyday life. I once saw a woman running after her husband with a chopper; when she caught up with him, she chopped the umbrella that he was carrying, rather than the man himself. There was another woman who told her husband that if he left the house she would strip herself naked on the street, and she did. My father once took a beggar from the street and offered him a job to help me with my homework. On his second night, he tried to take on one of the servant girls, who punched him flat on his nose. He was back to the street in no time, but whenever I got stuck with my homework, I would still shout my questions at him from the balcony, and he was always happy to provide me with an answer. My childhood experience was of a theatre of confusion, where the roles people chose to play and the rules that went along with the play could change and interchange into all sorts of forms and shapes, with or without boundaries, until they reached a state of harmony. Bateson would say this is just the theory of cybernetics. I prefer to call it life.

My love for chaos and the excitement of the world has saved me from many a lonely and miserable moment in my life. When I was about eleven, a man jumped from our fourth floor and landed in a pool of blood right outside my window. From then on, I began to see a ghost and could hear his sorrow.

When I immigrated to Canada, I did not leave those scenarios behind; I only expanded my stage into a larger world. But like many other immigrants, I put away my treasure from the past and locked the chest with a key. I did not see the need to bridge the two worlds. When I looked out from my window, I saw only the snow.

Therefore, life made perfect sense for me when I started my career as a reporter. My experience even gave me a sense of depth when I learned psychoanalytical work. But for someone whose sense of family is always a little bit out of focus, it seems strange that I decided to become a family therapist.

Professional Context

I worked for many years as a psychotherapist in the field of mental retardation, which people prefer these days to call that of the "developmentally delayed" or the "intellectually challenged." No matter how many times the name changed, however, the mental deficiency field was known to be very mundane and reflective of a history of institutional care. It was really a field about control and countercontrol and a hilarious slice of the human drama when the two were mixed together.

Again, this time looking through my professional window, I revisited the absurdities of my childhood stage. I saw a young woman, weighing two hundred pounds, who had soaked her mother's designer shower curtain with her own urine and then stripped naked at the bathroom window to draw attention from the rich neighborhood. Because she was "dumb," nobody thought that she was capable of rage. I saw a middle-aged man who could never forgive his father for putting him down as he was growing up, so he adopted the job of abusing himself and those around him. I also saw rescuers who trapped their victims while proclaiming that they were there to set them free and institutions of helpers running around offering dreams that they themselves could not pursue.

As I was seeing more and more, the crowd of ghosts outside my window grew. I began to identify with the world of the mentally retarded. We are all just imperfect and incomplete creatures coping with the restrictions and impositions of the world. I saw that our cognitive maneuvers to solve behavioral problems were only our desperate attempts to find solutions in a world that has none.

It became clear to me that one cannot deal with the mentally retarded in isolation. So I moved on to work with the families and provided staff training. I promoted ambiguity and ambivalence in a field that is usually restrained and restricted by an overabundance of explanation. All those times when I was seen as a family therapist and systems consultant, however, I was really focusing on the patterns of interaction in the system. I treated families in much the same way as I was treating the larger system. I could not differentiate the boundaries between the two.

From childhood to adulthood, my stage has always been the larger world. I was good at making total strangers connected, but I had no idea what to do with family members when they turned into strangers. I began to feel bored with myself and saw a need to expand my horizon.

First I went to Milan. I was right at home with the Milan team's distant stance and its grand way of using language, for I was also a narrator with years of practice in seeing things either through a window or from a detached stance. When I returned and went to work with Minuchin, all of a sudden the limelight was on me. I embarked on an apprenticeship of training that for the next two years, put my work and consequently my own self on center stage.

The Family

The family that I brought in for supervision had a twenty-four-year-old Down Syndrome man who had smeared his own feces on the bathroom walls. The case was referred by the mother as an urgent matter. I arranged to see them quickly, but on the day of the appointment only Bill came with his group home counselor. I asked Bill why he was there to see me. He said his mother sent him. This response is very typical in the field of mental disability, where therapy is seen as a way to fix the problem presented by the identified client's family and workers. I sent them away with a message that I would only see them if the family came with Bill.

At the next session, the rest of the family—the parents and a 31-year-old brother, Michael—came, but without Bill. This was an English-Canadian family. The parents had both served in the army and still carried the same no-nonsense atmosphere of the military. The mother explained that they did not want to talk about Bill in front of him. The family conversation was centered around Bill's behavioral problem, which apparently had a history of repeated occurrences. The family had taken many different measures, but the problem persisted.

This couple shared the characteristics of many parents who have adult children with developmental handicaps. Parents who have given birth to a handicapped child are often described as mourning the loss of the perfect baby of their dreams. I have seen this mourning persist and, as the child grows, take on the form of continuous coaching and correcting in the name of love and protection. The tragedy of disabled persons is that they are often treated as children, even when they have reached adulthood. While remaining childlike, they rage about living in a world of infantilism.

Bill was a highly functional young man who tried to lead a normal life, even growing a beard. He was able to hold down odd jobs in restaurants, but whenever he became frustrated, he would go into the washroom and smear his feces on the wall. This behavior made his family question his intelligence even more. Every problem was attributed to the fact that he was mentally retarded. Their way of helping him enraged him even further. His brother Michael tried to relate to him as a good brother should. But their worlds were miles apart, one being a successful architect living in an intellectual world, the other leading a restricted life in a group home and living by whatever odd jobs he could get.

The sense of failure that Bill was coping with was foreign to the rest of his family, for whom his rage was unthinkable. Thus, everybody focused on changing Bill's behavior instead of facing his pain and protest. Although professionals have long identified the need to involve families in the treatment of persons with disabilities, their methods too have focused on support and understanding. Often there is an unspoken ethic that one should be gentle with those who have suffered greatly from the unfairness of life. It is politically incorrect to rock the system, even if the rigidity of the system is creating or maintaining the problem.

How, then, does one provide a more complex therapy to families with a chronic illness or disability? It became the quest of my training.

The Supervision

By the time I brought this case in for supervision, I had already studied with Minuchin for one year. My first year of supervision was both dazzling and full of puzzlement. The language he used in supervision was very different from anything that I had been exposed to. He talked about creating discontinuity, both in the family's interactive patterns and in the style of the therapist, even though most of us held dear to our hearts the value of consistency. He taught his students to be "unfair" and "irresponsible" for therapeutic benefit, whereas for many of us that was a cardinal sin. His stances were strange, and yet there was something curiously liberating about them that touched a part of our inner psyches that was dormant and longed to be awakened.

With intensity as his mode, punctuation and challenge as his tools, he used a relational language reflective of a systems thinking. It was also a language of change and movement, consistently delivered with a mixture of challenge and nurturance. To Minuchin, his signature "kicking and stroking" were inseparable twins, one having no use without the other. He created disorder and tension, believing that out of discomfort people would access their strength to create change, particularly when support is provided. Without conflict there is no conflict resolution. You have to allow yourself to be captured before you can set yourself free. This style of supervision is far from cognitive coaching, although it contains an element of the cognitive. It involves a full range of interpersonal intensity that puts all your faculties to work. When I brought in the case of the shit painter, suddenly my therapeutic style and my work with families with chronic problems began to pull together. The family became a stage for the transaction of learning.

Jumping into Unknown Territory

At their third session, the entire family came at my insistence. It was through the videotape of this particular interview that I first introduced this family to Minuchin for supervision.

This was a conservative family that subscribed to logic and yet had produced a son who had given them the most irrational and absurd problem to deal with. Even though they came as a family, they insisted that I should talk to Bill without involving them. Their insistence activated my sense of absurdity, so I decided to enter into a ludicrous conversation with Bill. First I called the smearing his "signature" and asked him to describe in detail what he was painting, which finger he used, and whether he needed to smell his finger or not. Such a conversation was, of course, making the parents very uncomfortable.

After listening to my description of the family session, Minuchin offered an elegant explanation to my intervention, "To ask which finger do you use and do you smell or not smell, is problem solving. Wai-Yung is saying that the problem that people are trying to resolve is organized in ways that are not solvable. And if you are adding to the dimension of the problem, the solution needs to be different." He turned to me and continued, "If you want to expand further, you might ask if he wants to draw the face of his dad, or is it his mother he wishes to draw? Do you want to put a penis there, or do you not want to be anatomically correct? At the point when you are trying to expand the symptom, the people need to deal with the problem differently."

Going into the details of my work, let alone having my style and limitations pointed out, was not as easy as I thought it would be. At one point I was showing a segment in which I was talking to the family about Bill without involving the young man in the conversation. Minuchin was determined to track me down; he said, "Does Bill talk?"

WAI-YUNG: He does very loosely—
MINUCHIN: How do you know?
WAI-YUNG: Not here, but he talks—
MINUCHIN: He had talked before?
WAI-YUNG *(mumbling):* Yes.

I had no other choice but to show him a segment in which Bill was participating in the discussion. In this segment, I was leading the family to talk about how they might have silenced Bill with their highly verbal skill. I was the leader of the discussion. A couple of times Bill tried to participate, but I was more concerned with the topic. Subtle gestures from a disabled person simply did not register with me as being important. It became more poignant when at some point the family described Bill as a "curtain man," one who dropped the curtain whenever the limelight was focused on him. Instead of using the opportunity to draw him out, I asked the family to think about how to expand the "repertoire" of the "curtain man." Bill asked, "What does repertoire mean?" His brother started to explain. In my opinion his explanation was not very clear, and I took over the explanation of the meaning of repertoire.

Minuchin interjected, "I would make a diagnosis of the way in which these people talk with the young man not by telling them what to talk about but by saying 'Talk with him.' In the process of listening to the ways the people talk with him, I would call for an experience of trying to communicate and not being able to. I would be helping and criticizing, pushing and modifying. Then at some point or other, we would come to some kind of understanding of the process of silence." He then turned to me. "Instead, you talk about silence and talk about language. From the point of view of your content, you are challenging the silence; from the point of view of form, you are doing exactly what they are doing."

Shit! I cursed to myself! To defuse Minuchin's focus I moved on to show him another segment, in which I was telling the family a story: "Every week I go to New York for supervision, and my teacher always tells me that I believe too much in words. If he thinks that I believe too much in words, I wish he'd met you guys here." The family laughed. My classmates laughed.

Minuchin had no expression. He sat down and looked right into my eyes, "My feeling is that you will be very successful with the family. My problem is how can I be successful with you?"

"You force me to be abstract and I want to force you to be concrete, and you are winning."

Then he said softly: "What you are doing is not wrong. It is partial, and I want you to have the freedom of doing something different. I want you to include in your repertoire things that you are not including—the concrete, experiential, and relational."

He got up to mimic the session and started shaking two students' hands, pretending that they were the brothers: "Michael, I think you are wonderful. Bill, I like what you did." Then he turned to me and concluded his demonstration: "There is no elaboration, no language, just the understanding of what they were doing. You are too intelligent. I want you to fake it. Pretend you're stupid."

As we were walking out Minuchin suddenly spoke to me: "All I want you to do is to learn how to do an enactment. I don't know why we have struggled for so long and are not getting it."

I walked away experiencing great discomfort, anxiety, and a strong sense of messiness. Many thoughts stirred up inside me. It was true that I had never used enactment in my interviews. In the past, when I watched the way many so-called structural family therapists told one family member to talk to another, it seemed artificial and arbitrary to me.

Since my style was in question, it also became clear to me that I was not always a passive observer. I would do things like take off my shoes and hand them over to a man with a shoe fetish, while his parents and probation officer watched in shock. Or I would try to get a rabbi to become mischievous. When given my own stage, I too would dance with the families. But an active therapist who cannot create an enactment in a family is easily kept in a centralized position, controlling the flow of all conversations and activities. The story she extracts is basically from her own thinking, even though she would have described it as a collaboration with the family.

This option of taking a less centralized position was a new one to me, and somehow it took a year for me to understand it. The strange thing is that if Minuchin had said this to me right at the beginning, I would probably have treated it simply as an instruction about technique and would not have given it enough thought. I now found myself in a position of either inventing another technique to yield the benefits of an enactment, which I could not, or following one that had been developed and learn to use it creatively.

The ABCs of Family Therapy

I waited impatiently to see the family again, but when they came back I was at a loss as to what to do. I only knew that I had to escape from my dependency on words. But without language I was stuck in a strange position of turning a talk show into a silent movie. The lively conversation that had held a session together was now absent and replaced by a tension. In my anxiety, the only thing I remembered about structural therapy was its signature handshake. So I kept shaking hands with them. It was, at the beginning, awkward and almost comical. As I was doing it, however, I began to understand what a small break during a session can do to disrupt continuity. I started to pay attention to small movements. I discovered gestures and began to see pictures of family organizations with their own idiosyncratic transactions, as in a play.

In the last session, I had told the family that they were very square and could not understand anything about absurdity. Thus, they could not understand the meaning of Bill's shit painting. To prove me wrong, the father came wearing his wife's wig and was in a very playful mood. Michael was obviously embarrassed and angered by the father's behavior until he seized the wig from him and put it on his own head. Then, strangely, he was also in a giggling mood.

Recalling the scene from my last supervision when I had failed to capitalize on the brotherly connection, I purposefully restaged the act and restrained from interfering with any words. I asked Bill to show us how he might paint his brother's face. Bill took it seriously and with one hand held Michael's face, while symbolically drawing a picture on the wall.

BILL: I'm using a big brush.
MICHAEL: What if you were in the bathroom. Would you be using shit?
BILL: No! I won't do that.
MICHAEL: How come? You have done that thought before.
WAI-YUNG: It's very nice that your brother is saying that he wouldn't paint your face with shit.
MICHAEL: Yes, it is nice. I am glad he said that.
WAI-YUNG: Whose face would he paint with shit?
MICHAEL: Good question!
BILL *(annoyed):* I won't use my ass for that.

As this conversation was going on, the mother looked very tense. To complement her husband's playful mood, she came wearing a straw hat and was in slacks, but her relaxed outfit looked out of place as she sat straight against the chair with both hands grabbing the arms tight. I commented on her being so tense.

MOTHER: It was the subject. It wasn't the manner. I agree with you—it was a very nice conversation. I have never heard Bill give us an illustration of how he thought, or whatever it was that he was doing.
WAI-YUNG: It was the 'subject' that brought you to therapy.
MOTHER *(slowly):* It's the connotation of the washroom, and he, rightly so, connects it with something he did that is bad, and he does not want to repeat it, and hopefully he will never repeat it.
FATHER: It is one of those things that pops up every so often, like a volcano. It gets there and boom! That's the way he is. If he carried a palette with him, then he might well use color on the wall. But he doesn't have a palette, so he uses whatever that is nearby . . . for whatever reason.

Calling attention to the tragedy of this young man, Minuchin said, "He has parents who demand from him a higher level of functioning and at the same time treat him as a child. So the father is correct to say that there is a volcano, and the volcano can be shit or can become whatever it is. If I thought like that, I would join Bill in the expression of his feeling of impotence and rage to be put in that position in which whatever he does, he does not reach the mark."

Although he continually shifted my focus to relationships, Minuchin was obviously pleased with my attempt to get out of my usual centralized position. It became clear to me that before a therapist can make use of an enactment effectively, she needs to understand the application of space and movement in much the same way as a designer utilizes the stage. As Minuchin once put it, "An enactment acts much like a merry-go-round. Once you put it in motion it turns on its own, which allows the therapist a chance to observe, to think and to decide whether she should come closer, stay away, or take whatever position that is deemed useful at the time."

I had certainly found this to be true. When I mobilized the family to act among themselves, not only did it allow me to use my energy differently, but most amazingly, Bill began to talk!

In the next segment, I asked the mother why it was so difficult to face the washroom situation.

MOTHER: Because this particular behavior is down in his records. If he is going to try to get jobs or things, if anybody knows about this kind of thing, or if he should do it again, he will lose another job.

WAI-YUNG: Don't you think he knows that?

MOTHER: I don't know if he knows that or not. He's been told enough—

BILL *(interrupting):* Of course I know!

Everybody was surprised at such a clear statement coming from Bill. The mother was not able to believe what she had heard.

WAI-YUNG: He is telling you now.

MOTHER *(to Bill):* What, honey?

BILL: Of course I know.

MOTHER *(in disbelief):* You do know that?

BILL: Yes.

MOTHER: So when you did it the last time you knew it was going to cost your job, did you?

BILL *(nodding):* U'-huh!

MICHAEL *(to Bill):* Is that why you did it? So that you would lose your job? Or did you do it for some other reason?

The plight of a disabled person is that when he is able to come forth with a clear statement, nobody quite believes it. We have to check with him over and over again to make sure that his statement is based on understanding and not just a matter of coincidence, until he reaches a point where he resolves to give it up. After putting up an assertive front for a little while, Bill started to wobble. He said that he would not do it again. Fortunately Michael was able to correct himself.

MICHAEL: No, no, no, that is not what I meant, Bill. The last time when you did it, it was at your last job placement?

BILL: Oh, yes, it was down at Queens Park . . .

MICHAEL: That was where you last did it?

BILL *(slowly)*: I believe so . . .

MICHAEL: Did you know then when you did it that they were going to fire you?

BILL: Yes.

MICHAEL: You knew you were going to lose your job. Is that what you wanted?

BILL: All of a sudden it started to become boring.

MICHAEL: It started to become boring, the job? How come, didn't they give you different stuff to do?

BILL: Oh, they did!

MICHAEL: What was so boring with it?

BILL: They wanted me to do it twice or three times.

MICHAEL: Of the same thing?

BILL: Over and over.

MICHAEL: Why? Because you did not do it right the first time, or—

BILL: They said it wasn't clean enough.

MICHAEL: Were you washing dishes?

BILL: No, I was cleaning leaf lettuce.

MICHAEL: You did not clean it properly?

BILL: That is what they think!

Whoever invented the technique of talking to disabled persons in such a concrete and explicit manner, had no idea how they deprived these people of their chance to develop spontaneity and unknowingly made them flat and mechanical. Normally, I would have taken over the conversation and coached Michael in how to talk to Bill in a more natural style, but my thinking had changed. It did not matter how they talked, as long as they were talking together. They continued to explore the reason for the "washroom painting." Then the mother, who originally did not want the topic to be brought up, started to talk about how Bill also did it at their friend's home when visiting there with them. It was the end of the session, but the father insisted that I should know about that. Before I left I said to the family, "So Bill made a 'poo poo' of all of you!"

MINUCHIN: Why did you say that?

WAI-YUNG: I think the parents really rejected Bill. They are looking at Bill as though he is the problem, and I was trying to give the problem back to them.

MINUCHIN: To transform a symptom into a relational message gives the symptom a different meaning. Then, it is not any more "I make a poo poo"; for Bill, if he shits, he shits on father, he shits on mother. From the point of view of the family, it is a recognition that it is relational. But this is only the first step; the next is, How do you produce that shit? Do you control, stimulate, organize his symptoms? Then you can begin to deal with the rejection. I would deal with the rejection in concrete terms. We have here the brother, who is talking with Bill and clearly doing a very good job. I would ask the father to talk with Bill and the mother to talk with Bill. Then I would ask the brother to look at how they talk to Bill. Do they talk to Bill as if they are talking *with* Bill? Do they talk *at* Bill? Do they talk *over* Bill? Can they talk with Bill in such a way that there is a dialogue, and not an act?

Minuchin was obviously interested in watching the tape I presented, saying, "You are showing the process of depersonalizing this young man, and you are doing very well. It's very nice, I'm enjoying it."

I now view this session as my ABC learning in systems thinking. I began to expand my therapeutic posture in the session and to activate the system to do its own work instead of playing the role of a teacher or problem solver. There were uncomfortable moments, but I learned that in struggling through this discomfort, I was actually joining the family in a more meaningful manner. I felt I was now part of the family, as I experienced their dilemma and they also experienced me in a more personal manner.

THE EAST MEETING THE WEST

At the next session I had planned to deal with the question of rejection. Bill was late, however, and when he finally showed up at the session, his father confronted him immediately for being late. I saw that it was a good chance to begin an enactment, I asked Michael to explain to Bill what they were talking about.

MICHAEL *(to Bill)*: You know, when Dad and I talk, we talk very fast, we use big words and we are howlers. We thought, maybe when we are doing all that you find it hard to be a part of that conversation. *(Bill, not used to dealing with such concerns, looked uncomfortable.)* That was what we were talking about. I don't know, you can tell us if we are right or wrong. You said that you did not feel that you were being left out?

BILL *(his voice subdued, his head down)*: Not that I know of.

FATHER: Do you think that we love you?

BILL: In my heart, yes.
FATHER: In your heart. What about our hearts?
BILL *(putting his hand across his heart):* Okay, the family heart.
FATHER: We love you.
BILL: That's right.
FATHER: Do I love you?
BILL: Of course you do.
FATHER: Is that an honest answer? Or did you think I am kidding when I said I love you?
BILL: You meant what you said.
FATHER: What happens when I get angry, do I still love you?
BILL: Yes, you do.
FATHER: I love you even though I am angry. You know that because it is true.
WAI-YUNG *(to Bill):* How old are you?
BILL *(cheerfully):* I am 26, going to be 27.
WAI-YUNG: 26 going to be 27. For a moment, when I saw your father talking to you, I thought you were six. *(Michael responded yes; Bill was offended by my remark.)*
WAI-YUNG *(to Bill):* Ask your brother. Your brother agrees with me.
BILL *(looking at Michael):* Do you think I am six years old?
MICHAEL: When Dad was talking to you, it sounded like you might have been six years old.
FATHER *(caught off guard):* Why? Why did you say that?

Michael mimicked his father as he repeated the exchange between father and Bill. They continued talking, and Bill fell silent.

Indeed, the family was back to a two-man show of Michael and his father. To get them to deal with their own pain and resentment, I thought I might create a scenario in which each of them had to address their relationship with Bill. I said, "Kenneth Clark, the art historian, said that real art is not what pleases the eye, but what touches the soul. . . . If you were to take Bill's painting out from the washroom and frame it like those in the modern art museum, what is that picture telling you? Does it touch your soul?" I asked Bill to face his family and asked them how each of them would be affected if Bill became the painting himself.

FATHER *(to Bill):* When I see that, it makes me very angry, It touches my soul to see a son of mine would do that.
MICHAEL: It bothers you because you are ashamed of it.
WAI-YUNG *(to Michael):* Aren't you ashamed of it, too?

MICHAEL *(looking at the floor):* I am ashamed because he is my brother. Such a strange way to express something, by painting shit on the wall. There are better ways to do it than that.

WAI-YUNG: What is so strange about it? He is using real life ingredients to paint. *(There was a charged atmosphere in the room. Everyone was silent.)*

MOTHER: I don't think we ever pretend that it is easy.

FATHER *(directing her to look at Bill):* The painting is here. He is the painting. That is what we're shooting at.

MOTHER *(looking intensely at Bill):* It is just one big question mark to me. I don't understand it; how can you do such a thing?

FATHER: Okay. There is abstract art that we don't like. *(The mother, annoyed, began to argue with her husband, then sat back in silence.)*

WAI-YUNG: What is it doing to her? This painting that—

MOTHER *(angrily):* It isn't the painting, it is the interruption. I am not being allowed to say what I want to say. That is irritating me. *(to Bill)* I don't give a damn whether it is abstract art or not. As far as I am concerned, it isn't art in the first place. It is an expression, and it is a terrible expression. It is something I don't understand. Therefore, it scares me.

FATHER *(to Bill):* Is the shit on the wall art?

BILL *(embarrassed):* No. It is not.

FATHER: What is it, then?

BILL *(solemnly):* That everything is a big mess!

WAI-YUNG: He is telling you that his life is a big mess!

MOTHER: That's the best answer I've heard.

Here Minuchin commented, "Wai-Yung is a wonderful story-teller, and she is able to make out of shit a painting. . . . She then changes the meaning, and Bill is a piece of shit, and the family is ashamed, and so on. One story! There is another story that one can tell here, and the story follows from Michael's comments that 'It is a strange way of making a statement'. And out of that story comes a confrontative statement: 'In this family there is no other way, and you are part of the creation of a story made of shit. There must be a reason why in your family you cannot use oil, that you cannot use water colors. Probably, your family stops you from doing anything but painting with shit.' It's a different story." He turned to me and said, "It is a story that pleases my aesthetic sense and not your aesthetic sense."

"What are the differences in these two stories?" he asked the class. "In the story that Wai-Yung tells, people will own a feeling of shame, embarrassment, guilt. In my story, what I want is that Bill should be angry with the family. My story is a story that elicits transactions. Your story (turning to me) is a story that elicits understanding and emotion." Then he said, "She has a style that is quite effective, but it is incomplete."

I had known that Minuchin's compliments were always followed with a new challenge. By now, it had become an adventure to meet his challenges. I felt nurtured and energized from the intellectual and interpersonal exchange, which in turn drew out every ounce of creativity in me.

Minuchin continued, "The avoidance of aggression does not come just from the family. It comes from Wai-Yung, who presents a picture of life that does not have aggression and hostility, and that is nicer than life is." Looking at me he emphasized his point. "Your pictures about families are benign, and families are killers. Unless you accept that you are in the field of family therapy and that families are conservative, constraining organisms that cut people to pieces, you will not be able to help people to expand the niches that the family creates for them. Your sessions are like birthday cakes with too much sugar on them. You manage to give to sessions a benign spin."

The Sweet Taste of Aggression

I began my next supervision by telling Minuchin, "From the last supervision session, what hit me most was when you said that my session had no aggression and hostility. And you think maybe it is because of my background as a Chinese person. I walked away and said no, because China, like any other old nation, knows about hostility and aggression."

The truth is that I was furious for the two weeks following my last class. Coming from an unconventional family background, I would not have minded being seen as unreasonable, irrational, or irresponsible. I would even have enjoyed being seen as cranky and unpredictable. But sweet and sugary! It just blew my mind. For two weeks, I kicked dogs and walked with a two-by-four, hitting anyone in sight. I waited for the family to come back, and when they did, I tied them up with a roll of string that I found in my office. Like a spider, I set up my web and waited for the moment to attack.

The family was surprised as I began weaving a web around them with a roll of string. I walked around them quietly while tying them up, first their bodies and then their hands and feet. The father and Michael seemed to enjoy it and saw it as yet another game that I would play with them, while the mother and Bill were uninspired, as usual.

When I began this tactic, I did not know where the confrontation was going to be. I only knew I had to draw out the aggression in this family to show its connection to the shit painting. I struggled to find ways to upset their equilibrium.

WAI-YUNG: How often do you say that you love Bill? That you love each other?

MICHAEL: You don't believe it?

WAI-YUNG: I'll tell you what I believe in. I came from a different culture, as you all know. Love is not a word we used very commonly. And your way of using words makes me think about the army. It's almost like after you have done a successful killing, you pin a medal on your uniform, and you call it love.

FATHER *(frowning):* This is very strange!

MICHAEL *(ill at ease):* I think it's mainly kind of harsh. I felt implicated in the way you sort of accuse us of being false about our feeling for each other.

WAI-YUNG: I don't know what your feeling is, but I sense that you kill Bill with words—

FATHER: We may do that, we may well have done that!

WAI-YUNG: You kill him with words, and then you adorn the body with love.

MOTHER *(shouting):* What? What did she say?

FATHER: We adorn the body with love!

Minuchin stopped the VCR and said, "I think this is an expansion of your style, and you are working at a higher level of complexity. I think that before, you were much more in need of taking control of the process, and you are abandoning that. That's very good."

In the session, I continued to provoke the family.

WAI-YUNG: Michael, you know, the dance between you and your father has been a dance that goes on all the time. As long as you both dance like this together, everybody else is being cut out of it. I wonder what it would be like for your father and mother, if you were not in that picture?

MICHAEL: Oh, I don't know. Do you want me to speculate?

WAI-YUNG: Can you come out and see how they deal with that? Because it's interesting, it's almost like you have become the mother of this family in dealing with Bill. *(Bill laughed.)*

MICHAEL: Well, I think I'm closer to him. I think I relate to him better. That doesn't mean that I mother him.

WAI-YUNG: Why do you have to do the job for your mother?

MICHAEL: Well, I think my mom's from a different generation. That has a lot to do with it.

WAI-YUNG: Are you trying to protect her?

MICHAEL: No, I'm not trying to protect her. I'm trying to give Bill maybe a more honest vision of what life is like.

WAI-YUNG: You don't like her vision? You doubt her vision?

MICHAEL *(with some anger):* No, I don't doubt her vision!

Minuchin stopped the tape again and remarked, "This is completely new for Wai-Yung. It is a completely new experience for her! She didn't work like that. Working at that level of relational messages, it is the first time I've seen it."

It was a moment of discovery! Up to this point, I had only understood relationships at a self-reflective level. I was good at giving my thinking but not my guts, and certainly not at sticking my neck out. How did this change come about? It seemed as though everything that had happened during and outside supervision had something to do with it and that finally it just came spontaneously without thinking.

The heat continued to turn up in the session. Michael tried to untie himself from the string, which by now had become tangled. He announced that he needed to go to the washroom, but the string had restricted his movement.

FATHER: And you are not going to paint the wall?

MICHAEL: No, I'm not that angry. I won't paint the wall. *(Bill gave a thumbs-up sign.)*

The mother was getting more and more agitated. The tension in the room was intolerable.

FATHER *(shaking his head in confusion):* I am not sure where we are taking this to.

MOTHER: I am not sure, either. I don't know exactly what we are trying to achieve . . .

At this point I was desperate for Michael's assistance. After working so hard to get him out, I unwittingly drew him back into the session.

WAI-YUNG: Michael, it is so funny that conversation comes so naturally between you and your father. And conversations do not come between your father and your mother.

MICHAEL: My father and I are both outspoken, and my mother is not very outspoken, so . . .

WAI-YUNG: So how is life for them? Like two tombstones without you?

BILL *(happily):* Oh, yeah!

(Michael looked attentively at his mother, who had reached a boiling point. Her look pierced my eye for a moment.)

MOTHER: I don't know why, but you are painting us very badly today.

WAI-YUNG *(to Michael):* Have you always been an eavesdropper on them as you were growing up? You always listened to the way they talked? I think you are going to dedicate your whole life to them, to make their relationship work.

FATHER: Oh, come on. You must be kidding.

MICHAEL: No, I can't do that.

WAI-YUNG: Is that why your two wives walked out on you?

FATHER: He hasn't got two wives . . .

MICHAEL: Just the one. No, I don't think it was my family.

WAI-YUNG: If you dance so closely with your father, how is any other person able to dance with you in your life?

MICHAEL *(confidently):* I can dance with a lot of people. I can get very close to a lot of people, and that is not a problem. *(His voice softening)* My wife left me because she could not be close to me. She just didn't care for me. So that's really another issue. I don't think it was because of my relationship with my family that she could not have a relationship with me.

Bill listened carefully while both brothers were working to untie the knots in the string.

WAI-YUNG *(to mother):* As much as you seem to have more disagreement with me, I feel that you are the only real person here. Because you have aggression, you have anger. And these three men here—I don't see much of the aggression in them. How do you explain that? *(Father laughed.)*

MICHAEL: I don't know. I am not an aggressive person. It scares me, aggression.

WAI-YUNG: Aggression scares you? *(Michael nodded.)* What do you do with your own share of hostility?

MICHAEL: I don't know. Maybe I direct it on myself.

Minuchin commented at this point, "So we are here at a very interesting crossroad. It is clear that Wai-Yung is exploring new modalities of working. *(Turning to me)* You are using two modalities. One is familiar to you—the use of language—and in that you are very good. The metaphor of love as a medal to dead people is just beautiful. It carries all levels of metaphoric intensity, but that is something that you know how to do. But you are doing it in a different way. You are working personally with people in a one-to-one confrontation, and that is new. And because it is new, it is more difficult, but you are doing it. Clearly, Michael is experiencing this session as a therapeutic session for him."

If supervision is a story of experiences, and following Bruner's thinking, "stories become transformative only in their performance," no doubt my family session was only an enactment of my supervision. However, the concept of story seemed flat and distant at a point when I was experiencing a peak emotion, a sensation only achieved from the depth of an interpersonal encounter. Through a first-hand experience, I discovered that even aggression could be an act of intimacy. Wasn't it Satir, the goddess of love, who once told a distraught wife that the reason her husband was running after her with a knife was because "he is trying to get closer to you"?

It is the human relationship that gives life its meaning, purpose, and magic. Strangely, the relationship between teacher and student is not a highly popular theme in Western culture. On the contrary, teachers are like Buddhas; they belong to the realm of illusion. You need to kill them if you meet them on the road so as to prove that you are worthy on your own.

I had learned from many people in my personal and professional life, but I never had a teacher who journeyed with me through a process of learning. Someone, who within a particular time frame and in a specially staged scenario, pushed me when he felt I became banal, challenged me when he found me to be limited, nurtured me when my struggle was wasted, and valued me when I was able to make small gains. Ultimately, I took full advantage of being a student.

The Height of Intensity

Minuchin had considered his supervision of me to be complete after the last session, but the saga of the family continued as the aggression heightened. Eventually there was an explosion.

In the following session, Bill came to see me before his family arrived. He said he felt rejected by his "folks," adding, "My father treats me like a piece of dirt." I encouraged him to let his family know how he felt.

Bill was a different person, however, when the family joined us later. He turned into a young child again and became evasive as usual, bringing up unrelated things and losing all credibility.

With my encouragement, Bill finally told his parents that he felt rejected at home. His mother immediately implied that this idea was implanted by me during the time Bill and I had been alone.

MOTHER: When Bill spoke to you before we got here, did he say "I feel rejected by my family"? Were those the words he used?
WAI-YUNG: Those are the words he just used here.
MICHAEL: Yes, that's the words he used here.
FATHER *(pointing at Bill):* Ask him!
MOTHER *(acting much like a judge):* Right! *(to Bill, enunciating word by word):* Do you honestly understand what you mean when you say rejected?

Both father and mother insisted that it was very important for them to be sure if Bill knew what rejection meant. Bill began to mumble.

WAI-YUNG *(to Bill):* No wonder you don't want to open up yourself. When you talked about rejection today, it was like you dropped a bomb in the family. It is very hard for them to hear it. That's why they are angry—
MOTHER: Yes, we are angry. Because we don't think he understands the word.
WAI-YUNG *(to father):* You are a man with tremendous capacity. Why is it so hard for you to face his emotion? I guess it is hard because this is your own son, isn't it?
FATHER *(abruptly):* To face what?
WAI-YUNG: To face the fact that you might have rejected him.
FATHER: Not might have—I am sure I have. But again—
WAI-YUNG: That he is a wrong product for you, maybe?
FATHER: Well, sure, disappointment maybe. I am sure I got over it a long time ago, but there is still . . . there is still an element there of . . . of . . . shame. I would use the word "shame." There should not be, but there is. So what the hell can you do? *(Changing the subject):* Listen, I admire Bill for having the guts to speak up and say his mind.
WAI-YUNG: Then congratulate him. Say, "I am really happy, Bill, that you can tell me that."

The father leaned forward to Bill. He gave Bill his hand and proceeded to hug him. But I saw that as soon as he had done that, he patted Bill on the shoulder in a chummy gesture, indicating that the whole thing would be over. It was at that point that I said, "Don't sweeten it."

As if hit by lightning, the father jumped up, pointed his finger at me, and started to yell.

FATHER: Don't tell me what to do. I will deal with this, but don't tell me what to do, or how to act.

WAI-YUNG *(trying to remain calm):* Why are you directing your anger at me?

FATHER: Because you are the one who made the statement. Bill is not offended by it. And there should be no offense by it. *(Michael tried to intervene.)* Yes, I am emotional now, I am emotional! If the bloody Chinese are huggers or not, it doesn't matter . . .

MICHAEL *(jumping up and shouting):* Hey, listen! Don't get abusive. Shut up! *(They started pushing each other.)*

FATHER *(shouting):* Don't point your goddamn finger at me!

MICHAEL *(continuing to point):* Listen, what I was going to say before you got loud and obnoxious was, when you reached over to hug Bill, you were really upset, close to tears.

MOTHER: He was very upset.

MICHAEL *(pounding his hand on the chair):* Okay, that's fine. Accept that!

FATHER *(shouting emotionally):* I accept that . . .

MOTHER *(pointing her finger at me):* She was the one . . .

MICHAEL *(ignoring his mother):* Before all this aggression started off, you hugged Bill. And I could hear a choke in your voice. *(Father nodded in agreement.)* Why can't you just hug him?

This question triggered another outburst in the father, who insisted that everything was spoiled by my statement. Michael's face was also choked with anger. There was a great deal of confusion and tension in the room. The father and son were engaged in a shouting match, with the mother's voice echoing in the background.

WAI-YUNG: Today is the first time Bill is able to raise his point. And look at the intensity. Look at how hard it is for you to get closer to him. When I say don't sweeten it, it is because I think what you did was very nice when you went to hug Bill. And then, when you were trying to laugh and get over it quickly, that's when I want to—

FATHER *(seizing the chance and picking up the fight with me again):* You didn't see my face.

MOTHER: You didn't see his face.

FATHER: Now, I am pleased that Bill was able to state what he has. And Michael is quite right that the choke was in my voice and tears in my eyes, as it is now. But it pisses me off when you do that, and you do it very often. You spoiled a moment that was developing. End of story. Let us proceed.

WAI-YUNG *(to the family):* Now, I have an issue with it. When he insulted me, my nationality and everything, I felt that I might not be able to work with him. That is the abusive part that I cannot accept. Bill has accepted it, maybe.

BILL: Yes, I have!

WAI-YUNG: You have accepted it? But I will not.

BILL: If this goes on, I am going to leave.

WAI-YUNG: I do feel one thing with your family. It is so hard to take on heavy stuff without sweetening it. Today there was a change, and I wanted to warn you, don't repeat the pattern. And you became angry with me. I am going to leave you for a moment so that you and I can repair our emotions. Otherwise I would find it very hard to continue working with you.

I left the room. The truth was that I needed badly to find my breath again. The father was in tears, and the entire family was talking together as I was leaving.

This session also created much chaos at supervision. When I saw that I had created so much rattling in the class, I knew that I had surpassed what Minuchin had once considered to be my low tolerance of intensity!

Minuchin was thoughtful. "What she did was quite extraordinary," he said. "She insisted on intense affect, in a family that had already gone beyond its usual threshold. The fact was that he attacked her, and she survived. She survived, and she left saying, I will not let you shit on me, but you do shit on other people in your family. And that was a nice moving out. It was a very important moment. Because she says emotionality is acceptable." Then he shook hands with me and got up.

I still persisted, "I think the man did more when he attacked me. I think it was an important therapeutic moment. . . ." Minuchin smiled, "Absolutely. You moved the family to a level of emotional exchange that they are absolutely not accustomed to, and you are not accustomed to either."

The Process of Healing and Learning about It

With every move I made with this family, I felt I was in dialogue with Minuchin. Similarly, when I was interacting with Minuchin, the family was my platform. Soon I could not see the two layers of encounters as separate. They began as two parallel lines, but as training was taking its effect, they overlapped, the one extending over the other, further and further into yet another level. As supervision was drawing to an end, the two lines met and became one. I did not understand until much later that what I had actually learned from Minuchin was a therapy of movement. From the first day I came to study with him, he had invited me to move with him. No wonder I became intolerant of the benign and restrictive atmosphere at the family sessions and felt compelled to activate motion. Looking back, I see that my entire process with the family was moving from one plateau to another, like a mirror image of my supervisory experience.

Four months after my last supervision, I finally removed all obstacles and roadblocks and arrived at the mother's position. While the two brothers continued to be present in the family sessions, they were able to sit back and let the parents deal with each other. The father was able to resume his role and comfort his wife, who at this point was adjusting to letting go of Michael. Like other parents whose children are ready to leave home, this couple was learning to console each other.

When therapy ended, the mother gave me a water color that she had painted. It was a fine image of a bunch of wild flowers, which she labelled "Beside the Stream." I took it as her gesture that all of us had to find new colors in order to get the family out of shit.

I visited the family for the first time three years later. I met only with the parents. They told me that Michael had left home and was travelling abroad. Bill had settled in a group home. He had not painted with shit any more and continued to stay out of shit; he only pulled the fire alarm once or twice.

Chapter 15

Filling the Empty Vessel

Andy Schauer's Story

Wai-Yung Lee

I asked Andy to write a headline for a sensationalist tabloid, describing his therapeutic style. Without hesitation, Andy wrote on the blackboard: "Human therapist describes self as empty vessel."

I replied, "I don't want the responsibility of filling up an empty vessel. They have no bottoms."

Thus started my encounter with Andy, a process that was enriching to both of us.

Andy was one of the most committed students I've ever had. He would come to the office whenever he had time to watch tapes. By the end of his training, he had seen hundreds of my sessions. The quandary of supervising an extremely bright and self-effacing student is how not *to teach. Every statement I made could be transformed into a mantra, a road to explore, or a direction to follow.*

The problem with Andy's work was that it was efficient. He had mastered all the techniques that I had written about. Then he went to Jay Haley, and then to Whitaker, and he could do a reliable facsimile of each of us. And families, recognizing an expert, followed his direction. In families with children, he had a gentle way of talking with children and encouraging parents for better parenting. But when encouraged to talk about his goals of therapy, he would return to his "I don't know," which I paraphrased as "Tell me what I know." We did share the Confucian saying "If he knows, and doesn't know he knows, he is asleep. Wake him up."

ANDREW SCHAUER was a clinical social worker, who, during the period described in this chapter, was working with families at Queens Child Guidance Center in Jamaica, New York. Following his studies with Dr. Minuchin, Schauer relocated to Boston, where he planned to continue his work as a family therapist. He died suddenly and unexpectedly not long after the relocation.

Since I was respectful of Andy's effort to be like me but knew he would be better if he were himself, my supervision with him always had a teasing element. I would predict that he would start his presentation by declaring his ignorance or confusion. I would suggest he start showing his tape, because I knew it would be better than his presentation of himself. But the teasing was benign and always accompanied by an expectation, enveloped again in gentle teasing, of a future when he would not need to do it.

I don't remember a conflict with Andy. He always accepted my statements as an indication of my interest in his growth. And my personal response to him was to wait patiently for the time when he would integrate his knowledge with the ownership of it. When he presented a case and I wanted to make a comment, I would frequently preface it with a qualifier, "I know I shouldn't teach you, because you will believe me, but. . . ." Or I would ask the class to comment on Andy's work without teaching.

The goal was to make Andy accessible to Andy. The road was how not to teach.

The story of Andrew Schauer's supervision is different from the other stories, because to our deepest sense of loss, he is not here to speak for himself. Andy had begun to write a chapter for this book, but he died before it was finished. Wai-Yung Lee, who was a member of one of Andy's training groups, based what follows on videotapes, private conversations, Andy's written notes, and that chapter.

As I was reviewing Andy's videotapes of supervision over the course of two years, I could not help but wonder how much you need to know about a person's history in order to know the person. Without Andy to verify his reflections and inner thoughts during the process of training, what could we make out of his experience? Could we identify with his quest for knowledge, his need for validation, his anxiety on failing, his pain, joy, fantasies, wishes, fear of rejection, and search for a mentor?

Family therapists depend on the pattern of interaction in the here and now to provide important clues to the past and predictions for the future. Andy's here and now was captured on many hours of tapes that provided us with important clues to the mystery of Andy. As the story unfolded, Andy began to emerge, taking on a multitude of personas, appearing in one mask after another, until all parts of him manifested themselves and evolved into a rich and complex entity.

Andy's chapter began:

> After three years of studying family therapy at Family Studies, I was finally going to be in Salvador Minuchin's class. The year before, I had come in at 9:00 AM on every Tuesday for my 2:00 PM class with Jorge

> Colapinto and spent the entire morning watching videotapes of Minuchin doing consultations and therapy, teaching classes, and giving presentations at conferences. I was like the kid in the candy store. Each handwritten label promised a new adventure of viewing the work of someone whom I increasingly saw as not only a master clinician and seminal figure in the therapy field, but as an artist.

During Andy's first training session with a new group of students, Minuchin asked the supervisees to describe their style as therapists. When it was Andy's turn he went to the blackboard and drew a picture of a vessel. He then said, "I am an empty vessel!"

This was a direct challenge to a teacher. An empty vessel is a paradox. Its very shape and form invite action, but any attempt to fill the vessel takes away from its space. If you accepted Andy's picture of himself, you were put in a position of maintaining him in a one-down position. If you rejected it, you would be seen as rejecting Andy. If you asked him how he obtained such an impossible view of himself, you were led into a benign self-reflective mode, failing to see the powerful tactic of "he who is down need fear no fall." Any effect that enriched Andy would also disempower him.

Andy presented a case of a couple who had problems coping with their two children. His presentation carried the same quality of pleading ignorance and requested help. He began, "I am going to show you a first session of a family that I saw last night at my clinic. I am not sure what is going on with them, so what I would like is for you to give me feedback on what *you* think is happening." Contrary to what he normally might have done, Minuchin did not say anything about the style of Andy's presentation. Andy was to be left waiting for feedback from a teacher who chose not to be there. We could feel his anxiety mounting as we kept the group session going, providing different opinions and suggestions on his videotaped session.

Finally, at the end of the class, Sal told us why he was not offering feedback to Andy. "Andy created an organization in his presentation that made what I say useless. He said, 'I am an empty vessel, fill me up.' If I fill up an empty vessel, I am not helpful. So I am stuck!"

Then he told the class that it was not helpful to interpret Andy's thoughts, "because if he is an empty vessel, and I tell him what he is thinking, then the wine that will be produced will not be good wine." Minuchin delivered his statements briefly. His voice was as gentle as Andy's, and his face showed no affect. But everybody in the class was struck by it. Caught off balance, Andy struggled to ask the teacher what he meant. "I don't get it."

"You may get it later," Sal replied. "You may get it next week, or you may never get it!"

Two years later, when Andy was writing about his learning experience with Minuchin, that first session was still the one that had had the most impact on him:

> I felt humiliated, embarrassed, and more than anything, dismissed. Some of my colleagues felt moved to come to my defense. . . . In spite of some class members' obvious attempts to steer us away from the discomfort of this scene, Minuchin stayed his course and reiterated what he saw. When I said that I didn't understand how I was tying people's hands by how I presented myself, Minuchin's answer was that maybe I'd understand it in the future, or maybe I wouldn't. He was saying that he was not going to accommodate to me and my preferred way of presenting myself, and that it would be me who would have to change. This was similar to his stance in therapy.
>
> I left the class after my first presentation in a state of shock. I felt as though my worst beliefs about myself had been ratified in the court of the High Commissioner of Therapy and Human Worth. But at the same time, something began churning in my mind. I started thinking about the first class, when Minuchin had given some introductory remarks about the class and what we could expect from it. He said that therapy was, among other things, an invitation from the therapist to the family to jump into the unknown. The family comes with a problem. Overtly, this problem is a symptom. But they also have a usually unacknowledged problem in that they are hobbled by overly limited views of themselves as individuals and as a family. These limiting views are expressed in loyalties to preferred ways of acting, seeing, and thinking that constrain and impair people's ability to solve problems. Yet to change these loyalties means jumping into the unknown. It means that the familiar must be abandoned in favor of untested alternatives. The stronger the loyalty—the more ingrained the familiar ways of being—the more difficult it is to make the jump.
>
> As I thought about this, I realized that if I wanted to become a family therapist, I had better become familiar with the feeling of letting go of preferred patterns and jumping into the unknown. But at what point do you feel you can do it?

Thus Andy entered into an unspoken contract with his supervisor. In his notes Andy wrote, "I was there to expand, and he was going to push, support, kick, stroke, criticize, joke, implore, and do whatever was necessary to help me do that."

The Transformation of a Structural Family Therapist

After the persona of the empty vessel was discarded, Andy began to show himself as a solid person who was far from not knowing. He had dedicated a number of years to becoming a structural family therapist and was very familiar with structural concepts. He was conversant with the techniques and seemed to be doing everything that a structural family therapist was supposed to do. Therefore, Sal found himself facing an interesting dilemma in his supervision: how to transform a mechanical structural family therapist, who just followed maps and road signs, into a more complex therapist operating at higher interpersonal levels.

Minuchin has told his students, "Every now and then I have a nightmare. And the nightmare is that people who read my earlier work become my students, and I have to supervise them. I cannot tell them that what they are doing is wrong, because I wrote the books myself. And supervising such a person is like supervising myself twenty or thirty years ago." As he began to look at Andy's work, Minuchin's nightmare came true, this time in the form of a handsome student, six feet tall, who was a devoted admirer of his teacher's life and work.

One case Andy presented was a family with a Moroccan husband and a Colombian wife. They had two young children who would not respond to their discipline. There was a great deal of conflict between the husband and wife. Andy described how the couple would eat dinner in the bedroom where the TV was. The wife would ask the husband to serve her dinner and he would become angry. Then, when he asked her to switch the channel, she would refuse. The man was self-righteous and aloof, while the woman was explosive. The more he dismissed her, the more she demanded attention. There was no mutual accommodation between the couple, and the children learned not to listen to either one of them.

Andy was showing a segment in which the couple had an argument. Andy was unbalancing the couple by challenging the husband and supporting the wife.

ANDY: Can you tell her you didn't mean that and say you're sorry?

HUSBAND: Well, I didn't mean to . . . tell you what. I'll get down on my knees *(laughs)*.

ANDY: No, no, no! You did it so beautifully, then you undo it! *(Goes behind the man to support him.)* Say sorry to her. That's all you need to do. If you can do that, you will be okay.

At this point, Minuchin stopped the tape and asked a female student to take over the supervision. The peer supervisor told Andy, "You were supporting the wife, but your way of supporting her dismissed her in much the same way her husband does." The rest of the class also felt that Andy had fought the battle for the wife instead of helping her fight for herself. One student suggested that the husband's cultural background would not allow for the kind of maneuver that Andy was trying to introduce. The group concluded that the session had victimized an already victimized woman.

Andy was obviously made uncomfortable by the feedback. He looked for Minuchin's reaction. Minuchin was ignoring him. He was sitting, chanting *sotto voce,* "The mother will change. The mother will not change." Finally he noticed Andy. He said that Andy had managed to enact a conflict in the session, and by supporting the wife he had increased the intensity of that conflict. That might turn out to be useful. "But when I do something like that," he continued, "I always feel uncomfortable. I want to call the family during the week, and say 'Did anything happen?' This kind of operation requires an ability in the therapist to endure uncertainty. It is because Andy cannot tolerate uncertainty that he insisted that the husband should apologize."

Again and again during that year, Minuchin engaged Andy in a tango of ambiguity. His strokes and kicks sometimes came separately. At other times, they occurred together. The strange thing is that at the time, a student can feel only the blow.

When I was writing this chapter, I asked Sal why he was so mean to Andy. He said, "I loved Andy. He was a typical structural family therapist. If there is such a person, it was Andy. He was good in joining and structuring. He was charming, and he could be therapeutically authoritaritive as well. But he was too concrete. He was too good at following maps. I wanted to move him out of that security, so that he could tap into other resources and use himself at a more complex level. To achieve that, I had to hit him hard and create a personal experience for him. He had to experience complexity, hands on."

I wanted to say, Why not just tell him instead of making such a big production when he did not even know the changes that you had in mind? But I refrained from asking, as I knew that Minuchin's answer would probably be, "I did not know what the changes were at the time, or how to get there. Andy had to figure it out by himself. My job was only to get him moving."

I suppose training is at times like gardening. You plant the seeds. After that you can water them, but they have to do their own growing. You really have very little control.

Andy wrote about that time:

> I never lost faith in the contract. I saw Sal work with two groups of therapists and watched him have greater or lesser success with particular individuals, but he was always committed to peoples' growth. His contract was always clear to me. His stance was that you are more than you think you are. His supervision was in many ways like his therapy. He saw what we did not see and put us in a position of dynamic tension between what we said we wanted (to be better therapists) and what needed to change. Implicit in this was that he believed we could change.

Andy's description of his teacher's commitment to his growth was also a description of his commitment to learning from Minuchin. Their joining was so perfectly crafted that in this learning environment, Andy became a different person. I saw him enter supervisory sessions with a new energy that I also saw in his videotaped sessions. His face, losing nothing of its open sensitivity, became animated. Of this time, Andy wrote:

> I changed on several levels. I slowly absorbed the value that people are more competent and capable than they think. . . . While people in my clinic were talking about clients' limitations, I found that I was thinking about their unaccessed strengths. . . . I came to realize that Minuchin put me in a context where I needed to access those parts of myself that are capable and unafraid.
>
> My focus shifted away from myself to much more of an interest in understanding the therapy process. I watched my own conflict of wanting to expand but also remaining loyal to my old maps. It was sort of like a jack-in-the-box—wanting to get out but needing the right context in which that energy could be released.

As the empty vessel began to fill, Sal began to joke with Andy more. He even "defended" Andy's position. When any other student in the group tried to de-fuse criticism by making a self-deprecating remark, he would say, "No, you can't take that position. Andy has that space reserved. You'll need to find a different approach."

The middle phase of supervision is the most difficult period of learning. What one knows so well from previous learning needs to be re-examined, or even given up, to make room for the new. Yet what is expected is no clearer than a glimpse of the promised land.

Late in his second year, Andy reviewed a case that he had already presented once. A family composed of a single father and his two sons became the canvas for portraying the process of making a complex family therapist.

An estranged Italian American couple had two young children, twelve-year-old Michael and ten-year-old Emilio. After the separation, the children had lived with their mother until she had declared that she could no longer cope with them, at which time the father had returned to the house and the mother had moved out. The identified patient was Emilio, who was described as extremely difficult to manage at home and at school.

The case was referred to Andy when Emilio, who then lived with his mother, came to school with bruises. There was a great deal of confusion around the case; nobody seemed to know what had happened, except that there was "a lot of physical stuff" in the family.

Andy described the couple's marriage as eleven years of fighting. Despite the separation, the father was still at his wife's house quite a lot, and he continued to have a sexual relationship with her. He was very involved with Little League and coached his son's soccer team. Emilio was one of those angelic terrors, a beautiful small boy who smashed anything in sight when he got into fights with his mother. He had broken her antique china lamp with a tennis racket and then run away in the middle of the night. The mother got very upset with the kids and became abusive, both verbally and physically. The father complained that his wife "fucked him through the kids." The family was full of tension, and every small thing triggered an avalanche of defiance and rage.

Structural thinking highlights the importance of hierarchical and boundary issues. Adults should be adults so that children can be children. Yet Minuchin has often been shocked by the mechanical ways in which some structural family therapists impose hierarchy and authority. Observing tapes of some students' versions of structural intervention, he has asked in horror, "Did we teach you to do that?! If we did, then there is certainly a limitation in the model!"

Andy was well equipped with maps, but a competent therapist has to be like a competent actor. It is not enough to learn the lines. You have to live the role on stage, from beginning to end. Otherwise you are not serving art; you are, somehow, serving yourself. Now, Andy's artistry could become the focus of supervision.

> *I watched Andy, on tape, sitting in his office like a benign and knowledgeable teacher. He intervened with gestures that exactly mimicked my own. He would extend his arm like a traffic cop to stop a family member from intruding on another's turf. He would invite two family members to talk to each other with a gentle gesture. He was comfortable with children and always found a way of talking respectfully to them. After seeing many hours of my work, he had developed a softer, gentler version of my style. The problem was that while each of Andy's movements seemed okay, he lacked certainty about the therapeutic goal. Therefore, his sessions zigzagged, depending on the mood of the family and Andy's need to please.*

The Problem Solver Reorganizes

Since Andy was a problem solver, he always looked for problems to solve in the family. Working with a child who had a great many behavioral problems suited him, because there were always problems to solve. Minuchin was taken aback by Andy's tendency to dissect small details and his failure to see the larger picture. He began to realize that all his efforts to help Andy examine his interventions in a microscopic manner were only resulting in Andy's becoming more entangled in his thoughts. Minuchin introduced the idea that perhaps Jay Haley would have been a better supervisor for Andy. He said that Haley would have sent him into the room with the family to achieve a goal, without necessarily asking him how he felt or what he did. Such focus on the end result might have given Andy a proper perspective on the larger goal and free him from his preoccupation with minor maneuvers.

By the time Andy presented the Italian-American family at supervision again, the two boys had gone to live with their father. Therefore, Andy was seeing the father and his two sons. This time it was the father who claimed incompetency in dealing with the children, particularly with Emilio. Andy explained to the class that the two boys had been fighting while their father was in the bathroom. The father yelled at the boys, who did not hear him. He threatened to break their radio. As the boys did not respond, the father got so upset that he came out of the bathroom and did indeed break the radio.

Andy decided to support the father. Minuchin complimented him for having done this. He said, "The father was not violent, he was only destructive. Maybe he doesn't need such a big bang to make them hear. But in the beginning you support that and say 'Clearly they can only hear a big bang.' Later on he will learn that smaller things work also. What you want is the father to be competent and nurturing. But he cannot be nurturing if he is incompetent, because he's so angry in his helplessness. Okay, that's good."

In the next segment of tape, Emilio was shouting at his father for taking away his baseball cards.

ANDY: Emilio, time out, let's focus on what's happening.

EMILIO *(only thinking of his cards):* He's squishing them!

ANDY: Emilio! Last time you were here, we talked about seeing your own part in it, and that's what we need to understand.

EMILIO: I had a part in it. But Dad had more of a part.

ANDY: What was your part in it?

EMILIO: I pulled away when he asked for the cards. I was looking at them when he was talking to me, and I wasn't paying attention to him.

ANDY: So that's very important that you understand that. That's part of it. Now you're right he has a part in it too. The other person has a part in it. You're absolutely right.

Minuchin stopped the tape. "That's very good, Andy. But in this situation I think you could have complimented the father. Haley always insists that when you are successful, the family should leave feeling that they were successful and that you did nothing. It is very unfair, because you want them to know that you did the work. Haley says that they should not think of you at all. That can make for a very depressed therapist."

Andy continued with another segment:

FATHER: You just had a discussion with Andy, Emilio, and you said you understand. So take these cards out again, let's do it over again and see if you really understand. It's become a battle of you against me, and you're not going to win. You're not going to win because you're ten years old and I'm your father and I'm not going to have you be so into whatever you're doing that you can say "Dad, the heck you say." I'm not going to let you win.

ANDY: What you're saying is that you care about these kids so much that you're going to have them dislike you at times.

FATHER: Yes, that's right. They can even think "My dad is so mean."

Minuchin stopped the tape. "Here Andy is putting a positive spin that is absolutely not necessary. Because what the father is saying to his son is, Goddamn it, in issues of power operations, I will win. And that's good. Andy is a gentle soul who loves children, so he says to the father, What you really mean is that you love them. What the father *really* means is, In a power operation I must win, so stop it. Andy tries to make him reasonable, when he is saying, I have the authority, I am bigger than you, I eat more, I have more muscles, and I will kick your ass. The father is enjoying a new sense of competence, and Andy modulates the change just when the change is beginning." He restarted the tape.

FATHER: I'm not your pal, I'm your Dad.

ANDY: You see, Tom, I think that's an important part of parenting that you know better than me, because I'm not a parent. You do have to help the kids learn to be responsible for themselves even if they don't like that. And I think that you're willing to help them that way. They're going to grow up.

FATHER: All those other things that you say I have, my good qualities, my strengths, my love—they know that they've got that already. But the other side of the coin is that it takes character, it takes guts on their part and mine.

Stopping the tape once more, Minuchin commented, "This man is so uncertain about how to parent that he needs to explain it. Andy has a similar approach as a therapist. He needs to explain, I'm doing therapy.

He cannot say, That's great! He says, That's great because . . . He cannot resist providing an explanation to everything.

"Actually this is very good session. Your sessions now are part of a therapy where people are changing. But it would be much more economical if you learned how to increase intensity and decrease your tendency to teach and preach."

> *At this point in the supervisory process I was feeling comfortable with Andy's change. I knew he was seeing the family in a complex way. He established therapeutic goals and entered the system with a sense of participating in the process. When I made a comment, I had a sense of participation in a collegial dialogue. The effect of our changed relationship was exhilarating.*

Hierarchy and Nurturance

The issue of the next session Andy showed was Emilio's constantly missing his school bus. He was also doing poorly in school. Andy described how, as he was discussing with the father how to guide the children with good study habits, Michael listened but Emilio did not. Emilio started crying and put his coat on his head. The father kept talking, and the child got more and more upset, saying "Shut up! shut up!" But the father kept scolding.

ANDY: What do you do as his father to help him through those times when he's acting like a three-year-old?

EMILIO *(whining):* Let's go!

FATHER: That's my challenge. I know Emilio has a problem. But what is his problem? Is he afraid of something, that he doesn't do his homework, or is he fighting some invisible ghost inside him? Come on, Emilio, what is it that you cannot do your homework? What's the ghost, Emilio? What's the fear?

EMILIO *(screaming):* Nothing!

FATHER: That you won't make it, that you can't make it?

EMILIO: Let's go!

ANDY: You're working hard on the—

FATHER: Understanding side?

ANDY: On the verbal side. You see what is happening when he puts his coat over his head and says "Don't talk to me." He induces you to talk more, and then he refuses to hear you.

EMILIO *(burps)*

FATHER *(coaching):* Excuse me.

EMILIO: Excuse me!

FATHER: His boundaries have to be more clearly laid out.

ANDY: What does that mean?

FATHER: There's got to be moves and obvious punishments and consequences to his behavior. *(Emilio is sitting calmly now, coat off and his feet on the floor.)*

ANDY: He will eventually start taking responsibility for himself so there will be less burden on you to make choices. See, he doesn't respond to lecture.

FATHER: I know.

Clearly the dialogue with the father was part of Andy's strategic thinking. He was working both sides of the family street. While he was engaging the father in an adults-only conversation, he was also interrupting his powerless haranguing and giving Emilio space to organize himself. I felt Andy was ready for a more nuanced understanding of how to engage two family members involved in a conflict.

MINUCHIN *(to Andy):* Tom could have encouraged Emilio to control himself while you were supporting the father in controlling him. You could have engaged both of them in different ways. To the father, it is, Be comfortable with control. To the child, it's, How can you get your father off your back?

The truth is that you cannot control a ten-year-old if he does not want to be controlled, so it is important for the child to participate in the process of self-control. While you were able to support the man and connect with the child, you did not actually engage Emilio.

It's a question of esthetics. Your esthetic sense should have arisen and said to you, Andy, don't you see that this is skewed? You have so much space, yet you choose to work in only one corner.

ANDY: Yeah, I felt that, but somehow I was constrained because I didn't know how to do it.

MINUCHIN *(shaking his head in disbelief):* I don't think that's the problem, because you know how to do it. I'm not telling you anything that you don't know. What moved you to be narrow?

ANDY: I guess my feelings, when I was sitting there, were twofold. I responded to the father and the son, and both the responses that jumped out of me were negative. I felt the father talks a blue streak and doesn't hear his son. I didn't like that. At the same time I felt irritated with the boy for screaming and telling his father to shut up. So I was sitting with two dislikes, and I wasn't able to sit back from that and use it in a constructive way.

MINUCHIN: I want to continue talking about an esthetic sense, a sense of what feels right. I clearly don't know how to teach that, but it is an alertness for silences, for pauses, for inactivity. I'm not talking here about what to do. At this point you don't have it yet, Andy. You kept going with the control, but at this moment I would have talked with the child even if I didn't know how or what to say. I don't have the slightest idea how to teach that. The use of space is not taught in language.

ANDY: I felt stuck in the session. I felt something wasn't right, and that's why I'm showing it. I didn't go further with it than that. Maybe that's a good question to ask myself: What am I sensing?

Suddenly I realized that while I was talking to Andy as a colleague, he was responding to me as the teacher. I started laughing and began throwing coins out of my pocket to the other students. The class laughed and began throwing coins at me and each other. I thought I had made the point but was not certain.

MINUCHIN: Did you ever see Carl Whitaker's office, Andy? It was full of toys. Do you use toys?

ANDY: Once I spent most of a session playing dice with a mother and her children.

MINUCHIN: Sit on the floor while you talk.

ANDY *(complying):* I had so much fun I didn't think I should charge them.

MINUCHIN: No, that's your mistake. You were doing therapy.

"Walking and Chewing Gum at the Same Time"

Andy came to the next presentation looking as though he had something cooking. He maintained his usual subdued and restrained posture, but there was a hint of discovery waiting to emerge as he began describing a session with the family.

"I think I'm sort of doing it," he said. "I'm walking and chewing gum at the same time. I'm not blowing bubbles yet. But something clicked with me, with your throwing things at me during the last session. They were arguing, and Emilio was feeling angry and misunderstood. He was more oppositional by the moment. I did a number of things, and they're spaced throughout the tape, so I thought I'd tell you some of them and show you what happened at the end."

Andy cleared his voice, creating suspense about what he was about to show. "They were arguing over homework," he said.

As Andy talked, it was obvious to the class that he was also changing his usual way of presenting. Instead of reporting a long sequence of facts and events, he now became an interesting storyteller, and the class was captivated.

ANDY: This time when the father was being critical of Emilio again, I thought of Carl Whitaker and his parallel play. So I exaggerated the idea of punishing Emilio and brought humor into it. I said to the family, "Why don't we beat Emilio up?" I got up out of my chair and I playfully roughed him up, and he laughed. Then I got out the batakas—you know, those big, heavily padded bats? You can whale the tar out of people with them and not hurt them a bit. So I said, "Let's all beat Emilio!" And we all started beating him up, and he was laughing. Then I threw him a bataka and said, "Defend yourself!" It just broke the whole atmosphere! And there was no point to it! You know, my tendency is to want to teach something and make a point of it.

MINUCHIN *(obviously pleased):* This is not Andy's style. This is an interruption of logic to create an affect. And he is operating out of a freedom of intervention that is absolutely new. Andy, you've watched more tapes than any person I know. This time you finally put what you know into practice.

ANDY: Yes! I wasn't going my usual route from *a* to *b* to *c* to *d.* I had my usual route, but I felt freer to just do something else and see.

MINUCHIN: To do that you need to have the confidence that you can follow the process. You have to know that you can control it at any point, wherever it goes.

ANDY *(fast forwarding the tape):* Here is another segment I wanted to show you. The father is in Little League, so I used a baseball metaphor, and they locked horns over that. I had them do a family sculpture. I haven't read that much about it so I don't know how it's done formally, but again I wanted to get out of the normal track that they fell into again. So that was another intervention that was nonverbal, that was discontinuous. Then at the end of the session they finally talk to each other. I saw that the father could listen and the son wasn't disrespectful, and I thought this was a good ending.

FATHER *(frustrated):* I tried to tell him. But he wouldn't listen.

ANDY: Why is this happening? *(Father and son begin to argue.)* Stop the talking. Do you see what's going on here? I want you to make a sculpture about the family. No words. When I say make a sculpture, you put yourself in a position that demonstrates what's happening.

The father did the first sculpture. He placed Emilio's hands against himself and he had his arms around Michael. Then he placed Emilio on the floor. Emilio put his feet against this father while the father and Michael pointed in an accusatory manner at Emilio.

Then Andy asked Emilio to do a sculpture. Emilio asked Michael to sit down. Then he put his hand up against his father and the father's hand up against him, in an oppositional manner.

Andy commented on the similarity between the father's and Emilio's sculptures; they were in agreement as to what was going on. He then invited Michael to make a sculpture. Michael asked the father and Emilio to hold hands and to push against each other. He then stood back and with an amused expression he commented, "Yeah, that's what I see is going on." Andy stopped the tape.

ANDY: Right after that exchange, they started talking to each other about what was happening.

MINUCHIN: How do you think Andy moved from a purely structural, dry, middle-distance type of intervention, to incorporating the voices of Carl Whitaker, Virginia Satir, and Peggy Papp? He's been contaminated! *(The class laughed.)* But when do we get the transformation? Maybe, in order to throw the book away, you need to graduate. You can jump only when you've graduated. You have always worked from middle distance, Andy. Your therapy has been controlled by internal maps of sequences. Now you are working with discontinuity. How did that happen?

ANDY: Well, it goes back to when I started in your class last year. In my first presentation I was very, very cautious, to the point of falling all over myself and saying that I knew nothing. But you didn't accept that. You said I can't help you if you present yourself as an empty vessel. I can't help you. So I went away from that very upset, and I felt dismissed. I thought it over very carefully and put those things together and said, If I'm going to invite people to jump into the unknown, then I have to be able to do that myself. So for the last two years I've been trying to do that.

It's been painful and hard because I am a cautious person. It's been a series of jumps. You make one jump, and you're at the next level and say, Well, can I jump this far? So I think there's a whole process of understanding what the next jump is and getting the nerve up to do it. I've seen you for two years throwing things at people on occasion as a sort of demonstration of being discontinuous and nonverbal and playful. There was a sense of looseness that had no point to it. But it kind of crystallized a jump that I could take, and it came together.

MINUCHIN *(smiling):* What you are saying is very disappointing, because you are saying that it takes two years.

ANDY *(laughing):* Well, it took me two years!

Epilogue

The current Dalai Lama said something that reminded me of Minuchin's teaching. It was something like, I have not told you anything that you don't already know, and I have not taken away anything that you really own. He also talked about the two practices of Buddhism. The lower level practice is for people who need rules and road signs to follow, whereas the higher level is for people who can go beyond all restrictions, eventually reaching a freedom of being.

Andy wrote in his draft of this chapter:

> In looking back, I see this achievement as a complex interaction between my desire and dedication, the group process with supportive colleagues, and contact with a unique and powerful teacher who lives his beliefs in terms of affirming competence in his students at a profound level.

The paradox of the empty vessel is a lot more intricate than I initially understood, for when Andy described himself as such, perhaps it was not so much a put-down as a call for a special teacher to enlighten him. When Minuchin dismissed Andy's statement at the first session, he was in fact engaging him as a partner embarking on a challenging journey.

At the end of the training year, I asked Andy to sum up his experience with Minuchin in one sentence. He answered, "I am very lucky!" I took it as a humble way of expressing his gratitude, but I did not agree that luck had too much to do with it. As I followed Andy's epic to its last session in order to write this chapter, I was again struck by the unblemished form of student/teacher relationship in which the pursuit of knowledge was crystal clear in its transaction. This simple elegance renewed for me a desire for learning.

After observing Minuchin doing supervision for over five years, I see that students will map out their own journeys even though they are traveling with the same teacher. They start out together, but they soon show their different paces and ways of proceeding. Some go very far, but others seem to get stuck at some point and cannot quite break free. One might say that Andy was stuck during his first lesson. As I watched, I was worried for him and wondered if he could go the course. Like his fellow students, perhaps I did not have as much faith in him as his teacher did. I projected onto him a lot of my own anxiety and resentment at being in a position to be criticized and therefore failed to understand that a student like Andy is free of the emotional baggage that many of us adult students carry. He was able to place his trust in a supervisor whose vision would take him places.

Andy himself offered this graceful explanation: "If you are close with your ego and the teacher reaches you to open up, it will be very painful. But if you are open, then it will be a bliss." From that point of view, the empty vessel certainly contains an open space for learning to take place.

A vessel is also a boat; after it has been loaded, it sails away. Andy died suddenly of a heart attack shortly after he had completed his training. Teacher and fellow students alike, we mourn his loss.

As I carry away my image of Andy, I wonder about the other missing pieces of his story that may have escaped my detection. Is this the true Andy story, or is it my imagination that this was someone free from restraints and messiness in the pursuit of knowledge and wisdom? Could there be someone so much more pure than what we could be? Or is it just an illusion of those who wish for the persona of a perfect student? We can never be sure. But who needs an absolute answer, as long as we are touched and enriched by the spirit of his quest?

Epilogue

Salvador Minuchin

So here we have stories and storytellers. They are all more human than otherwise; they all speak the same language, share the same cultural limitations, may even have similar dreams. But the storytellers are different from each other, and they proclaim their uniqueness. If we listen carefully, we can hear regional dialects, ideological phrases, klezmer music, Tennessee Williams plots. And each one carries a personal belief system that has shaped the core of their therapy.

The stories of Margaret Meskill and David Greenan are modern American. They talk about gender confusion and about gender rights. They are spokespersons for larger groups. Margaret tells about the unintended stereotypical dismissal of men that goes together with the feminist rebalancing of injustice. David, who sees himself as a flagbearer, offers a cautionary tale about the blinders of proximity.

We can see Israela Meyerstein's father, perched on the green roof of a Chagall painting, reading his poems, and Israela's difficulty in balancing her aesthetic heritage with her need for certainty.

Hannah Levin comes from a responsible and vanishing world that dreamt of social justice. Her stories speak of people's unmet needs, and of the passions and limitations of personal effort in the world of managed care.

Gil Tunnell brings the perfection, without the fragrance, of magnolias. A world where conflict is submerged in form, where surfaces are graceful, confusions postponed, and where one reins in the scream and talks softly.

Adam Price's stories are written on the glossy paper of the successful middle class, where nothing is correct or incorrect since the pain has been tamed. From this world of examined truths, Adam meets the rage of the Jacksons, who use words not to explain but to explode.

As a child, Dorothy Leicht was given a caretaker's job, and she started to collect details. Responsible for keeping dark clouds away from home, she developed a large number of solutions that left her too close to the immediate to see the horizon.

Wai-Yung, like Harold with his purple crayon, constructed her world as she went along; realities and dreams comingle, periods and paragraphs are exiled, and Buddha's shadow smiles.

Andy Schauer was the most "American." He had the optimistic belief that achievement comes from accumulated effort. In his world there was no space for doubts, except, perhaps, about himself.

They were a segment of the privileged world of healers. We had agreed that their voices were too compelling, and that they needed to hear and own their tangential thoughts. Their chapters document their journeys of transformation, and the struggle that accompanies a therapist's expansion.

I am a tinkerer, a meddler, a storyteller, some kind of a playwright. Throughout my life I have collected voices. Some have the flavor of my Argentinian roots; the romantic poets of my childhood and adolescence, the feel of my small town. Some reflect my Jewish identity; the customs and passions of my family, my early Zionist readings. Some reflect my first experience in Israel—as a doctor in the war that established the country, and in work with the children who had come as refugees without their families. And some reflect my intimate circle: wife, children, and grandchild, who have told me about closeness, confusion, mistakes, and repair.

In my professional life, Freud's ideas were challenged by what was to me the more satisfying complexity of Sullivan's thinking, and by the cultural school of psychoanalysis. Some of my voices came from my anthropological reading, which gave intellectual underpinning to my experience of being an immigrant in more than one culture.

As a family therapist, my talmudic and stubborn rationality was conquered by Carl Whitaker's appreciation of the irrational, and his freedom to give in. Braulio Montalvo lent me passion and compassion; Jay Haley showed me that the goal is what matters, and that the possible pathways are multiple. The voices of Peter Urquhart, Barbara Bryant Forbes, Jerome Ford, and Paul Riley guided me into the Black-American culture, and others, within my family and outside, helped me to understand the feminine perspective.

I still collect voices, and some are very clear. Lester Baker talks to me about science and sick children, Don Bloch about collaboration among healers. I am refreshed by Carlos Sluzki's mixture of intellectual quest and humor. And Michael White invites me to engage in polemics.

In the end, I carry my voices in a teacher's pouch and I lend them freely, as long as they are transformed in the process of assimilation. From the younger colleagues who have written these chapters, I demanded what I think I have achieved for myself: an acceptance of their basic beliefs and style, a challenge to their certainty, attention to their peripheral voices, and an open enjoyment of learning from others.

References

AAMFT Founders Series. (1990). Videotape produced by the American Association for Marriage and Family Therapy, Washington, DC.

Anderson, H. (1994, November). *Collaborative therapy: The co-construction of newness.* Workshop presented at the American Association for Marriage and Family Therapy Conference, Chicago, IL.

Anderson, H., & Goolishian, H. A. (1988). Human systems as linguistic systems: Preliminary and evolving ideas about the implications for clinical theory. *Family Process, 27,* 371–394.

Badinter, E. (1980). *Mother love, myth and reality.* New York: Macmillan.

Bateson, G. (1972). *Steps to an ecology of mind.* New York: Ballantine Books.

Bell, N. W., & Vogel, E. F. (Eds.). (1960). *A modern introduction to the family.* Glencoe, IL: Free Press.

Boyd-Franklin, N. (1989). *Black families in therapy: A multisystems approach.* New York: Guilford Press.

Brown, L., & Brodsky, A. M. (1992). The future of feminist therapy. *Psychotherapy, 29,* 51–57.

Coontz, S. (1992). *The way we never were: American families and the nostalgia trap.* New York: Basic Books.

Donzelot, J. (1979). *The policing of families.* New York: Random House.

Falicov, C. J. (1983). Introduction. In C. J. Falicov (Ed.), *Cultural perspectives in family therapy* (pp. xiv–xv). Rockville, MD: Aspen.

Fisch, R. (1978). Review of problem-solving therapy, by Jay Haley. *Family Process, 17,* 107–110.

Foucault, M. (1980). *Power/knowledge: Selected interviews and other writings.* New York: Pantheon.

Gergen, K. (1985). The social constructionist movement in modern psychology. *American Psychologist, 40,* 266–275.

Gorin, G. (1990). *Life on edge: Poems by George Gorin.* Chicago: Adams Press.

Hoffman, L. (1985). Beyond power and control: Toward a "second-order" family systems therapy. *Family Systems Medicine, 3,* 381–396.

Maturana, H. R., & Varela, F. J. (1980). *Autopoiesis and cognition: The realization of living.* Boston: D. Reidel.

Mazza, J. (1988). Training strategic therapists: The use of indirect techniques. In H. A. Liddle, D. C. Breulin, & R. C. Schwartz (Eds.), *Handbook of family therapy training and supervision* (pp. 93–109). New York: Guilford.

McGoldrick, M., Pearce, J. K., & Giordano, J. (Eds.). (1982). *Ethnicity and family therapy.* New York: Guilford.

Minuchin, S. (1974). *Families and family therapy.* Cambridge, MA: Harvard University Press.

Minuchin, S. (1984). *Family kaleidoscope.* Cambridge, MA: Harvard University Press.

Minuchin, S., & Fishman, H. C. (1981). *Family therapy techniques.* Cambridge, MA: Harvard University Press.

Minuchin, S., Montalvo, B., Guerney, B., Rosman, B., & Schumer, F. (1967). *Families of the slums.* New York: Basic Books.

Minuchin, S., Rosman, B., & Baker, L. (1978). *Psychosomatic families: Anorexia nervosa in context.* Cambridge, MA: Harvard University Press.

Nichols, M. P., & Schwartz, R. C. (1991). *Family therapy: Concepts and methods* (2nd ed.). Boston: Allyn & Bacon.

Papp, P., & Imber-Black, E. (1996). Family themes: Transmission and transformation. *Family Process, 35,* 5–20.

Pirotta, S., & Cecchin, G. (1988). The Milan training program. In H. A. Liddle, D. C. Breunlin, & R. C. Schwartz (Eds.), *Handbook of family therapy training and supervision* (pp. 38–61). New York: Guilford.

Schnarch, D. M. (1991). *Constructing the sexual crucible: An integration of sexual and marital therapy.* New York: Norton.

Selvini Palazzoli, M., Cirillo, S., Selvini, M., & Sorrentino, A. M. (1989). *Family games: General models of psychotic processes in the family* (V. Kleiber, Trans.). New York: Norton.

Simon, G. M. (1995). A revisionist rendering of structural family therapy. *Journal of Marital and Family Therapy, 21,* 17–26.

Skolnick, A. (1991). *Embattled paradise: The American family in an age of uncertainty.* New York: Basic Books.

Stone, L. (1980). *The family, sex and marriage: England, 1500–1800.* New York: Harper & Row.

Thomas, F. N. (1994). Solution-oriented supervision: The coaxing of expertise. *The Family Journal: Counseling and Therapy for Couples and Families, 2,* 11–18.

Walters, M., Carter, B., Papp, P., & Silverstein, O. (1988). *The invisible web: Gender patterns in family relationships.* New York: Guilford.

Whitaker, C. A. (1976). The hindrance of theory in clinical work. In P. J. Guerin (Ed.), *Family therapy: Theory and practice* (pp. 154–164). New York: Gardner.

Index

D

M

N

O

S

U

V

W

Y

Z